36 17 12 22 .5 4 8

39 35 25 26 17 24 8

SUGAR IN THE GOURD

EVELYN HANNA

SUGAR

IN THE

GOURD

E. P. DUTTON & COMPANY, INC.

NEW YORK   1942

DEDICATED

TO SOUTHERN WOMANHOOD

wherever it may be

SUGAR IN THE GOURD

There's sugar in the gourd
But I can't get it out;
The way to get it out
Is to roll the gourd about.

—Old Negro song

CHAPTER I

Say that it is a late June afternoon in middle Georgia; that the year, for no reason at all, is nineteen hundred and twenty-two; and inevitably, immediately you have before you hillsides and valleys of shimmering green, green with peach trees and golden with the precious fruit. Since it is early in the season there is not yet the sharp odor of fermentation from cull dumps but only the fragrance of the ripening fruit throughout the long serpentine rows.

Looming high above the orchards, glittering like a synthetic jewel in the late sunlight will be the owner's home, sometimes new, square of line and pragmatic, more frequently a graceful old "mansion" that has stood there since ante-bellum days.

The orchards are heavy and slumbrous with their rich yield; overburdened limbs have been propped to prevent their breaking. The air is thick with the dust of many wagons; the streets of the adjacent town are equally thick and turgid with darkies who are spending their week's wages for tobacco and raw corn liquor. Saturday afternoon is theirs; they line the sidewalks, the courthouse steps, and obliterate the shop windows; they greet one another with high shrill cackles of delight; they spit tobacco juice and gather about the Holy-Roller preacher exhorting them from the base of the Confederate monument.

Up in Washington, D. C. an orator cries, "Now you take the South—"; and a wit answers him, "Not me, *you* take it! I don't want it!"

Very well, then, let us take it, since it is being given away.

Say that on this particular Saturday afternoon in June the orchards in general were deserted. Yet in Frost Haven, Georgia, between the endless rows of Ellison Frost's trees a young man plodded ahead of a girl, pushing back the branches that stung his cheek. The dirt kept getting into his shoes but he thought a little more would not matter; soon they would come to the spring where he could wash his feet, or wash his whole body if he had a mind to. As for Daisy, the dirt did not bother her, she was as barefoot as on the day she was born. She had a way of breaking up the clods with her toes as she walked along, crumbling them to powder under her short, broad feet. It seemed to the young man that this was not mere sensuous enjoyment from the feel of the soft dirt, it was rather a delight in breaking something.

Daisy, yes, that was her name. As if that mattered, either. At the top of the hill he paused and looked back toward the big Frost house, hoping that he could no longer see it. But it was still there, gracious and dominant, and he would have to go farther yet to get away from it. Its proud silhouette overtopping the green trees haunted him; it might be badly in need of a coat of fresh paint, the roof over the kitchen sagging for want of repair, but to him it represented the South of which he had read and dreamed as a boy in the North, just as Sabina Frost represented the Southern Girl. How small and delicately made she was, how cool and beautiful; the gray eyes were always still in her pale face, her dark hair never ruffled.

His body grew hot at the thought of her as he hastened on toward the spring, not because the spring was in itself desirable but because it was as remote a spot as he knew, out of sight of Frost Haven, and in no way connected with Mr. Ellison Frost's peach orchards.

Now Daisy, of course, was connected with them, she was the daughter of Mr. Frost's overseer, Sam Cummings, but she was as incidental as the spring and as elemental as the earth. "Ain't it been hot today?" she complained. "Seems like I ain't done nothin' but sweat. I bet you been busy as a yearlin' in fly time."

When he did not answer she ran to catch up with him. "Matt, Matt, why won't you talk to me?"

He looked down at her flushed, stupid face. "I'm sorry, Daisy, I didn't hear you. How much farther is it to the spring?"

"Hits just over one more hill. Papa wants to build him a pond there, he says we'll have more fish than John saw."

"John who?"

"I don't know—hits just a sayin', 'more fish than John saw.'"

"Oh. I suppose it's from the Bible."

"I reckon so."

He was conscious now of her thick, stolid body beside him, of the sting of the peach leaves, the dirt in his shoes and of that driving something, somewhere in the core of his being that never left him. Walking downhill between the rows, straight into the face of the setting sun, he did not stop to ask himself what it meant. He was afraid he would find the answer. It was cooler in the hollow, the air was suddenly fresh on his burning face, and when the rows of trees came to an abrupt end he stood for a moment breathing deeply. "So there *is* an end of the Frost orchards," he said bitterly. "I should never have believed it."

"Everything ends sometime," she answered, and he looked at her quickly.

"Does it? I've often wondered."

"Hits an old sayin'," she responded.

"And you're full of them as an egg is of meat. I presonally distrust them, do you hear? I don't believe any of them!"

"I don't know why you're so cross, less it's because you're hot. I reckon hits always cool at Mr. Frost's house, bein' up on a hill, like, and the rooms so big."

"How do you know?" he asked. "Were you ever in the house?"

"No. Was you?"

"Of course!" (Once, just once, when Mr. Frost had sent for him to help work on the books.)

"Are they?" she asked.

"Are they what?"

"Are the rooms big and cool?"

"My God! I didn't notice. But I should think they

would be, just from contact with Mrs. Frost and—and Miss Sabina. *They* are cool enough, I can tell you."

"Miss Sabina," said Daisy, "she goes out of her way not to speak to me."

"That's where you're mistaken," he laughed shortly. "She doesn't pay you that much attention. If she went out of her way not to speak to you, it would indicate that she knew you were there—which is entirely fallacious and likewise presumptuous." He did not expect her to understand what he was saying, he was talking for his own pleasure—or pain.

"She don't never do nothin', I reckon that's why she stays cool."

"She reads," he told her. "She reads all the time. One day she came down to the packing house with a message for Mr. Frost and she could scarcely stop reading long enough to tell him; she kept her place in the book with her finger. She's sitting on the front porch reading now, I dare say." It made him feel cheap to be discussing her with Daisy, yet he wanted to go on talking about her, go on thinking of her sitting on the porch reading, undisturbed, tranquil.

"Look a-yonder," Daisy said. "You can see the spring from here."

"In that clump of trees?"

"Yeah—springs is always at the foot of hills."

He wanted to cry out, "No! Once I saw one at the top of a mountain!" It wasn't true, but her generalities and platitudes were enough to goad a man into braggadocio or lying. Yet why should he get angry with her? What did he expect of a common field daisy?

The soil underfoot, he observed, was no longer red

dust, it was mountain dirt, white and sandy. Now there were sassafras bushes everywhere, blackjack oaks, and along the terraces rhododendrons grew in profusion. The fading sunlight hovered over bay trees making them as silvery as they would presently be by moonlight. He would lie beneath them, watching the stars come out and making his peace with them.

They walked along a crumbling old stone wall, past pine trees that bristled like Fuller brushes and all at once, it seemed, they were at the spring. Here again the soil was different, black and marshy at the water's edge, blackened probably by rotted leaves.

"Oh, it's pretty!" he cried. "I had no idea it would look like this!" He stared down at the crystalline water, watched the sand bubble up in small fountains and felt the cool air soaking into his body.

The color and variety of the stones in the water amazed him: there were crystal quartz, flint, some red, some green, others cream colored, but the loveliest were of robin's egg blue. Toward the head of the spring there was a newly cleared spot untouched by sunlight where the twining white roots made a network in the water. By the base of a holly tree he saw lizards, water puppies and crawfish. Farther up on the hillside were wild flowers, black-eyed Susans, lavender blossoms that looked like sweet peas and starry red flowers.

Daisy had already waded into the little stream that flowed from the spring and was holding up her skirt gingerly. He smiled wrily at that and began stripping off his shoes and socks, then he rolled his trousers up to his knees and followed her. It was cold, icy cold, and he loved it. He picked up stones from the bed of the stream and hurled them at Daisy's feet. "Don't," she said, "you're getting my skirt wet."

"Take it off."

"Think you're smart, don't you?"

"No. But I'm having fun. Come here, Daisy."

"Hit ain't dark enough yet."

He laughed. "God, the simplicity of the one-track mind! I only wanted to show you a stone I'd found—"

When she came closer he saw that the unbecoming moisture was gone from her face, in the late twilight she was losing her identity as Daisy Cummings and taking on a symbolism that he neither loved nor hated but accepted without analysis. "What is that in your hand, Daisy?"

"Hits a crawfish. I love to take their eyes out, they look like opals—"

He drew away from her. "Daisy! How can you?"

"That ain't nothin'; I been doin' it all my life. Hits nice here, ain't hit? We can come here all summer, and next summer, too."

Repelled, he went over to the bank and began drawing on his socks. "No. I won't be here next summer."

"You ain't mad at me, are you, Matt? I done throwed the crawfish away." She came up and sat beside him. "Why ain't you comin' back next summer? Your papa comes every peach season."

"I know, but I'll be through the university then and I'm going to Europe. I'm not going to be Mr. Frost's bookkeeper all my life."

"Where's Europe?"

"On the other side of the Atlantic."

"I bet hit costs money to git there. And you ain't got no money."

"All right. I haven't any money, but I can get there just the same. I can work my way over on a cattle boat; I can wash dishes or scrub decks. Nothing on earth can keep me from going."

The moon was coming up over the bay trees now, slipping in and out of the clouds, then riding triumphantly higher. Nothing could stop the moon either.

"You won't be no better off," said Daisy flatly.

"Perhaps not." Oh, he would though. He'd no longer be the son of Mr. Frost's packing superintendent; he'd be Matthew Cox with an A.B. degree and a European background. He could sit on the front porch at Frost Haven with Sabina and say, "Did I tell you about seeing Goethe's home at Weimar? And Flaubert's at Rouen? You really must go over sometime; drink absinthe at a sidewalk café in Paris, tea at the Cheshire Cheese in London, Pilsen beer in Munich—" or did ladies drink absinthe and beer?

"Perhaps not, Daisy. Perhaps I won't be any better off but I've got to find out. You don't know what it's like to have something inside you that drives you on, never lets you rest. As soon as you get what you wanted it doesn't mean anything to you any more because there's a new something, much bigger and more important ahead of you then. And so it keeps on. That's why you never think you have got anything. Whatever it is inside you is hard and relentless, it never lets up. It makes you do things that you know are wrong, but you have to be doing something."

"Is it anything like a tapeworm?"

He laughed shortly. "Why yes. Yes, I suppose it is."

But how to name the nameless or define the boundaries

of the limitless? How could he tell her what it was when he himself did not know? How name something at once vague, complex and unattainable? Was there a word for the dark burning force within him, the hunger for learning, the shame of being simple Henry Cox's son, of being so inferior to the Frosts, particularly Sabina Frost?

He knew that Sabina was indolent, spoiled, arrogant but he did not know whether he loved her or despised her. He could almost see her pale tranquil face before him now, the small perfect body that had never been stirred by love and he wanted to hurt her, humiliate her as she had humiliated him.

He moved back where the ground was higher and dry, and the girl beside him moved, too. Daisy, that was her name.

"It's dark now, Daisy."

"Yeah. I reckon hits dark enough."

CHAPTER II

BETWEEN EXISTENCE AND NON-EXISTENCE THERE WAS, Sabina Frost believed, a vast world in which an individual could live and have her being. Non-existence, of course, encompassed the milleniums prior to birth and following death—pleasant enough states, but over them a person had no control. Existence, on the other hand, had many disagreeable connotations such as struggle, doubts, possible or actual penury, humiliations, failures, which seemed to predominate greatly over any hypothetical joys and triumphs.

Consequently she had evolved for herself a world of unreality that was nothing so positive as a fabricated life of make-believe, but rather a denial of things that were. When events threatened to come so close as to besmirch her consciousness, or sordid facts obtruded upon this precious state of negation, she drew back mentally in order that they should not touch her, particularly her emotions. This withdrawal had been at first deliberate, conscious, but was now a psychological nervous and cerebral pattern and she noted with pleasure its obvious rewards.

Whenever she looked into the mirror (as she could do now if this early morning rain were not so soft and conducive to day-dreaming that she preferred to lie in bed) she saw an unlined face, fresh, and younger than its actual years. Presently she would throw back the linen sheet, rise, and discover anew the purity of her untouched body. On Sunday mornings she liked to look back over the week just passed and count the hours, days which had left no mark upon her. Where other people singled out events, happenings to remember, Sabina treasured the absence of memorable moments.

The rain drummed out its muffled staccato beat on the worn shingles of the old Frost house and through the windows the leaves of the oak trees appeared crisp and glistening. Why should she get up and look out when she knew so well what she would see?

The house that had been her grandparents' was set far back on a hill in a handsome oak grove and looked on the south toward the town of Frost Haven, on the north toward negro-town. It faced westward, looking down upon the rolling acres of peach orchards which made her father alternately rich and poor, exuberant and morose, but were frequently beautiful and always symmetrical—such a cool, planned symmetry of trees and rows, such an orderly clipping of branches that they were identical in design and shape and doubtless varied not a pound in production.

They were now heavy with ripening fruit, too heavy—the rain would ruin them for shipping. And all the roof tops of the town were black and sodden, as were the packing shed, the overseer's house, the barns, and all the darkies' cabins on Happy Hill. The sound of the freight train switching endlessly as it picked up the yellow refrigerated cars at various sidings was thin and hollow on the morning air.

But Sabina's patterned reflexes turned back the consciousness of the rain, the noisy freight cars and the spoiling fruit; her thoughts came, circuitously, by long habit, to rest upon herself.

She liked being Sabina Frost (descended from the Frosts of Maryland by the pre-revolutionary migration of her ancestors to Georgia), twenty-six years of age, lying in a canopied old "tester" bed, regarding life with the objectivity which she considered essential to a tranquil existence. To be "in the world but not of it," a condition Lord Byron had recommended but not practiced, to be amused by the industry of human ants building up little hills only to see them crushed, to consider the futility of men allowing themselves to be hurt by business failure and of women who were slaves to their emotional or social desires, to refuse to allow one's self to be involved in the petty struggles: these things made up the proper philosophical approach to life. She admitted, however, that not every one could achieve it.

Her father had laughed uproariously over a conversation between two of his cousins on the subject of flowers. "Yes, I have a beautiful garden," said the wealthy one, "but I give so much to it. Flowers require love and sympathy and understanding."

"And they also require niggers and money and manure," the poorer one had retorted.

Sabina saw nothing amusing in this, she considered

that both cousins had been right. Likewise she granted that the ability to practice the objective approach presupposed intelligence, breeding, disciplined emotions—and niggers and money and leisure. She had achieved this detachment slowly and on occasions painfully, and she had no intention of giving it up.

There were times, of course, when it became a bore: when the opinion of the Fine Arts Club that "Sabina is such a lovely person" (and she liked to think of herself as a lovely person) was insufficient, when reading the minutes at the meeting of the Daughters of the Confederacy did not seem to be the *summmum bonum* of existence, and there was a noticeable lack of drama in playing the accompaniment to the singing of *America* by the Colonial Dames; but these were the penalties of being a lady.

"Delicacy of mind" had been one of her mother's paramount precepts, and so obediently had Sabina followed it that her mental processes were of the most crystalline purity. If Will Rogers never met a man he did not like, it could be truthfully said of Sabina that she had never seen a disagreeable fact. This is not to imply a lack of perception, intelligence, or comprehension, for she possessed those qualities in abundance. But owing to its habits of deliberate evasion, her mind resembled an ancient English village with its intricate system of winding, circular streets set off on either side by tall, old brick houses. The resemblance was further borne out by the rose vines clambering in profusion along the front, and the absence of bathrooms in the rear. Her father once said in his dry, pithy way, "Sabina had the makings of a scholar, but she was afraid she would get her mind dirty."

And then he added rather superfluously, "She is a lady in the worst sense of the word."

Her mother's complete precept might have been phrased in this way, "a delicate mind in a delicate body," for she had encouraged Sabina to think of herself as being exceedingly fragile. A woman should not lift heavy things, she must not get her feet wet, she must not take violent exercise (and any kind of exercise was violent), she must "take care of herself" or she would "be an invalid the rest of her life." These vague euphemisms were never explained and Sabina never asked for an explanation because she knew they involved disagreeable functions of female anatomy; and it was easier to accept them and be physically indolent. Consequently she had evolved gracefully into a state of perfect ladyhood and perfect hypochondria enucleated by that amazing facility for denying anything approaching reality. Over her desk hung a quotation from Epictetus, "You are but an appearance, and in no manner what you appear to be," but she construed this as a commentary on others, and one which in no manner concerned herself.

Sometimes when the unwelcome thought forced itself upon her consciousness that life was slipping through her fingers like sand on the seashore, that she might soon be an old maid as well as a lady, she had moments of sheer panic. It was true that she was "indifferent," self-sufficient, but she felt that to a man of the right type, assured and able, her remoteness would be a challenge.

The rain had thinned out into long silver needles that glittered in the now brilliant light. There were Lila May's heavy steps as she waddled from the kitchen to the dining room, the smell of coffee and bacon and batter cakes.

Sabina dressed slowly and found her mother and father awaiting her in the library. The Sunday newspapers which would not be read until after dinner were placed neatly on the long table.

"Good-morning, Mother. Good-morning, Father."

"Good-morning, Sabina. You are late."

"Sorry. I overslept, I suppose."

As she walked into the dining room she knew perfectly well that she had delayed coming down because at breakfast she would have to face a fact: today, the twenty-fifth of June, nineteen hundred and twenty-two, her half sister, Clarissa Frost, was coming home—again.

CHAPTER III

AT TIMES IT SEEMED TO ELLISON FROST THAT THE LIFE OF his household was compressed between anachronistic traditions and equally threadbare quotations. While he yielded to none in his admiration for the South's picturesque and flamboyant past, his years in the North had given him a sardonic disrespect for a great many of the intangible things his wife cherished and, indeed, lived by. As a Southern gentleman he acquiesced in their predominance in his home, as a man he despised them.

When Clarissa's mother had died at the child's birth in Massachusetts, he had given up his law practice there and returned to Georgia where he soon afterward married the handsome and vivacious Janie Lee Regis more as a matter of convenience than of passion. He knew now that whereas almost all Southern women were vivacious, their vivacity frequently cloaked a mind that was banal, pragmatic, narrow and opinionated. And although he knew that Sabina was largely the product of her mother's upbringing, the girl was a constant bewilderment to him.

[26]

He believed that if she had belonged to anyone else, he would have understood her. But when, as she grew older and became more exasperating to him, he remarked one day to his wife, "You must have looked in the wrong head of cabbage when you found Sabina, my dear," her lips set in a thin line and she replied, "Motherhood is not a subject for levity, Mr. Frost."

"I assure you, my dear, that I never thought it was, but the workings of the Mendelian law leave me at times completely confused."

"You have never been confused, Mr. Frost, since I have known you."

"Thank you, my dear."

He would have liked to cry out, "But ah, you see, you have never known me. I am a man of the most violent contraditions. I like to give orders—and have them disobeyed. The well-ordered routine of your house is pleasant enough, it is the life to which I was born, but frankly, madam, it bores me to distraction. Only Claire understands me, Claire is my own child. If she wants to jump over the moon, I will hold it for her while she jumps."

She was mercurial, yes, a creature of many and varied enthusiasms, but life with her was interesting. With Sabina you could only guess at what was going on. Both his children had talents, but neither had any conspicuous one. When Sabina was younger, she had played the piano very prettily, "with imagination and much expression" her mother said, but the girl had lacked the diligence to achieve accuracy and perfection; and after hearing concert artists like Paderewski and Rachmaninoff she had vowed that she would never play again. She wanted to excel but was unwilling to work for it.

Now that she was playing with words as previously she had played with notes, he suspected her of ambitions in the field of poetry. She would take her notebook off to a remote spot where the landscape was charming, not too rugged, the hills not too high, the trees not sufficiently thick to conceal lurking wild animals or snakes. (She always seemed to prefer mere prettiness to beauty.) Then she would seat herself on a tree stump, her skirts spread out smoothly about her in Gibson-girl fashion, a parasol shielding her face from the too exuberant sunlight, and look at nature: a discreet, not too prying look that said, "Isn't it pretty," as a well-brought-up child would stand before a Vermeer and give it her polite approval.

But there was never any poetry in the notebook, for she was too impatient to bother with form. Sometimes there were bits of sad, singing prose in the minor key of the Chopin she so much admired. But more frequently there were only arrangements of words, "beat, beat, beatitude," "symposium, symbolism, sympatico, synthesis," "catacombs, catnip, cataract, catastrophe, catechism." Once there had been a sharp observation that startled him: under the quotation, "Vengeance is mine, saith the Lord," she had written, "The Lord is selfish."

Was that what she thought about in church, rather than the clothes of other women? If so, he didn't mind, for it bespoke a hardness and inflexibility which he sometimes feared she did not have. In all justice to Sabina he must admit that she did not bother about other women's clothes and she was no meddler in the affairs of others. But this was somehow, he felt, not a virtue in Sabina; it was a fault arising from a profound disinterest in other people.

He sat now watching her at the breakfast table, waiting for some indication that she was perturbed over Clarissa's coming. He knew that in a few moments his wife would ask when she was expected, and he had his answer ready for her.

"Sabina, you look pale this morning," she began. "Don't you feel well?"

"Just a small headache, Mother, I'll be all right if I keep quiet."

Ellison Frost stifled a smile. "Shall I get you an aspirin, Sabina?"

"Oh, no," exclaimed her mother quickly, "aspirin is bad for her heart. I never let Sabina take aspirin. When did you say Clarissa was coming, Mr. Frost?"

"About eleven, I think. Perhaps," he suggested hopefully, "we had best not go to church. I'm sure she wouldn't like it if no one was here to greet her."

"Nonsense," replied Mrs. Frost. "On the contrary, I'm sure Clarissa is much too sensible to want us to stay away on her account. And after all, Clarissa is always coming and going."

"Perhaps you would like to stay at home and wait for her, Sabina?" he said.

"Of course, father, if you want me to, but I may have to play Mrs. Nixon's accompaniment in church—"

"In that case you must go by all means," he said, folding up his napkin. He pushed back the old Hepplewhite chair, resolving that he, also, would go—to see if she played Mrs. Nixon's accompaniment. At times Sabina was almost as interesting as Claire.

At ten minutes of eleven Clarissa had not arrived and Mrs. Frost announced that if they waited any longer they would be late for church. Her tone invested the phrase with such opprobrium that it immediately took its place in any category of Federal offenses punishable by fine, imprisonment or even death. The colored boy was hurried into his white duck coat and cap, and sent to bring the car to the door.

"I'm so glad it rained before seven, so that it would be fair before eleven," Janie Lee Frost remarked as her husband helped her into the car. "It's so convenient for church."

"Not so convenient for the poor devils who have to go to work, Janie Lee," her husband replied.

"Oh, Mr. Frost, you talk like a socialist, I'm sure you think it's smart. Where is Sabina?"

"Here she comes now." He watched his daughter's deliberate approach with amusement, she always walked as if it made no difference where she went or whether she went at all, but as if only the manner of her walking were important. It was typical of Sabina, he thought, to be more concerned with the manner than with the deed. And it was one of the reasons why she would never be able to write. He was reminded of one of Carlyle's essays, possibly the one on Dante, in which the Scot declared that where a thing is beautifully said, there is also a deep and universal meaning. It was a *non sequitur*, and he did not believe it even though Carlyle had said it.

"Such a nice day," Janie Lee Frost said with approval. "How is your head, Sabina?"

"Better, thank you, Mother."

The car rolled past the orchards and Ellison Frost looked back from his seat beside the driver at his two women: Sabina looked as fragile and delicate as a dream, there was a haunting, Botticellian quality to the picture she made in her pale pink dress and wide leghorn hat; but his wife looked exactly what she was, the capable state secretary of the Daughters of the American Revolution, church woman and civic leader. He had a moment of panic. "Janie Lee, you are *not* wearing your D.A.R. pin and bars to church?" The ladder of golden steps, each bar denoting a fighting ancestor, hung from her shoulder to her waist.

"Well, I know I shouldn't, but the dress is so plain, it's a last year's one—"

"For God's sake, take the damned thing off. I'm sure it's against the rules—"

"If you think so, Mr. Frost—" She reluctantly unpinned the decoration, folded it carefully and put it inside her purse.

Janie Lee and her ancestors! It was possible that she was descended from fighting stock, the bars proved it, but what a travesty it seemed now as he thought of her indigent family, "the Recumbent Regises" he called them when he had to write out monthy checks for their support.

His irritation passed gradually as he looked out at the shimmering leaves and the soft translucence that bathed each familiar object. The flower gardens which they passed were fresh and vivid with color; the half-moon of last night and (he hoped) tonight was a blurred steely gray against the noonday sky. It pleased him to recall a remark about himself he had overheard yesterday, "When Ellison Frost says it's going to rain, it rains. It's scared not to." But he did not want rain now, he wanted peaches.

When they reached the church the service had begun and they had to wait in the vestibule until the minister's prayer was concluded. His wife's subdued breathing was reverent beneath her last year's blue chiffon, his own white linen suit seemed to vibrate with the influx of each breath, but if Sabina breathed, you did not notice it. The minister's nasal monotone droned on, picturing a *nouveau riche* conception of heaven which was evidently to him analogous to eternity. Ellison Frost softly quoted from the *Religio Medici*, "For who can speak of eternity without a solecism or think thereof without an ecstasy?"

"What did you say, Mr. Frost?" whispered his wife.

"Nothing, nothing, my dear. I see the regular pianist is here, so Sabina won't have to play. I am disappointed."

"Yes, the child plays with so much expression."

But she doesn't keep good time, he thought rebelliously.

Sabina wished that the services were more elaborate, the furnishings of the prosaic edifice more glamorous. Religion, she thought, should be an anaesthetic since it had nothing to do with reason; its only appeals were emotional and sensuous. There should be more form, more "trappings" to keep the audience from thinking. Actually, there was so little in this drab little Protestant church to distract the attention that sometimes one could not help hearing what the preacher said. The intrusion of that strange man's disagreeable voice into the sanctity of her mind was a form of mental violation. What right had he to force his opinions and beliefs upon others? The entire service should be in Latin so that while one murmured with one's lips, "*Pater noster, qui es in coelo, sanctificetur nomen tuum. Adveniat regnum tuum; fiat voluntas tua sicut in coelo et in terra*—" one could embark upon any chosen peregrinations of fancy.

She, Sabina, could forget her present state of non-entity, could go back to the childhood dream of being a princess in disguise, or advance to some concrete outline of her mature ambitions; she was going to be famous for something, she was not quite sure for what. She would be a painter of world note, living in a Park Avenue penthouse; a great writer digging elemental and powerful stories out of humble lives in far-off lands; or she would be the wife of a great person, pouring tea for diplomats and directing the course of world events. That, perhaps, would be the easiest, to wear satin tea gowns, order flowers for dinner parties and be very careful not to seat the Consul from Megalomania next to the wife of an isolationist senator. And since Great Britain had probably the greatest empire in the world, she generally decided before the offertory was played to become the wife of the British Ambassador.

But there still remained a half hour to be passed after the collection had been blessed and consecrated. Sabina knew the minds of the congregation so well that she could tick them off individually, summing up their thoughts in a word or a phrase: the minister's wife, food; her mother, pride—pride in having fulfilled her obligations as a Southern woman; young Matthew Cox was probably thinking about bookkeeping or the peach crop; Mrs. Nixon, her voice—which made up in fervor for what it lacked in quality. The mind of the professor's wife was on her hips and never rose above that position; and on the contrary the mind of the wife of the hardware dealer was on her hair and never went any lower. Perhaps it was nice to have a stationary mind that never slipped off into the index-file marked *Verboten* and brought up subjects that left one quivering and torn with self-doubts.

One of these forbidden subjects was her father's kindness and tolerant leniency that masked disapproval of all she did and thought. There was his obvious preference for Clarissa in flat contradiction of her mother's statement that "Parents have no favorites. They love all their children equally."

As for her mother, there was her possessiveness which seemed little less than octopodan, though she called it "protecting my daughter." Clarissa had never allowed herself to be protected. To Sabina, yielding had seemed the better part of expediency as well as a saving in wear and tear on the emotions.

And especially there was the subject of Clarissa herself, but Sabina thought of this card as being entirely blank. It was not that she lacked knowledge of Clarissa and of their relations to each other, it was rather that she never allowed herself to put this knowledge in concrete form. It remained a vague hostility, a subdued animosity —in a word, it was jealousy, based on fundamental differences in character, attitude toward life, aspirations, differences even in physical make-up. And yet, it may be that the last phrase should have been first, that the other disparities were the direct outgrowth of that fundamental one. For Sabina was small-boned, delicately made, and her self-doubts might never have been known to one who was physically more robust. Where Sabina was languid, reserved, her half sister was antithetically exuberant and gregarious. Where Sabina considered long the advantages and disadvantages of doing a thing, had the desire and ability to do it but was unwilling to make the attempt lest she fail, Clarissa rushed into it headlong. As Mrs. Frost had said at breakfast, Clarissa was always coming and going. Her enthusiasms were as endless as they were unprofitable, but they kept her occupied—usually in New York. Each new project was an orange to be sucked dry, then discarded and she had never admitted coming upon a lemon.

Clarissa would come home today as she always did, refreshed by her latest expensive failure, her brown eyes bright, her red curls soft and smoothly shaped by the best hairdresser on Fifth Avenue. She would lift up her strong freckled arms and cry, "I fight all my battles for nothing. But I fight."

Nobody had ever told Claire, Sabina reflected, that somebody had to pay for those battles, and that the somebody was always their father.

Clarissa would greet people on the street in so polished, so charming a manner. "Why, Mrs. Alderberry, I'm so *happy* to see you! How *have* you been? I've thought of you so frequently and wondered how you were getting along. But I don't have to ask, you are looking simply marvelous. Yes, I'm fine, thank you, but then I always am, strong as a horse, you know—you simply can't kill these country gals. It's been *so* nice seeing you, do come to see me. Yes, I'll be here some time, at least until I hop off again. Good-bye, Mrs. Alderberry." And then when the woman was gone she would turn to her father. "Is that old buzzard still hanging around here? I thought she was dead long ago—oh, it was her husband. Well, I don't blame him for dying. She looks simply atrocious,

I bet he bought her at a rummage sale. What does she
do? Oh—yes, I'll go up and buy something from her,
poor soul. She just adores me. Where's her shop? Isn't
that where Mr. Elkins used to be?" And a week later
Claire would go a block out of her way to avoid the
woman. "There's that awful old Mrs. Alderberry again,
she's such a nuisance, let's stop in here until she goes by."

Claire's friendliness depended on her mood, and
Claire's mood depended upon how long she had been at
home and how long it would be before she was going
away again.

Her father would laugh and say, "Claire, you simply
ought to be shot," but he knew that people liked her and
it pleased him—particularly since it was nobody's secret
that Sabina had the reputation of being unfriendly and a
snob.

She had never explained to him that this accusation
was true only to a certain extent. Frequently she would
have spoken to people, indeed, she had every intention
of doing so, but she would discard, because of their
banality, the remarks she first thought of making; and
then, before she could think of anything at once appro-
priate, personal and original, the persons she had encountered were gone, saying, in all probability, "Sabina
Frost barely speaks, and she looks as though it hurt her
to do that." And so she was damned for her pains.

Too late she would realize that it would have been
better to say, "Hey, how're y'all?" in accordance with
local custom, and damn the weather as being too hot, too
cold, too rainy or too dry. Or she could even break a
precedent by saying, "It's a fine day, isn't it?" and evoke
a reply, "Yes, but we need rain terribly, don't you

think?" (It was a rare season indeed when Frost Haven did not need rain.) And then the man or woman thus addressed would go his way singing her praises, "I tell you that second daughter of Frost's is a fine girl, she's as plain as an old shoe."

The minister must have finished speaking, for there was a brief silence broken only by the flutter and chirpings of sparrows in the trees outside, then the notes of the organ rose and swelled, pealing out richly, sonorously, and obliterating all else. The congregation rose heavily from its stupor and the men ignored the wrinkles in their coats but the women gave little surreptitious pulls at the back of their skirts lest their appearance of consecration and spirituality be belied.

The air of June was itself a benediction but the man in the pulpit superimposed his own, then hurried to the door to greet his flock before they departed. He would leave his pulpit voice inside the church, and use in the vestibule his semi-professional or man-to-man voice. "So glad to see you this morning, Mrs. Moreton; we missed you last Sunday." There was likewise an air of restrained hurrying as if the people behind would like to push forward, as if the smell of fried chicken were already in their nostrils and they could hear the tinkle of ice in the tall tea glasses.

Mrs. Frost was nodding to a friend, "Wonderful sermon, wasn't it, so human and yet so—"

"Divine?" suggested her husband.

She looked at him suspiciously. "Well, not exactly divine. Of course, only Christ was divine—how do you do, Miss Taylor, is your mother better?"

Sabina felt herself being pushed against someone and she murmured, "I'm sorry."

"*I'm* sorry," the man said and stood back for her to pass. He was obviously a stranger, handsome, and a Yankee—perhaps not handsome, but certainly of striking appearance. What could he be doing in Frost Haven?

Then she saw that with him were a woman and two small boys. Married. She might have known.

Her mother was shaking hands with the minister. "Oh, Mr. Wilhoit, such a lovely sermon." There was her father's insincere, "Yes, indeed. Well, good-day, sir." And her own, "How do you do, Mr. Wilhoit?"

"Good-day, Mr. Frost. Good-day, Miss Sabina."

Then swiftly came the minister's warm greeting, "You are strangers, but very welcome. Your family, sir?"

"My sister, Mrs. Page, and the two little leaflets. My name is Barrett Page."

"I'd like for you to meet some of the members of our church. This is Mrs. Frost, Miss Sabina and Mr. Frost. Mr. Page, his <u>sister</u>, Mrs. Page."

"How do you do?"

"How do you do?"

As they went down the steps they could hear the minister saying effusively, "So happy to have you. Will you be here some time? Come whenever you can. Delighted to see you. What was that you said about the 'two little leaflets'? That's very good. Good-morning, *good*-morning."

When they were in the car Mrs. Frost looked back over her shoulder. "A fine-looking man. Very fine-looking. I wonder what he is doing in Frost Haven."

"I am amazed, my dear, that you didn't ask him," said her husband.

"He looks as if he might not tell you if you did ask," Sabina remarked and her father nodded. "You are quite right, Sabina. Nevertheless, *I* wonder, too."

And Sabina thought, So do I.

He wasn't the British Ambassador, but he looked as if he could be.

The June afternoon seemed like any other, and Clarissa's homecoming no different from all the others. She had come and gone so many times, always with a flourish as if it were an event; and yet when she alighted from the car in which her Atlanta friends had brought her, Sabina stood by a window watching, thinking, Is this going on forever? Some day there will be a last time. You'd think that some day she would bring home a husband, and babies. I hope she has six babies, all crying at once and waiting to be fed. I'm tired of her coming in like a conquering hero. Perhaps this will be the last time—

The friends drove off, the colored boy brought in her bags and her father kept his arm about her. "Ah, Claire, it is so nice to have you home again. We've been expecting you since morning—"

"I know, but the Moultons were at the station when I got into Atlanta and they insisted on my staying to dinner with them. Where is everybody, mother, Sabina?"

"Your mother hasn't finished dressing, but Sabina is around; she was here only a moment ago. Sabina—here's Claire—"

Yes, I know, thought Sabina, how could I help but know? But there's no use going in until I have to.

"I'll be there in a moment, Father," she called. "How are you, Clarissa?"

"I'm fine. What are you doing? Why don't you come on down?"

"I can't make my hair look right."

"Oh, your hair is always beautiful, Sabina. Do hurry, I'm dying for a drink."

But even when you were not with Claire, you couldn't get away from her. You always felt as if she was in the exact center of the house, or as if the center of the house was wherever she happened to be. Her intense voice came floating upstairs. "Father, I'm not criticizing, you know I'm not, I love this place, but it's always such a shock to come back to it. It seems so dark and cold and lifeless, like the inside of an old church. The paneling is nice, your old furniture is handsome, but it looks as if you had already sold it to the Daughters of the Confederacy for a museum. Why don't you let me do it over? Paint the woodwork ivory, put up some gay chintzes; color, that's what you need, light and color. I could just go mad over color—it's the most entrancing study in the world, and I just have to have it about me. Magenta and lemon, wine and French blue, cerise and apple green—"

"Sit down, Claire," laughed her father, "and un-lax. You needn't bring your job home with you. By the way, how is it?"

"Fine. Fine. How are the peaches?"

"Suppose we get that drink you mentioned. Where's the boy?" He went into the kitchen calling, "Grover? Grover Cleveland Smith, come here, you black ape, get some ice and crush it fine, I don't want a lump in it. Wait a minute, get me some mint from the garden first, break it off about eight inches from the top."

"Yassuh. For how many, suh?"

"Two. Mrs. Frost and Miss Sabina won't have any."

"Three, Mr. Frost."

There was her father's laughter again. "All right, you black rascal, make it three."

Sabina was brushing her hair when her mother came in, sat on the edge of a chair and began whispering, "You see, she wasn't in the house five minutes before she had him drinking. You see what she does to him."

Sabina was recalling her father's laughter. "Yes, I see. It doesn't seem like the same house."

Her mother sniffed. "It isn't. It isn't my home any longer. She takes it over."

"Oh, Mother, please; she doesn't mean to, it's just her way." Sabina shrugged. "After all, it's father's house and Claire is his daughter. I suppose we'll have to go down."

"Drinking!" Mrs. Frost said it so violently that her nose glasses were agitated. "Drinking in my house on Sunday afternoon! I shan't go down until they finish."

"If you don't she'll come up here, bringing it with her."

"If she has to drink, why can't she do it in her own room where nobody could see her? I'm ashamed for the servants to see her."

"Oh, Mother, she's not a dipsomaniac. Are you ready to go?"

As they walked slowly down the worn steps of the old mahogany stairway, Sabina noticed that her mother was wearing her oldest, most faded cotton frock, intended, probably, as a subtle rebuke to Clarissa. And strangely enough, she herself had done exactly the same thing.

But if Claire noticed, she ignored the reproach. "Oh, hello, darlings, how sweet you look, as clean and shiny as angels! I'm simply filthy. How are you?

"Hello, Clarissa," said Sabina, "It's nice seeing you again."

"Welcome home, dear, we're always so happy to have you. We expected you this morning; in fact, we waited for you so long that we were late for church."

Clarissa took up her glass off the hall table. "Church? Mother, you are simply priceless. Do you know I had heard that people still went to church in the remote rural districts, but it scarcely seemed plausible."

"Claire," laughed her father, "you are just trying to show off."

"No, Father, I really did hear it, I assure you I did."

She took off her hat that had a band of printed silk to match her dress and threw it on the sofa. The silk outlined just enough of her supple body to suggest the enormous vitality it concealed; her short, loose curls were moulded to her head and the sunlight gleamed brilliantly on them. But she did not sit down, there was a new restlessness in her face and she walked about peering at the titles of new books.

"How was your trip, dear?"

"Oh, fine. Fine, thank you."

There was a silence, her father was watching every move she made and waiting for her words.

"You had a lovely day for it," said Mrs. Frost, "though

it rained here early this morning. Was it raining when you left New York?"

"No, I don't think it was. There may have been a slight drizzle." She turned then with a slight laugh and said, "Well, we have asked after everyone's health and we have discussed the weather. Father says Lila May has a new baby, she has one every time I come home; perhaps I had better stop coming. Isn't there any other news?"

"News?" said Mrs. Frost. "No, I can't think of any. Miss Lucy Taylor's mother has had a stroke."

And there was a strange man at church this morning, thought Sabina, a most arresting strange man, but I would never tell you that. You'd take to going to church in these "remote, rural districts."

"Hasn't Sabina any new admirers?" Claire was turning the pages of a 1788 edition of *Evelina* as carelessly as if it were a book of the month.

"We don't allow Sabina to receive the attentions of the local young men," said Mrs. Frost. "And of course we can't receive strangers in our home; we don't know anything about them."

Clarissa laughed. "Gee, kid, that's tough! I'll have to take you back to New York with me."

"Well, don't take her to the Bowery with you." But Ellison Frost smiled as if he had enjoyed hearing unladylike words. He took the last sip from his glass and put it on the tray. "Finished, Claire?"

"No, I've scarcely started. It's much too nice to hurry." She moved about the room carelessly as though she were accustomed to having everyone wait for her words. Sabina felt as if she were being pushed back into the wall, they were talking about her as if she were not in the room. But what could she say that would interest Claire? Should she tell her that she was invited to attend a bridge luncheon at Seven Pines, that she had recently become convinced that Bacon did not write Shakespeare and that neither did the seventeenth Earl of Oxford? Should she say to Claire, There is a lovely spot down by the pond on Father's Hilltown orchard where white lilies grow and the birds come to drink in the evening?

But Claire's voice broke through urgently, "Why are you all so quiet? It's so quiet here, like another world. Whenever I come back to Frost Haven it's as if time had stopped and nothing had happened since I went away—except Lila May's babies. I am surprised that the air of this house hasn't made her sterile. It is always the same, with a few more shingles gone from the roof, same old rugs, vases, same massive dull furniture. And you sit there as if you, too, were museum pieces. You seem to be just marking time."

Mrs. Frost sat still but her face had the look of one who has left the room. "You are tired, dear, and nervous. You need a rest."

"Perhaps, my dear," said her father, "it isn't we who are marking time, but time who is marking us."

It was the drinks, of course, that made them talk like that, thought Sabina; nevertheless, a little shudder passed over her shoulders and was lost in the faded rosewood chair. Where was the gaiety she had heard just a few minutes before?

"Would you like a bath, Clarissa?" she asked.

"Yes, yes, I'd love a bath."

"I'll ask Grover to make a fire in the coil heater."

"Oh, I had forgotten you had to do that. I'll unpack while it's heating."

Sabina could hear the tinkle of the ice as Claire took the glass with her up the steps.

Yes, Clarissa was back home again, but she was not the same. Sabina's mind said over and over, "Not the same, not the same." The sunlight lay in a glittering pool on the old Aubusson rug as it lay every bright summer afternoon at five o'clock; but Clarissa was different. How did a person become different?

Her mother and father went out into the garden and Sabina stood looking at the room trying to see in it what Clarissa had seen. She recalled that when she had returned to the house after months of college and subsequent visits, it had struck her forcibly, but living continuously in a place over a long period made one unable to see it.

It was old, yes, for her great-grandfather had built it just before the Civil War and there had scarcely been any money since then to make improvements. When her father infrequently made large profits on peaches, there was a trip to New York or Cuba for the entire family, then former debts were paid and if any money remained it went into more trees, new machines, bigger orchards.

Sometimes the house was painted on the outside (to preserve it) but nothing was ever done to the interior. The great high-ceilinged rooms spread out over the hill-top, and there was no way of getting them warm in winter except by large open fires where oak and hickory wood were burned. The library was paneled in native walnut and was therefore dark; even the heavy red velvet curtains only made it seem more pompous and less cheer-

ful. In the massive secretary were the big leather-bound
books that had belonged to its original owner: Shakespeare, Byron, a dictionary, Gibbon, Macaulay, Thack-
eray, Josephus, Plutarch, the Bible, *Crown Jewels*, Boswell, some textbooks of the seventies, her father's law
books. There was a smaller walnut secretary on the
opposite side of the room where Ellison Frost kept his
important papers and the letters that had remained unanswered over a long period of years. The late afternoon
sun, coming dimly through the stained-glass windows,
made a feeble glow on the yellowing envelopes, the rusty
pens and the moth-eaten felt which lined the desk panel.
A long table with carved legs hid the worn spots in an
Oriental rug and there were two chairs, both straight,
with graceful fiddle backs. Yes, it was a room in which
life had stopped.

Sabina went slowly into the dining room where the
Hepplewhite chairs were pushed back against the wall;
it was perhaps a coincidence that their seats came at
exactly the point where the wainscoting ended, and
against their lacy backs was the original wallpaper as
fresh as on the day it was shipped from England. Those
ships, of a deep rich blue, had sailed serenely on the walls
for some eighty years and not one of them had ever
moved outside its enclosing rose circles, or been ruffled
by a wind. The heavy silver tea service (which Clarissa
had said was Sheffield plate), the soup tureens, water
pitchers and candlesticks seemed to bulge out over the
break-front sideboard; and a thin linen damask dinner
cloth obscured the oval table. The dining room looked as
it always had, but perhaps that was because Clarissa had
not been in this room since her return. And surely she

would have admired the crystal chandelier which had been expected to fall every day for the past twenty years. Sabina looked at it steadily, as if by looking she could cause it to fall—she realized suddenly that for a long time she had been wanting it to, she could not explain why. Perhaps it would put an end to something. She went up to it and touched one of the low shining branches, wondering why she considered it symbolic, and what it was that she wanted to end. It could not be considered a sword of Damocles threatening death, its fall could hurt no one; and yet it had a perverse significance for her, she wanted it to fall because it would mean the end of something.

She could hear the water for Clarissa's bath running upstairs; and her father and mother would be coming in soon. Quickly she went into the living room where the tall grandfather's clock was chiming the quarter hour. Instead of seeing the handcarved mantelpiece she seemed instead to see Claire standing before it, smart, assured, sophisticated, as alien to the old carved love seat as she was to the swan's-neck rocking chair. Even the grand piano that stood open, filling the southeastern corner of the room, had no relation to Claire for she gave no indication of ever remaining still long enough to take notice of music. Claire would be at home in a hunting lodge, or in an extremely modern apartment—a place where there was physical activity, or brilliant surfaces, where no one ever sat thoughtful or quiet, drinking in the past and absorbing it until it became a poison, inducing lethargy and negation. Small wonder that it irritated Claire; it was not her proper background, but it was Sabina's. Let Claire be Clarissa Frost of Boston and New York. She,

Sabina, was Miss Frost of Frost Haven—except when Clarissa was at home. And then she was nothing.

The strange man at church would see Claire, and then he would never look at Sabina again. Rebelliously she went to the great gold-framed mirror that hung in the hall and stood before it. She was lovely (Sabina is such a lovely person, so many people had said it); her blue-gray eyes looked contemplatively back at her between heavy black lashes, her features were delicate, her skin ivory. Soft and dark was the hair that fell in a loose roll almost to her shoulders. She was as beautiful as Lady Christabel, or La Belle Dame Sans Merci—or the Lady of Shalott who sat looking in a mirror watching life go by.

Perhaps it was true, as Claire had said, that nothing ever happened in Frost Haven. If by that she meant violent physical action, yes. But it seemed to Sabina that there was as much activity involved in reading Montaigne's *Essays*, or discovering what went on in a well-bred person's mind as there was in a drunkard's hurling a chair, a rider's taking a hurdle, or an officer's capturing a gangster.

Clarissa was the brightness of noonday, but she, Sabina, was the morning. Morning becomes Sabina—at twenty-six. Was it true that she was twenty-six, with that childish face and untouched body? Life should have written something on it, somewhere. Dejectedly she wandered out into the garden, wishing that Claire had remained in New York. Claire made her think about things that were best left unthought, made her feel unbearably inferior one moment and disproportionately, illogically superior the next. Claire left no stone, not even Sabina, unturned.

Mrs. Frost said that she was quite tired after supper

and went to her room early. So did Sabina. They did not admit to each other or even to themselves that they did not want to talk to Claire, and likewise they did not want to hear Claire talk. Mrs. Frost resented what she considered her husband's blind fondness for the girl, his partiality and indulgence. Sabina was unable to endure being placed in a secondary position. Claire knew such new and interesting things, there was about her the aura of the metropolis; she had stories of the smart and sophisticated literary circles (what George Jean Nathan had said when he damned a new play, or Henry Mencken's last word on the "Bible belt"); she described studios in Greenwich Village where furniture was made from goods boxes and painted to resemble—almost anything, where women made batik and everyone drank home-brew. She knew Russians, Poles, Scandinavians, Peruvians, men who wore flowing ties and berets, women whose hair was cut short in Dutch boy "bobs," who wore smocks, smoked incessantly and told dirty stories. These people were all very intense about something, said Claire—about art, about the ignorance and Philistinism of America, about how ridiculous Prohibition was, and the censorship of realistic books.

Claire did not live among those intense and almost unexceptionally impoverished artists (they were frequently dirty, too, she said), but she knew them, knew what Bolshevism was, and laughed about "parlor pinks." New York, Claire had said at supper, was the crossroads of the world: the richest rode in their limousines over roads made and cleaned by the poorest and the intellectuals wrote books about them. One's standing as an artist depended upon the layer of society one portrayed and

worked on a descending scale: the wealthy were tolerated only if they supported art (and artists), the
bourgeoisie were utterly hopeless, but the poor, the lower
classes would be the future source of all the art and all
the brains, as they were now the only people worthy of
being portrayed in oils, or in books.

Sabina had listened to her, mute and antagonistic, feeling herself immeasurably "provincial" (one of Claire's
new words), because her only contact with that world
was through the pages of *The Dial* and *The American
Mercury*. She had frequently puzzled over the queer
drawings in the former magazine, the seemingly sloppy
and untutored lines portraying sprawling fat nude
women, old shapeless men, indistinguishable wood cuts.
She had said to herself, This is art, modern art, I must
like it—and she had thought it was terrible.

Claire had looked at her at supper, over the baked
ham, Irish potato salad, and iced tea; had answered her
questions about cubism, impressionism and the pointil-
listes. Then Mrs. Frost had said firmly, "Claire, I'm not
criticizing, but after all I studied art at the Female College, I copied the masters. And all these 'isms' you speak
of are just a fad. They are not art but voluptuous, obscene, sordid things, or just abstract lines. Art must be
beautiful."

"Perhaps they are," her husband interrupted, "beautiful—but not pretty."

"At least," said Claire, "they are stimulating, they
make you think."

"Make you think about what!" snorted Mrs. Frost.

"Mother, if you mean sex, everybody has always
thought about sex and now they admit it. After all,

what is more important? Where should we be without it?"

It was only a short while later that Mrs. Frost had become very tired. Her strength had held out until she finished her dessert, then she went upstairs. Sabina had to go up to look for a book she had promised someone, and Ellison Frost and Claire went out on the veranda.

A little breeze from the north stirred down its length and there was the clean, sharp fragrance of tea-olive in bloom. Claire lighted a cigarette and stood by the steps that led down to the boxwood-lined walk.

"It's so quiet," she said; and her father answered, "Yes, no sound but the crickets, and just faintly the croaking of the frogs in the pond beyond the hill. Do you hear them?"

"I think so."

"Why don't you sit down, Claire? Do you mind if I do?"

"Of course not." She answered his last question first, then returned to the preceding one. "I don't know, it's so strange seeing trees and grass and rocks again. In New York you forget that they exist."

"Oh, yes, New York," said Ellison Frost vaguely. "It's unnatural, an anomaly. I can't understand why anyone lives there."

"You are just a born rustic," laughed Claire.

"Bucolic."

"Yes." Claire went on, "You're an anachronism, this whole place is, mother, Sabina—"

"You said that this afternoon."

"But it isn't fair to Sabina," Claire contended. "She doesn't seem to know what life is all about; has nobody ever told her? She can't just sleep her life away; this isn't the Middle Ages. I feel sorry for her."

"Sorry for her, eh?" said Ellison Frost quickly. "I don't think she will let you do that. Sabina doesn't want to be pitied. She'd rather be blamed," he finished with a smile.

"Nice epigram," said Claire laughing. "I like to talk with you."

"Either you are prejudiced, or you are pulling my leg. What's up?"

"Up? Nothing. You are a suspicious old man."

"You haven't told me what brought you home this time."

"You can guess, can't you? The business folded up and I sold it."

"At a nice profit, I'm sure."

"Yes—for the woman who bought it."

"Claire, really—" Ellison Frost looked away over the dark hills. They were softly curved and graceful, quiescent in the moonlight. And as he looked they took on a form that was familiar to him, the form of a giant woman with an arm flung there, breasts rising higher, then her great thighs, and the long stretch of her mighty limbs; it was a woman of the earth resting from her work and waiting, waiting not impatiently for the man who would come and take her. She was slumbrous, slow, yet smouldering; and certain, quite certain that eventually the man would come.

"Are you angry, father?"

"Angry? About what?"

"The money."

"Oh, the money. Why should anyone be angry when

money has been lost? It is gone, perhaps it can be recovered, perhaps not. You see, Claire, things have been rather bad here for the last few years. When the crop's a failure for several successive seasons, it's enough to ruin a man. Then I'm not quite sure about that overseer I've got, I don't trust him."

"I'm frightfully sorry, Father, I didn't know. But I still have all the money I got from mother's people. I haven't touched that, and I can pay you back."

"You keep it. You may need it some day." As hills they were beautiful and mysterious, as peach orchards they were a snare and a delusion; the woman was a harlot, that's what she was, a harlot waiting to lead men to their destruction. Bah! Such melodrama! "Do you see a light in that cabin far over to the right? That's where Cummings lives; I'll bet my bottom dollar the whole family is sitting on the front porch barefooted. Po-whites. Well," he brought himself up sharply, "so you've sold the interior-decorating shop. And now what is next?"

Claire lighted another cigarette, her rocking chair moved silently. "If I told you, you probably wouldn't approve."

"If I didn't approve, you'd go right ahead as you always do," he countered.

"Yes."

"When I tell Sabina not to do a thing, she doesn't do it."

"No guts," said Claire softly; and her father repeated smiling, "No guts."

"Wouldn't it be awful," Claire asked, "if either of us was like the other? Aren't you glad we offer variety?"

"Sometimes I get the strangest idea that you are both

part of the same person—perhaps you are, both of you are parts of me. I want to put you in a basket, shake you up together and take out one complete person. Sabina lacks certain qualities you have, and you, miss, would do much better to have some of hers. I don't mean that I want a perfect reproduction of myself, God forbid, or that I think I am an admirable person—I know my own deficiencies only too well. But I wish I could make you and Sabina over again, I'd combine you—"

"Siamese twins, I suppose," jeered Claire.

"No. One person."

"What an idea! You are the queerest father—do you ever talk this way before mother and Sabina?"

"Lord, no—"

"Why not?"

"You know well enough."

"Yes, you are afraid you'll shock their delicate sensibilities. Whom *do* you talk to?"

"You, when you are here. I keep fairly busy with those things"—Ellison Frost waved a disdainful hand at the orchards—"the rest of the time I'm afraid I'm like the darky who said, 'I just sets and thinks, but mostly I just sets.' "

"No, I don't believe that. You've been thinking, I suspect, more than you've been setting. Is it about Sabina?"

"Sabina? Oh, she'll get through all right—if it isn't too late. I find that the Lord generally gives us everything we want—after we have ceased to want it."

"But how do you expect Sabina to get married? She never meets anyone here."

Ellison rose and went to the edge of the porch to knock the ashes from his pipe. "She isn't ready for that yet. She may think she wants the status of a married woman, but marriage itself, with its physical indignities would appall her; there's no telling what it would do to her. She'll meet someone some time—what else do you think churches are for?"

"Oh, church—really now, Father—"

"Well," he contended, "there was a very fine-looking man there today, a stranger from the North."

"Yes?" said Claire.

"A man by the name of Page, Barrett Page. I haven't yet been able to decide what he is doing here."

"Why are you looking at me?" cried Claire. "Am I supposed to know him?"

"Do you?"

"Really, Father! There is a strange man at church in Frost Haven and your suspicious mind gets to work. Very subtly, oh, very subtly you work the conversation around to the point where you ask *me* if I know him. Do the men I know generally attend church? And how many strange men from the North do you think there are roaming the United States?"

"Now don't protest too much. I have eyes, you know, and ears, and I was once a lawyer. Here is my case: always before when you've come home there have been flowers, telegrams and letters waiting for you, there have been long-distance calls. Today there have been none of these things except a few letters—and you've been restless, nervous. So naturally—"

Claire laughed and put out her cigarette. "So naturally you put one and one together and made seven out of it. Listen to the frogs, you can hear them quite distinctly now."

Her father was looking straight at her. "You don't by any chance know this Mr. Page, do you, Claire? Mr. Barrett Page?"

"No, Father, of course not."

"Very well, I only wondered."

There was a moment's silence, then Claire spoke, "What were we talking about before we got off on that subject?"

"I think I shall ask him to come out for a drink," said Ellison Frost.

"Ask whom?"

"Mr. Page. He looked at Sabina with a great deal of interest."

"Oh. Yes, do, ask him by all means. It's a bit cool out here, don't you think?"

"I find it very pleasant," said her father.

The light in the overseer's house went out and the shrillings of the crickets were louder than ever. A bold and impudent moon rode the soft clouds across the sky.

"Do you know that you are a much nicer girl when you're alone with me," said Ellison Frost, "than you are when Janie Lee and Sabina are around? You seem to play up before them, try to show off—"

"Yes, they make me sound much more interesting than I really am."

"The trouble with you is, you haven't the courage of your fictions."

"The trouble with you is," retorted Claire, "you had rather make phrases than a living."

"Claire!" he said sharply.

"Oh, Father, I didn't mean it, I was just making a phrase myself—"

"It's true," he said unhappily, "it's true."

"It isn't, Father," cried Claire passionately. "Oh, dear, let's start all over, shall we?"

"Of course."

She pulled her chair close to his and began, "Once upon a time there was a little girl named Clarissa. She had brown eyes, red hair, lots of freckles and the kindest, gentlest father in all the world."

"A bedtime story!" exclaimed Ellison Frost. "I had no idea it was so late."

"The trouble with you is," grumbled Claire, "you are too understanding. It simply isn't being done."

He was looking out over the hills again, wondering what lay beyond the waiting woman, and if any man ever got beyond her reach. Between him and the hills now were two immediate problems: the orchards (exemplifying his financial troubles and the difficulties with Cummings), and Claire who had, he believed, lied to him for the first time in her life—and about a man, Barrett Page. A cold and intense anger shook him, welling up from a general dissatisfaction with life and centralizing in his own inability to conquer it.

CHAPTER IV

Sometimes when Sabina was walking she had the disturbing sensation that she was not walking in a straight line down the center of the street but was weaving from side to side like a drunkard. And frequently there was another equally annoying sensation that she was lifting up her feet, putting them down again and yet not advancing —it was the kind of thing that happens in dreams, when one is trying to get away from something, or trying vainly to reach something else. When she had first noticed it she had called it "locomotor ataxia" or "auto intoxication" because she liked the sound of the phrases, but once it became so pronounced that she consulted the family physician about it. "I'm afraid, Miss Sabina," he had said, laughing, "that you don't know a good case of biliousness when you see it. Calomel, Miss Sabina, and more exercise."

She had put the doctor down as a fool, an old-fashioned pill-dispenser, but she had taken the calomel and promptly forgotten to notice whether she walked better or not.

In front of the shop windows downtown she knew that she walked well enough for she was always glancing into them surreptitiously to see how she looked. She scarcely ever knew what anyone else was wearing, and frequently she did not see people she passed because she was so intent on her own appearance. She would be seeing her own pale cheeks and geranium-pink mouth in the window glasses, or trying to smooth out the frown over her eyes induced by the bright sunlight. She would never touch her garments on the streets even though the organdie bows on her gingham dress needed adjusting; she thought it better for them to stay as they were. After all, she was Sabina Frost, and she believed that other women observing a bow that was askance would think the angle premeditated and would conclude that it was a new fashion.

The town, that is the business section, inspired in Sabina her most exalted moments of superiority and egoistic inflation. At home she might be the victim of her father's unspoken criticism and her mother's sententious platitudes, at home she might suffer from comparison with Claire (whether Claire was absent or present), but on the streets of Frost Haven she was not only Ellison Frost's daughter, she was Sabina Frost, cultured, lovely, accomplished. She was Sabina Frost who went annually to New York or the West Indies, who read only the deepest and most "high-brow" magazines, and whom nobody really understood. Women whose minds were on the price of lard or coffee, whose thoughts centered on proper vitamins for their children at school were incapa-

ble of understanding anyone who lived completely in the
realm of mentality. Sometimes after she had passed shop-
pers on the street she would think, Why, that girl was in
my class at high school; I should have spoken to her more
cordially. But at the time she had faced her, the girl had
been only someone she knew vaguely and was unable to
identify; at any event, no one who should interrupt Sabina's thoughts of herself.

Walking home at dusk she would pass such people
pushing their babies in prams, or she would see their small
frame houses (in some instances the late sunlight would
cause a glare from a bright tin roof), and she would wonder how people could live like that. There would be a
light in the kitchen where a woman was preparing supper, the heavy odor of fried food would permeate the
cool evening air, and Sabina would think, How incredibly sordid! How can they be content to be shut up in
those small rooms, to eat, go to bed, sleep and raise babies?
Such little lives—little people. It sounded like the title for
a book.

Rarely, only rarely, a wave of humiliation and jealousy
would engulf her; in a moment of panic, self-abasement,
uncertainty could seize her. She saw herself not as a superior, cerebral person moving on a higher plane, but as
one who was shut out from the things other people had,
utterly alone, utterly useless, fortifying herself with sub-
terfuges. These moments passed as quickly as they came
and she put them down as unworthy of her, as a nun,
looking in upon a domestic scene might question briefly
the wisdom of her renunciation, then rise above the temp-
tation of the flesh.

The only analogy to those thoughts was an experience,

perhaps even briefer, that had befallen her one evening. She had come in late and walked up on the porch where Claire, her father and Mrs. Frost were sitting talking in the darkness. They had seemed so complete, a unit in themselves, and as individuals absolute strangers to her. It had been almost like walking into a strange house and she had looked at them, wondering what they had to do with her. Her thoughts had previously been so far away and she was now suddenly thrust into their midst, into an intimacy she did not want. She had gone to her room immediately and sat by the window looking out into the darkness. That moment when she had come upon them had been like a blinding flash of light, as if a shutter had been raised in a room that was perpetually dark. She had felt that for just an instant the veil which ordinarily obscured things had been lifted so that she saw them with a terrible clarity—and what she had seen had been chiefly her own alienism, her cruel loneliness. Loneliness, she knew, was the penalty of being an artist, but in moments such as these she knew also that she was not and never could be an artist.

Now that Claire was at home again, there was less time to think. Claire wanted to be doing something, going somewhere every hour of the day; she accepted invitations which ordinarily she would have scorned and returned from them saying, "Wasn't it terrible? Honestly, I don't see why people like that try to entertain; their houses aren't spacious enough for so many people; you are jammed right up against everybody else; the hostess has to borrow her neighbors' dishes and silver; and the food! Sabina, what kind of salad *was* that? The sandwiches must have been made the day before and kept

in a wet towel. And did you see the pictures on the wall!
Honestly—"

But most of all Claire wanted to ride, and although
the horses were generally needed in the orchards and
Sabina hated to ride with Claire, who was much the better horsewoman, there came an afternoon about a fort-
night after Claire's return when the last of the Hileys had
been shipped and the Georgia Belles had not yet "come
in." The horses were available; Ellison Frost insisted on
his daughters' going, and at five o'clock the animals were
brought up from the stables by Grover.

"Hits gwi rain, Miss Claire, sho's Christmas," he predicted darkly, "y'all go get wet to the skin, and Miz
Frost, she raise cain if Miss Sabina git a drap on 'er."

"We won't go far," Claire assured him and they set
off down the graveled driveway.

"Clarissa, do you think we ought to go?" Sabina asked.

"Why not?" said Claire. "What if it does rain? It will
feel good after all that heat. And I'm sure it's better than
sitting at home with a book."

Sabina was not so sure of that; she had listened eagerly
to the darky's prophecy, hoping that the ride would be
postponed. She always hoped up to the final moment of
departure that something would happen to prevent her
doing the things she did not want to do, and something
usually did. But Claire was determined to go, and any
difficulty which arose only made the act more enjoyable.

There was the sharp downhill grade where the drive
met the main road; Sabina felt as she always did at this
point that she was going over the horse's head, but they
were safely in the road almost immediately and Claire
cried, "Let's ride to Halsey's Junction!"

"It's six miles, Clarissa! We'll be late for supper—"

"We can stop somewhere and get a hot-dog and coffee!"

"I hate hot-dogs," said Sabina.

"Did you ever eat one?"

"No. They're so vulgar."

"We'll get back in time for your supper, Aunt Matilda," laughed Claire. "Come on."

There was just enough dust on the road to make it soft, and the black clouds that were piling up made the air pleasantly cool. Soon Sabina could feel its sting upon her cheeks and the heady exhilaration of rhythmic motion. "I hate exercise," she grumbled; and Claire called, "What did you say, Sabina?"

"I said I detest exercise."

"That's because it makes you feel too good and you don't like that. You'd rather think you were sick."

"That's absurd, Clarissa."

"No, it's psychology. I suppose another reason you dislike exercise is that it lifts you out of yourself, keeps you from daydreaming so much."

"I never daydream," said Sabina coldly; "it's so—so shop-girlish, like waiting for a Prince Charming to come along and marry you."

"Well, don't we all?" asked Claire. "You're a prig, Sabina."

"A what?"

"A prig."

"I thought you said a pig."

"Oh, you'd never be anything so vulgar as that."

Sabina watched her sister's easy motion in the saddle and wondered if she looked as graceful. She wished, too, that Claire had not such a good disposition; she was critical, but that was the worst of it. She had withstood Sabina's reluctance to go riding, her demurring and grumbling; now she was enjoying tearing past the farmlands and woodland stretches. Perhaps Claire was only happy because she had got her way.

Sabina reflected that she had done all she could to spoil the ride for Claire; her efforts had been a failure and she might as well make the best of it. She touched her stirrup to the horse's flank and felt his long legs stretching out beneath her. They were nearing the railroad crossing but it was unnecessary to stop since the only trains came early in the morning and late at night. Sometimes there was a special peach train but not often, and they were too close now to stop. When they had crossed she thought she heard a whistle; turning to look back she saw a train curving around the bend only a quarter of a mile away. For some reason the sight did not unnerve her; she cared now only for reaching the junction before Claire did. Overhead there was a sudden ominous roll of thunder, it roared in long protracted blasts, then in short, crackling ones and streaks of lightning began to splinter through the dark upheaval.

They came to Whipple's orchards which stretched for almost two miles along the road and Sabina was still leading but she felt uncomfortable about it. Claire had a new horse that would not do his best until the whip was applied and Claire was only using the spurs.

Sabina held out against telling her as long as she could, then she called, "Your whip! Use the whip!"

"Thank you, Sabina."

In a few seconds Claire was even with her but still

not ahead. The thunder rolled and crackled, the sky was split with venomous thrusts of lightning and the horses began to be affected by the sulphurous atmosphere; they plunged and snorted but Claire held the reins more tightly and Sabina did the same. The wind was springing up, a definite forecast of either rain or a sandstorm, but the junction was still two miles away. Sabina tried to call to Claire but her voice was drowned in a heavier roll of thunder than any which had preceded it. Her shirt, wet with perspiration, billowed out from her body. They passed wagons rushing homeward and cars came toward them with their lights making feeble round glows. A small farmhouse was left behind, a negro cabin, a country school; then the first great drops of rain spattered in the road. There was a small crossroads store with no one standing outside it, and now the junction was in sight. Claire touched her horse with the whip; the loose curls crept down beneath her hat; and she leaned forward, intent and intense.

The air was not so sultry now for the few drops of rain on the dusty road had brought a smell of freshness. Sabina was panting; she knew she was going to have pneumonia as a result of this ride, or one of them would run into somebody in the darkness, or one of the horses was going to stumble—but she had no intention of letting Claire win. She dug the stirrup into Jerry's flank and he nosed up ahead of Claire just as they pounded past the small settlement. But then he did not stop.

Claire's words came faintly, "We did it! That was fine, Sabina. Where are you going?"

She pulled so hard on the reins that her horse jerked his head angrily. If she pulled any harder he would rear and throw her. Pneumonia nothing! she thought. She was not going to be allowed to die in bed; she was going to be killed by this horse, and it was all Claire's fault. The wind was blowing the rain in mighty gusts; it beat upon her hat, her shoulders, her hands. She had now gone more than a mile past the junction; Jerry was pulling first to the right then to the left as if he might bolt at any moment, leave the road and plunge across the fields in either direction. Where was Claire? Perhaps she thought that if she came up from behind, Jerry might think the race was still on and run faster than ever.

Then there was a glare from the lights of an approaching car and Sabina was sure this was the end. Jerry was certain to rear and plunge—from sheer weakness her grip lessened; she was almost fainting with fright. The car came closer and she felt herself swaying in the saddle but it seemed to her that the horse was not going quite so fast. The lights came closer; she put one hand over her eyes and with the other pulled the horse over to the right side of the road. There was a blinding flash; liquid, opaque strips of light ran vertically before her eyes, and then the car was past. Her head drooped and the reins almost fell from her hands. Jerry had come to a full stop. The car had halted and was backing up, perhaps it was one of her father's friends though it seemed impossible that anyone could have recognized her in the heavy downpour. There was a man's voice, "Can I help you?" and someone was getting out of the car.

She said, "Please—" and found that her teeth were chattering. The reins were taken out of her hands and she was lifted out of the saddle but when she tried to stand her knees buckled under her; she was shaking all over. The man jerked her up sharply and said, "Here, this won't do!"

If there were only some place to sit down! She saw the running board of the car and stumbled toward it. "I'm all right," she said weakly.

"The hell you are!" the man said roughly. He was looking about for a tree or a post to which he could tie the reins. "Get inside the car out of the rain. Can you stand up for just a moment?"

"I'm all right," she repeated; "and besides, I think I hear Clarissa coming."

"Clarissa?"

"My sister. She'll be here in just a moment. Thank you very much, Mr.—"

"Page," said the man. "Here, you get inside, and when your sister comes, she can hold this animal while I give you a drink. Do you live in Frost Haven?"

"Yes, I'm Sabina Frost. I think I met you at church. But I don't want a drink, thank you."

"You are going to have it just the same. And you're going to get inside that car if I have to put you in."

"No," said Sabina. "I'm too wet, I'd ruin your car, I'm simply dripping." Page! Mr. Barrett Page *would* have to see her in a state of collapse looking like a drowned rat! She hoped Claire looked as bad.

"Sabina," Claire called, "is that you? Are you all right? What happened?"

"Nothing happened—except I suppose Jerry ran away." Sabina wanted to cry; she wanted never to see a horse again. She would phone her father to come get her. "And the more I tried to stop him, the faster he went. Oh, Clarissa, this is Mr. Page. Mr. Page, my sister, Miss Frost."

"How do you do, Mr. Page."

"How do you do, Miss Frost. I came along and saw this child—"

"She's not a child," said Claire dismounting and coming over to the car; "she's old enough to be able to manage a horse. You're not hurt, are you, Sabina?"

"No," she said coldly, thinking that it was just like Claire to pretend that she, Sabina, had made an episode out of nothing.

The rain was beating down in torrents but Claire seemed not to know it. She stood holding her horse's bridle and Mr. Page stood holding Jerry's. Sabina sat on the running board letting the rain course down her neck, deriving a sort of perverse pleasure from it as it soaked into her breeches and crept inside her boots down her legs. She would certainly have pneumonia.

"Well, what are you waiting for? Come on, let's go. It was nice of you to stop, Mr. Page. Thank you very much."

"I'm not going," said Sabina. "I'm going to phone father to come get me. I wouldn't get on Jerry again for all the horses in the world."

"I really think, Miss Frost," said Mr. Page to Claire, "that the child is right; she's had a nervous shock, and she's wet to the skin."

"Nonsense," said Claire. "Sabina, if you don't get back on Jerry right now and ride him home you'll get such a complex that you'll never get over it as long as you live." Claire wasn't bright and amusing now, she was angry, and Sabina grinned.

"I'd just as soon have a complex," she said, "as what I've got now."

There was no amusement on Mr. Page's lean face as he turned to Claire. "She sounds like an *enfant terrible*, Miss Frost. But I have an idea. You drive my car and take your sister home. I'll bring the horses."

"You'll bring the horses? How?"

"Ride one and lead the other. Can you drive on these slick roads?"

"Of course I can. But Sabina isn't hurt, there's no earthly reason—"

"I insist," said Mr. Page.

Sabina sneezed, and Claire said, "Oh, very well. Get in, Sabina."

"Thank you, Mr. Page," Sabina called. "Do you know where we live?"

"No."

"Just before you get to town there's a big peach orchard, and on the left overlooking it, an old dilapidated—"

"Museum," finished Claire. "You can't miss it." She turned the key, adjusted the gear and found the starter immediately. Sabina sighed; Claire was so clever about things, she could get into a strange car and start it without having to ask what this was and where that was. She wasn't afraid to be driving home in the rain over slick roads. She waved casually to their knight errant and drove off without grinding the gears or choking the motor.

Sabina began to wonder if her horse had really run away or if she had only thought he was going to. Should she explain to Claire? No, it would sound too much like an apology and she had no intention of apologizing. Claire could be as angry as she liked—the ride had been her idea, not Sabina's.

The car went straight enough on the level stretches; they passed the junction, then Whipple's orchards; but then the hills began to loom and as they started up the first steep one the car edged towards a ditch on the left. Sabina wanted to catch the steering wheel and jerk it back the other way but Claire let it slide, then she pushed the accelerator down and for no reason at all the car straightened itself out. Damn, thought Sabina, Claire has all the luck. As they reached the top of the hill there was another car coming but Claire held to her side firmly and the two crawled past each other with a good two inches to spare.

Sabina sneezed again, and Claire asked, "Do you have to do that?"

"I suppose I could put my finger on my upper lip."

"Perhaps there is a coat of some kind back there you could put around you."

"No," said Sabina, "it was bad enough to take the man's car, without ruining his spare clothes besides. We've already made puddles on the floor."

"Fortunately it's upholstered in leather," said Claire. Sabina touched the seat, and sure enough it was. That explained its being so cold.

"This won't give you a cold, will it?" asked Claire.

"No." A cold! Sabina felt like the soldier in the *Incident of the French Camp* when his commander asked him if he was wounded. " 'Nay, I'm killed, Sire!' And his chief beside, Smiling the boy fell dead." A cold! The rain was beating in on her from the west but then she discovered the rolled strips of isinglass and with stiff fingers she managed to fasten it to the windshield.

The car was crawling sidewise up another hill; it almost stopped halfway to the top, but Claire put it in low gear. The wheels churned for a moment, the most sickening sound in the world for it meant you were stuck; then the slow progress uphill began. Sabina was afraid to breathe or sit back until they should reach the top; she was leaning forward on the edge of the seat as if she were helping push the car forward.

"Another half hour and these roads will be bad," said Claire.

"That's what I call a masterpiece of understatement," declared Sabina. "Probably Mr. Page was afraid he couldn't drive over them, and that's why he took the horses and let us have his car." She was doubly annoyed with the man, first for seeing her when she was not mistress of a situation and second for calling her an *enfant terrible*. Doubtless he thought she didn't know what an *enfant terrible* was.

"Well, there's gratitude for you," commented Claire. "I suppose you've decided now that you didn't need help."

"I didn't need his. He's not a gentleman."

"Oh! He's not a gentleman! Why do you say that? It seems to me he did all anyone could have done and a great deal more than was necessary. He was kindness itself—I assure you I thought he rather overdid it."

Sabina did not explain that she had decided he was not a gentleman because he was more obviously a man —big and lean and hard. He had lifted her out of the saddle with one arm, holding the reins with his other hand, and when she was unable momentarily to stand up, he had jerked her roughly up against him—with more liberty, she thought now resentfully, than a farmhand would have taken. No man had ever held her like that before, and she hoped none ever would again.

"So you didn't like your Prince Charming," declared Claire.

"I thought he was detestable," Sabina said flatly. "Probably just a damn Yankee."

"I thought he was rather nice, but then I have a weakness for big men, and for Yankees. Give me Yankees any time in preference to these lazy Southern men." Claire was smiling as if at some secret joke of her own, and Sabina was conscious of the familiar sensation of being left out of something. How did Claire know so much about men that she, Sabina, did not know? Claire had thought Mr. Page attractive, and no doubt she would be dressed and waiting for him when he came in with the horses.

Sabina rubbed her cold arms and legs, trying to stimulate circulation in them; her feet felt like dead fish packed in ice. She would get a hot bath (the water would be hot because Lila May was cooking supper), her mother would put her to bed, and probably rub some of that awful-smelling stuff on her chest. In the morning she would be dead, just in time for the weekly edition of the Frost Haven *Herald*.

The rain was thinner now; those heavy, blinding sheets of water had lightened, and Claire was making a sharp left-hand turn. "Where are we going?" Sabina demanded.

"We're home, Aunt Matilda, and aren't you surprised. If mother's idea was to make a Victorian lady out of you, she certainly succeeded. You swoon with fright, you have to be rescued, you are about as helpless an individual as I ever saw. Probably you had better stay in the hothouse after this. If you want to know, I'm utterly disgusted. Utterly. I thought you were like that because it was forced on you, but now I know better." Claire's eyes flashed as she pulled up in the backyard. "You like it. It relieves you of any responsibility; you want to be a parasite because you don't have to exert any effort to cling. Some day, my fine young lady, you may wake up and find you no longer have anything to cling to."

The lights on the back porch were on and Mrs. Frost came running out. "Sabina? Claire? What on earth happened? I've been worried to death! Where are the horses?"

Grover came up from the stables. "Where the horses, Miss Claire? I told y'all hit gwi rain—"

"Where's father?" demanded Claire. "The reception committee seems incomplete." She was slapping the seat of her breeches to get some of the water out of them.

"He's downtown in the car," answered Mrs. Frost. "Whose car is that? Did you have an accident?"

Sabina got out, slammed the car door behind her and ran up on the porch; she tried to slap the water out of her breeches as Claire had done. "Sabina, really!" said her mother. "I wouldn't do that before Grover. Go upstairs and get those things off. Wait a minute; come here, Sabina. Your cheeks are flushed; you've got a fever."

"I have not got a fever. I haven't got anything, it seems, except a perfectly wonderful sister." She was shaking with anger and Claire was gazing stupidly at her. "I'm tired of it, do you hear? I've stood all I can of Clarissa's superiority. She knows everything, she can do every- thing—"

"Well, bless my soul!" ejaculated Claire. "I didn't

know you had it in you! Go on, Sabina, don't stop—"

"Oh, what's the use?" said Sabina turning and going into the house. She was afraid she was going to cry and nothing would please Claire more. At the foot of the stairs she called, "And when Mr. Page comes you can have him with my compliments; I wouldn't touch him with a ten-foot pole!"

"That's mighty white of you, Sabina," came Claire's amused answer. Then there was Mrs. Frost's sharp voice, "Clarissa, what does all this mean? What did you say to the child? What is this about a Mr. Page? I wish you would tell me what happened."

"Nothing, Mother," Claire was answering wearily, "except that I tried to make Sabina come to life and she won't come. I'm going upstairs. When Mr. Page arrives with the horses you might thank him for the use of his car and tell him that Sabina isn't very grateful to him for coming to her rescue."

"Why, Clarissa! I don't know the man—"

" 'You will, Oscar, you will,' " said Claire.

Sabina turned on the water in the tub but she left the bathroom door open; she was torn between the desire to weep with self-pity and the equally strong desire to find out if Claire really had any intention of not seeing Mr. Page.

She peeled off her wet shirt slowly and reveled in the warmth of the steam on her cold body; but she listened intently for Claire's steps.

The more she struggled with her boots, the more stubbornly they refused to come off. She thought of getting into the tub with them on, but that would only postpone and aggravate the ordeal. She went to the head of the stairs to call Lila May, and then she heard voices. "Oh, do come in long enough to have a drink, Mr. Page, Mother will be so disappointed if you don't." It was Claire, of course, Claire saying, "She wants to thank you for your kindness to my sister."

Sabina stood for a moment unable to assort her emotions or clarify her thoughts. Then she went back into the bathroom and looked in the mirror. Yes, she had never looked handsomer, her face was flushed and glowing, her eyes smouldering. Quickly she turned off the water and put the wet shirt back on. It felt like the kiss of death, and it probably was, but even a worm (a bookworm, she amended hastily) turned sometimes. She went to her room and got out a dry handkerchief to sneeze into, paused long enough to put a drop of perfume on it, then she started downstairs. When she saw the man and the two women standing in the hall she wanted to turn back, but she forced herself to go on. Mr. Page looked bigger than ever, and he seemed surprised to see her. "Hello," he said. "How are you feeling?"

"I'm fine, thank you. Are you very wet?"

"Not as wet as I'm going to be," he laughed, "when I get that drink."

"Well, look who's here!" cried Claire. "I thought you'd gone to bed with a hot-water bottle."

"Don't be absurd, Clarissa," said Sabina.

Her mother had been gazing at her with horror, but had said nothing; now she went into the kitchen and beckoned to Sabina to follow. Sabina hesitated, "Do you want me, Mother?"

"Yes, come here." Mrs. Frost's stage whisper was sibilant. "What on earth has got into you, Sabina? Have you lost your mind?"

"No, Mother—"

"Where did you get that awful stuff?" She sniffed at the perfume. "You smell like a hussy. And the way those wet clothes cling to your body—Sabina, I never knew you to act like this before in your life. Do you want to have pneumonia?" She turned to the cook. "Lila May, go upstairs with Miss Sabina and help her get out of those things."

Sabina made a last stand. "But Claire has hers on, why can't I have a drink with them?"

Mrs. Frost went out of the kitchen toward the living room remarking, "I think you've lost your mind."

Lila May said, "Hurry up, Miss Sabina; I done had interruptions enough and supper's late already. I got to git back to my rolls."

Sabina's shoulders drooped as she walked slowly to the staircase; the brief fire that had animated her had died down and she was shivering again. It wasn't her mind that she had lost, she thought bitterly, it was something else; and whatever it was, it would be a long, long time before she found it again—if she ever did. As she went up the steps she was conscious of Claire's mocking eyes watching her from the living room. It seemed a thousand miles up those stairs. She felt like Henry IV crawling on his bare knees up the cathedral steps in the icy snow to acknowledge his fealty.

To Claire, Sabina's incipient, short-lived rebellion had been both amusing and pathetic. She could not understand how her sister plucked up courage to begin an insurrection, then lacked the stamina to carry it through. Sabina's reasons for undertaking it were obscure: she had said flatly that she detested Mr. Page; it was obviously not physical attraction for him that had drawn her downstairs. Could it have been jealousy of her, Claire, or had her brutal words to Sabina on their arrival home stung the girl into action?

Barrett had thought the incident little short of tragic. He stood holding his glass thoughtfully and wondering how a woman like Mrs. Frost could be so blind as not to foresee the results of her domination and more especially of her humiliating treatment of the girl. He finished his drink hastily as Mrs. Frost came into the room.

"Won't you sit down, Mr. Page?"

"No, thank you, I must be running along. Good-bye, Miss Frost, I hope you and your sister won't be ill."

"I want to apologize," said Mrs. Frost, "for Sabina's behavior; I don't know what got into her."

"I saw nothing which called for an apology," Barrett Page said coldly. "Good-bye, Mrs. Frost."

"Oh, your keys," said Claire following him to the door; "I think I left them outside."

Janie Lee Frost sat down in the living room and took up a missionary society pamphlet which she pretended to read. She was glad the man was gone, he had not treated her with the courtesy to which she was accustomed. He had actually seemed to disapprove of her rebuking Sabina!

Her bosom rose and fell unevenly but she kept her eyes fixed on the pamphlet. It was about China, and she looked at the pictures of native children at missionary schools without seeing them. There was an article some-where in the book on which she had to give a report at the next meeting, but she was unable to find it now. Her heart was pounding distressingly; she must see the doctor about it before very long. How could Sabina have done this to her? What had got into the girl to make her so defiant, so rebellious?

She took off her glasses and wiped her eyes. Sabina would never know how she had hurt her. After all the love and care that had been lavished upon the girl, how could she have done such a thing, such a cheap, common thing as put perfume on herself and come downstairs where that man was, in her wet riding clothes that showed every line of her figure, and then tell her mother that she refused to obey her and go back to her room?

Mrs. Frost turned the pages in the book while she tried to decide which of the two things had hurt her most, Sabina's defiance, or her coming downstairs in the first place. Both had been so unexpected, so totally unlike Sabina.

Tears dropped from her cheeks onto the book. Sabina had never given her any trouble about men; she had never wanted to go riding at night or to dances without a chaperon as other girls did. Sabina was a lady, and therefore totally devoid of any impulses which could lead to—to so many things. A lady was supposed to be feminine but not female. What had brought Sabina downstairs?

Janie Lee Frost rose from her chair and put the book down. She wished there was someone with whom she could discuss the problem, but it would have to be dealt with in her prayers. Mr. Frost would not understand. He had told her once that good women were the worst women in the world; they saw in the simplest, most innocent deeds acts of downright immorality. There was nothing so dirty, he had said, as the suspicious mind of a thoroughly good woman. Mr. Frost didn't mean those things, of course, but he did have queer ideas about some things. She pulled her dress down smoothly around her heavily corseted hips and went into the kitchen to see if supper was ready. She didn't feel as if she could eat a thing, she was so upset, but the steaming rice, the fried chicken smelled very good. Lila May was putting little moulds of tomato aspic on lettuce and pausing between each mould to look at the hot rolls in the oven.

Sabina had hurt her terribly. But perhaps she would be able to eat a little something after all. She would try.

CHAPTER V

ONE OF ELLISON FROST'S GREAT WEAKNESSES (AND HE admitted that he had many) was his enormous curiosity about people, about trivia, about life in all its aspects. However, it was his wife who condemned this characteristic as a weakness; Ellison Frost was rather proud of it. He called it "appreciating the importance of trifles" and knew that it gave color to what would otherwise have been a much duller existence. If a man's life was bound up in trifles, as everyone's was in Frost Haven, it behooved him to make the most of them. He knew the history and background of each one of his migratory packers, and no solitary tramp or beggar who came to his home ever got his supper and departed without leaving his autobiography (whether true or fictional) in Ellison Frost's mind.

His wife scorned these simple and frequently sordid stories, and was ashamed of her husband's interest in them; yet she could listen for hours to the recital by a fellow clubwoman of the slow progress of Mrs. Burk-halter's cancer into eternity, or the circumstances and details of a young bride's miscarriage. Her interest in the poor and unfortunate was confined chiefly to a desire to improve their moral rather than their physical state; and her obsession with guiding Sabina's life was at bottom only the determination to see her own will enforced. She had never questioned the right of apostolic succession or of her own wisdom. If she read surreptitiously a letter Sabina had received, it was in order that she might tell Sabina what to do. If Ellison Frost read it, it was because he wanted to see what Sabina's own reaction would be.

When Barrett Page's flowers for Sabina arrived from an Atlanta florist two days after the ill-starred ride, her father was less interested in the blossoms than in the card which said, "I take it all back. You are not an *enfant terrible*." He was impressed that the man had learned so early that one was always having to revise one's opinions of Sabina—at least, that had been his own experience. It could be due to another weakness on his part, this fre-quent changing of his mind, or it could be due to Sabina herself whose character was not yet formed and settled, who was one person one day and seven others the next.

As he collected fragments of information about the afternoon of the ride, he mentally retracted the remark which he and Claire had previously agreed on, that Sabina had no guts. Well, call it courage—and wherever she might keep it, however remote and inaccessible it might seem at times, it was there; and, perhaps for the very reason that she used it so seldom, when she did bring it forth it had a singularly fresh and pristine quality, not like other people's bedraggled courage that was used every day. There was surely something to be said for conservation of the virtues, just as one did not use one's best silver or wear the family jewels every day.

He was immensely titillated by this thought and proud of Sabina for having inspired it. He was convinced now that the girl was not a coward; her hesitations that eventually resolved into inactivity were the direct outgrowth of imagination. Her mind conjured up so many dangers and evils which could befall that she drew back where a less imaginative person, foreseeing nothing, rushed forward. Likewise, as the opposite extreme of these dire forebodings, her mind swung to a glamorized conception of what life could be, infinitely lovely, scintillating and gay so that she lived always in a mental world of melodrama that was either more terrible or more beautiful than real life.

Ellison Frost had no sympathy with the so-called "realists" to whom sordidness was the only synonym for reality. To him the peach orchards in bloom, shimmering pink against the emerald of new-planted grain, rising and falling with the hills, was as integral a part of reality as tramps huddled over their fire in a ditch, or darkies slashing each other with razors on Saturday night.

This intensification of the two extremes of life in which Sabina seemed to dwell might be the result of the boredom of her own life; and yet she showed no wish or inclination to enliven it, she seemed rather to prefer to remain withdrawn, uninvolved. Since Claire's return she had obviously been more disturbed, more unhappy, but more alive—until the day of the ride. Since then she had retired once more to her ivory tower, leaving the impression that she had erased from her memory all the events of that day. Sometimes he thought that Claire's superior vitality had a depressing effect upon Sabina. At other times there were indications that the younger girl was storing up intangible things that she got from Claire, draining her dry as hay, and long after Claire had lost or forgotten them they would be discovered in the intricate labyrinth of Sabina's mind unblemished and also unimproved by any process of mutation.

The difference between the two girls was never more marked than at the dining table where Claire ate with gusto, heartily, as she did everything else, and Sabina nibbled and pecked at her food, eating, in her mother's original phrase, "not enough to keep a bird alive." It was possible that she had no appetite because she took no exercise, but he believed that it was rather a pose on her part: a method of attracting attention and possibly sympathy, and at the same time an implication that she was less earthy than Claire, more spiritual.

Ellison Frost, dwelling on the importance of trifles, construed this as having large connotations. Sabina's delicacy was as typical of the thin-blooded, dying, postbellum South as Claire was the product of the more vigorous North. The South had been bled white, sterility had set in, and with sterility the impulse toward introspection. Sabina seemed to proclaim the antithesis of Descartes' *Je pense, puisque je suis*. She thought, therefore she did not exist.

Frost Haven was certainly no place in which to practice thinking. Sabina had not one person to whom she could talk. Here, anyone who discussed ideas was ostracized by unanimous consent, and any unfamiliar word or thought was greeted by a jeering, "Maybe so, I wouldn't know," or "—whatever that might mean." The inhabitants prided themselves on being "low-brow"; ignorance, far from requiring apology, was set at a premium; and learning was a cause for ridicule.

This might be one of the penalties of living in a transitional period, but Ellison Frost contended that any and all periods were transitional, containing perforce the seeds of the past and the buds of the future. It was true that this was neither the old South nor yet the new, while it contained side by side, the antagonistic elements of both: crumbling mansions and idle, eroded acres, the frank and shoddy commercialism of a bright tin roof; old boxwood gardens and filling stations; cotton mills, country clubs and the Victorian tradition that what was kept out of sight did not exist.

As late as his father's day there had been Shakespearean clubs in Frost Haven. Now literature was dead, and long live the pulps!

If Sabina were an anachronism as Claire had said, she was as much out of place as out of time. She should have lived in New England in the days of bluestockings, where, if she could not have been a Margaret Fuller or an Emily Dickinson, she could have employed herself happily in embroidering carpet slippers for the dactylic feet of Lowell and Whittier.

It was unfortunate that he had suddenly begun to think of Sabina as a problem just when he needed to give all his thought and attention to the orchards. The physical ordeal of packing season was bad enough: the strain of long and uncertain hours, of getting the right number of cars at the right time, watching the market, getting up the money for the weekly payroll; these things went with owning orchards and he could deal with them; it was his personal relations with the Sam Cummings, the overseer, that made each of the necessarily frequent encounters a bitter and nauseating experience. It was impossible, in the light of developments, to understand how he could have been taken in by the man in the first place. Cummings had appeared one winter day (it was four years ago now) just before a freeze when smudge fires had to be built throughout the orchards and someone to help direct the darkies was needed imperatively. Cummings had not been a prepossessing figure: a small man with a disproportionately large and bulbous nose, colorless skin and hair, and pale gray eyes. He was a hunchback, and the hip-pockets of his faded overalls were ripped at the sides so that they hung down like mudguards on a Ford. The man had told the familiar story of having had hard luck, there was going to be a baby, of course, and Ellison Frost had felt sorry for him. Cummings' air had been docile, agreeable, and he had seemed immensely grateful for the job.

Ellison Frost knew now that beneath that docility was a stupid stubbornness; behind the agreeability had been desperation (the man had once served a prison sentence, and more immediately he and his family had been "run out" of an adjoining county); the gratitude had cloaked a sort of peasant shrewdness which recognized a proper field for its talents. Frost knew now, too late, about the family: Cummings' wife, a dull heavy creature, was more beast than human; his daughter Daisy, a fresh-faced girl of about twenty was a half-wit and a slut if ever he had seen one; and the baby had become the child, "Tippy," whose head bobbed foolishly from side to side and whose deformed hand hung down uselessly from his arm like a wounded bird fluttering about.

But that was only the beginning of the evils of the Cummings family. When Ellison Frost had found at the end of the first year that he had no money to pay the man, and the bank would advance him no more, Cummings had demanded stock in the orchards. In the succeeding years there had been curculio (worms in the fruit), flooded markets, and more shares to Cummings. On the one good year Cummings had taken a cash payment and refused to restore any former share. He now assumed the importance of a partner and the insolence of a blackmailer. Subsequently there had been many days when Frost was tempted to sell out to him, or hand over the orchards rather than have further dealings with the man; he felt more and more that he would like to return to his earlier love, the law. But he could not bring himself to part with the acres that had been his grandfather's and his great-grandfather's, that had known the songs of happy, and perhaps unhappy slaves, that had been white with the ungarnered wealth of cotton, black with the desolation of war and reconstruction.

What would become of them after his death he could not say, but he had no intention of dying for a good many years. He was only fifty-five, and longevity was a Frost tradition.

The law of primogeniture was on Claire's side but she had been born in New England, had spent so many years in the North that it was difficult to associate her with Georgia soil. With all his fondness for Claire, he had to confess that she had no roots. Sabina, on the contrary, did, though she would be the last to admit it. The idea of Sabina's managing a peach orchard was as fantastic as the developing possibility that Barrett Page was in love with her; but if Ellison Frost had learned anything during his swiftly accumulating years it was that the fantastic happened much more frequently in life than the logical did.

It was logical to assume that Claire and Page had known each other in the North and he was here now because she was. But her father had seen the two together often now and could discover nothing to confirm that suspicion. He could not and would not believe that Claire was having an affair with any man, she was too shrewd about getting what she wanted, and she had never wanted anything that was second rate. There had been one week end recently when he was genuinely worried: Claire had spent those days in Atlanta with friends, she said, and during that time Barrett Page had not appeared at the Frost home, nor had Ellison Frost seen his car in town. That could easily have been a coincidence; it had to be. For Page was a likable person; it was as impossible to suspect him as it was Claire of such flagrant deceit and improbity. He never violated Mrs. Frost's sense of propriety by asking Sabina to go riding at night or to attend a cinema without asking Claire, also. But it was to Sabina that he sent flowers, books, candies, the staples of incipient courtship. If it were not by their gifts that you knew them, then how were you to know?

One afternoon Ellison Frost came home from the packing house to discover the three, Sabina, Claire and Page, having lemonade and sandwiches on the north veranda overlooking the garden. That, he considered, was another proof of Sabina's influence, the substitution of

lemonade for Scotch and soda, and how Claire must have
hated it! The girls were in muslin dresses—no, not muslin, of course, but the modern equivalent, something
thin and soft, Sabina's of blue and Claire's of yellow.
They made quite a pretty picture and Page looked par-
donably smug sitting on the wicker settee between them.
Yet, as Ellison Frost stood in the doorway looking at
them, the moment took on a strange significance; it was
not that he thought, Here is a little hour lifted out of
time, a fragment of universal history passing before my
eyes, young girls entertaining their beaux on the front
veranda. It was not that he saw himself as an intruder, a
father watching over his two daughters; nor yet as an
older man whose experience, whose essential dryness will
inevitably suck up something of the freshness of youth.
It was nothing so simple as an older person feeling out of
key with young people, weary with the knowledge that
he, too, had once thought these things important.

As he stood there looking past them at the long, rec-
tangular pool that mirrored petunias and graceful urns he
felt that the impression he had got was no abstract or
general one but had to do immediately with the fact that
it was not young men his daughters were entertaining, it
was only one young man.

Then, just before Barrett Page saw him and came forward to shake hands the eidolon took shape: it was that
the young man had or was going to have some relation
to both the girls.

"How do you do, Mr. Page, I am very glad to see you.
Hello, Claire, Sabina—"

"I hope you don't think you find me here too often,"

laughed Page. "Won't you sit down and have a drink with us?"

"Do, Father," said Claire. "There's an extra glass here waiting for you."

"Thank you, thank you. It's very comfortable here, at least twenty degrees cooler than it is over at the packing shed." It was the strangest situation he had ever walked into: if Page were in love with Sabina he would be restless and impatient for Claire to leave. If there were some dark secret between him and Claire he would not be watching so intently the brooding, lovely face of Sabina. There was color in her cheeks this afternoon; she had never looked more fragile, more appealing, so completely a picture of tender womanhood. And Barrett Page was either in love with both of them or he was in love with neither—the clinging vine or the independent, vital, efficient Claire.

"Where is your mother?" Ellison Frost asked the girls, knowing quite well that Janie Lee would never absent herself from motives of tactfulness.

"At the D.A.R. meeting," answered Sabina. "Father, won't you have a sandwich? You know when Mother has refreshments in the afternoon we never have much supper."

"No. No sandwiches, thank you, Sabina." How could the little minx sit there looking so soft and yielding when in place of a heart she had a core of obstinacy and egocentricity of the size and texture of a petrified ostrich egg? It was perhaps one of the God-given deceits which descended upon women when there was a prospective husband around. Claire, he observed, was the most restless of the three, an indication that she was the most in love and ill-pleased at the ascendancy of Sabina's star.

"I'm afraid I've disturbed your conversation," he said, finishing his drink hurriedly. "I'll be running along."

"Don't go, Mr. Frost," cried Page. "It is only that we were discussing a very trivial subject, a dance at the country club on Friday night. I'm to have the honor of taking Sabina and Claire."

"Both of them? In my day we did those things differently."

"But you never had to choose between two such girls. I understand now how bigamy originated." Barrett Page's words sounded casual but the older man wondered if Page ever said anything casually, his jaw was too firm, the gray eyes in his lean face too forthright. Had this handsome stranger from the North felt the same thing about the two girls that their father did, that they were the antipathetic but integral parts of one personality? Or was it merely an echo of the old theory that every man needed two wives?

The ice settled noisily in the silver pitcher. "I used to think," said Claire, "that the word ought to be Brighamy out of respect to Mr. Young."

"What would the wife of a bigamist be called?" asked Sabina. And her father answered quickly, "A bigamistress, I should think."

"Oh," laughed Barrett Page, "you said that as if you had given some thought to it beforehand. But then I always suspect the makers of bons mots, it's because I'm so slow about them myself. Could I have some more lemonade, Claire?"

"Of course," said Claire, rising. "Will you have some, Father? Sabina?"

Why had Page asked Claire for the lemonade instead of Sabina? Ellison Frost told himself that this was a significant fact, and then almost angrily he determined that he would see no more significance in anything. He was like those people with hypersensitive ears who could hear the grass grow. It seemed to him sometimes that he actually saw the passage of time. This last feat had no moral effect on him; it did not make him increase his activities but rather depressed him with the futility of all activity.

There was a movement in the shrubbery outside, birds perhaps, and he roused himself to ask, "Who is giving the dance on Friday night?"

"You are, Father," laughed Sabina.

"I am?"

"The Fruit Growers' Association—of which you are president."

"Oh, yes, a nice bit of irony, that. But since I am, I want to make sure that Cox and his son are invited."

"Who are they?" asked Claire.

"Sabina knows them; the boy goes to the university and his father has had charge of the packing shed every summer for years now. They're from Ohio and have seen better days. They won't embarrass you."

"Really, Father, do you think we should? Suppose all the members of the Association invited their help—" Claire broke off laughing. "If you ask them, you'll have to ask the packers, and if the packers are invited, the wagon drivers and pickers will be hurt."

"And Sam Cummings," cried Sabina. "We'll have to ask him and Daisy!"

"Daisy would be the belle of the ball," said Claire. "We shouldn't have a chance; she'd wear her pink chambray and have a wad of chewing gum as big as a tennis ball—I think she's been collecting it for years. When her 'date' wants to show her a big evening he gives her a whole stick of gum. Most of the time she just gets a half."

"Girls, girls!" said Ellison Frost reprovingly. He was about to make a remark to the effect that any pretense of social distinctions in Frost Haven had long since become a farce when Sabina cried, "Here comes Daisy now. Let's ask her!"

Barrett Page was laughing with them. "I think I'll ask her to go with me. Then where would you two girls be?"

"You might take all three of them," Ellison Frost suggested maliciously and Page threw back his head and laughed. "You must think I am just a Mormon at heart, Mr. Frost."

Daisy came around from the drive into the garden, calling as she came, "Tippy? Tippy?"

There was a rustling in the big camellia bush but no other sound. Daisy's stocky figure moved nearer, her straight hair hung in damp wisps and her soiled gray cotton frock was limp against her body. "Mr. Frost, Papa wants to see you. He says them last cars you ordered ain't come." She stood for a moment looking at her reflection in the pool, then she asked, "Ain't none o' y'all seen Tippy, have you?"

"We haven't seen him, Daisy," Ellison Frost answered,

"but I think I heard him. Look behind the camellia bush."

"The which?" said Daisy.

"The big bush to your right."

"Oh. Yeah, I see him."

The child started running, his strange, misshapen little body moving like a gnome's in the early dusk. The girl watched him languidly, then surprised him at a turn like a dog lying in wait for a chicken. She shook him roughly and his abnormally large head bobbled loosely on his shoulders. "Git on home," she said, "you little ape, you. Git on now, or I'll git me a switch."

She reached out her arm and Ellison Frost suffered horribly at the thought of his Chandleri Elegans camellia being broken, but Daisy's threat was idle. She was too lazy to "git her a switch." Tears washed down Tippy's grimy face and in desperation the girl picked him up. "Shut up," she commanded sharply as she settled him under her sturdy arm, "shut up now. Ain't nobody go' hurt you. I swear—you'll be the death o' me yet."

As she turned to go down the walk Ellison Frost watched her curiously, wondering if there were really something sinister about the entire degenerate Cummings family or if he only imagined it. Then his gaze returned to his enigmatic daughter, Sabina. She looked bored enough to start reading the Congressional Record at any moment and he did not know whether to spank her or give her an approving pat on the head. Either she wanted to be alone with the young man, or she had decided to wait until something better in the way of young men came along. He wondered how long it would be before he knew.

Janie Lee Frost was in protest against the entire situation. She had been irritated for weeks and the irritation grew as her husband ignored it. The fact that Sabina had not caught cold on the afternoon of her ride was the source of her first chagrin: such flagrant disobedience as the girl had shown on her return deserved to be punished by illness; moreover, it made her own carefully fostered rules for Sabina's health and the fiction of the child's delicacy look rather silly. Naturally she was glad that Sabina had suffered no ill consequences since the Lord had willed it that way, but it was very hard to understand.

But the constant thorn in her flesh was the frequent presence of Barrett Page in her house. The man was a stranger about whom they knew nothing and wanted to know everything. He was not even a Virginian or a South Carolinian, in which case discreet inquiries could have been made through her relatives. He was a Yankee from Massachusetts, and although her husband contended that he had heard of the Pages in Boston, she was inclined to doubt this, to put it down as a pretext on Mr. Frost's part for obtaining the man's companionship for himself—that would have needed no pretext since he delighted in low company and listened to tramps by the hour—but also for his daughters. There was the rub. It was perhaps excusable for Mr. Frost to take the man through the orchards, show him how the peaches were gathered, graded and packed; it might be that he intended trying to sell the orchards to Mr. Page—Yankees always had money. But to allow him to be seen so often with Sabina and Claire was tantamount to approving the man as a prospective son-in-law.

And if Mr. Page was a Bostonian, why had he not gone to Harvard, or at least to Yale or Princeton? That would have given him some standing—but no, he said he was a graduate of an upstart university in New York and every one knew that those New York universities were just hotbeds of socialism and atheism.

Furthermore, the man had been in Frost Haven long enough. Why did he not go on back where he came from—wherever that was. His sister-in-law and two little nephews had left weeks ago and Janie Lee Frost was not at all sure but what they were his wife and children. She did not like it. It was simply ruining Sabina who was as flattered as any rural miss over the attentions of a handsome man with a fine car. And when she, Janie Lee, went down to breakfast, her eyes red with worry, sleeplessness and tears, the whole family acted as if *she* were being ridiculous!

Now Mr. Frost was insisting on her going to this dance when he knew how she felt about dances; but he had said that it was her duty to him and to her daughters and the word duty was a clarion call. She dressed slowly, protesting inwardly at each step of the process, pausing to rip out the old shields and sew new ones in the sleeves of her black chiffon, and lingering to pin an artificial gardenia on the shoulder. There were fresh ones in the garden but she had never been able to understand why women should ruin their best frocks with fresh flowers which always stained the fabric and left the imprint of corsage pins.

When she joined her husband who was waiting impatiently downstairs, she thought that he looked quite unnecessarily handsome in his black coat and cream-colored flannel trousers. He was as slender as when she had married him and though his hair was rapidly graying, his short clipped mustache showed scarcely any gray at all. But it was his eyes that made him look young, they were long and slanting, as frank and innocently curious as a child's, blue with flecks of black in the iris. His nose was small and classically perfect.

Mrs. Frost sighed. His slenderness made him look younger than she did. She was conscious of her hips controlled by heavy corsets that reached up and supported her pendulous breasts but also restricted her breathing. Many an ample meal had gone into the making of that flesh as it had flushed her wide flaccid cheeks, but she regretted none of them. Ellison Frost, she had known for many years, did not respect her, but he loved her—at least as much as was decent. If he chose not to respect her because she clung to old and pious beliefs and was not given to original thought or speech, if he chose not to eat the hot stuffed sausages, the mustard pickles, the country hams baked in cider, the fruit cakes and custards that she piled so bountifully upon his table, those were his prerogatives as a man. But she frequently thought he would be less inquisitive about life, less critical of her, if he ate more and weighted down those restless bones of his.

"Janie Lee, you are late; I believe you did it on purpose because you didn't want to go," he said.

"No, Mr. Frost, when I say I'll do a thing, I intend to do it."

"If it kills you. What's that thing on your arm?"

"My fringed shawl. You know I bought it when I went to the D.A.R. Conference in Washington. Do you like it?"

"No. But do come along. The president of anything, even the Fruit Growers' Association, ought to be on hand for the organization's festivities."

"You're afraid you'll miss something," accused his wife as he helped her into the car.

" 'It's no such of a thing,' as Miss Lucy Taylor says, it is merely courtesy, my dear. Besides, for all you know, one of your daughters may be sitting out in a car 'necking.' " He started the car quickly and turned out of the driveway into the road.

"Necking? What is that?"

"Use your imagination."

"Not my daughter," said Janie Lee Frost firmly.

"Well, mine then."

"Oh, dear, what a dreadful expression, necking!"

"For such a beautiful act. If there is anything lovelier than a young girl being kissed by the man she loves, I don't know what it is. He takes her face in his hands, and there is all the adoration and wonder that life holds in the look they give each other—"

"Ellison Frost," she interrupted, "I don't know what has gotten into you."

"It is something, my dear, that I hope will never get out. In your clubs it is probably known as 'appreciating the finer things of life.' "

"You know good and well, Mr. Frost, that kissing, or 'necking' as you call it, has never been mentioned in any club I belong to. You should have turned at that corner, Mr. Frost."

"Yes, I'll turn at the next one." He had forgotten about the streets because he was thinking of a passage from Byron, a stanza that began,

Ye stars! which are the poetry of heaven!
If in your bright leaves we would read the fate
Of men and empires,—'t is to be forgiven,
That in our aspirations to be great,
Our destinies overleap their mortal state,
And claim a kindred with you; for ye are
A beauty and a mystery—

"There is a nice moon," said Mrs. Frost, "over there to your left, right on the top of Jim Franklin's barn."

"Everything works together for the good of those who love God. A moon for the country club dance." He waited for her to say, "Don't be sacrilegious, Mr. Frost," and she said it. Then he went on, "I'd like it better if it looked less like a slice of ripe Elberta peach."

What was the rest of that stanza?

For ye are a beauty and a mystery
And create in us such love and reverence
From afar, that fortune, fame, power, life,
Have named themselves a star.

Possibly that was not great poetry; it did not give him chills and fever, but it made him forget his wife's bromidic conversation and think of her warm, mahogany-colored eyes, of what lovely white shoulders she had had when they were married. So it must be poetry of some sort.

As he turned into the road leading up to the clubhouse he saw that lights had been strung through the pine trees before the white frame building, and outlining the doorway were peach boughs prodigal with fruit. The soft, sad notes of a waltz hung like a threnody on the heavy air as if the South were unconsciously mourning its glory that was dead. Where were the gaiety, glamour, life that balls had had in the old South? This was such a cheap and unconvincing replica, and he thought how further disillusioning it would look in the morning when sunlight shone on the wilted boughs, on the scrambled chairs of the orchestra, the empty whisky bottles and cigarette stubs. He parked the car and went around to open the door for Janie Lee. The waltz had made him forget Byron and the stars (it must not have been great poetry after all), had raised in him a great protest against this new South. If there had been bitterness in the sadness of that waltz, he felt that there would have been hope; but it was too acquiescent.

"I'm going to feel like a fish out of water in there," said Janie Lee.

"Possibly you should have brought a good book to read," agreed her husband, "or can fish out of water read? I don't know a great deal about them." He opened the screen door and then almost drew back, for it was just as he had feared. The entire ballroom was decorated with boughs from peach trees. Golden and luscious fruit clung to them over the rustic mantel, over each window and doorway, and above the wooden chandeliers that were shaped like a wheel. Artificial miniature trees in pots were banked in front of the orchestra and the majority of the girls were wearing green, yellow or peach-colored frocks.

Janie Lee was nodding to some of her friends and saying, "Yes, so appropriately done, isn't it?" Henry Middleton came forward to say that there were chairs at the back of the room and as Ellison Frost followed, he saw Sabina dancing with Barrett Page. But where was Claire?

He discovered her then, on the opposite side of the room, dancing with the president of the bank, and he thought, How typical of Claire!

Henry Middleton unfolded two chairs from Pratt's, the undertaker, and held one firmly while Mrs. Frost was seating herself. It was a delicate moment, not unfraught with danger, but when she was established the chair lost its significance; her firm head and shoulders rose far above the white linen cover on the back, and the seat which seemed to be of the exact material and design as the carpeting at church, was lost beneath Mrs. Frost's black chiffon amplitude.

"We were afraid you weren't coming," said Henry Middleton pulling up a chair beside them, "but I didn't think you would let us down. How do you like the decorations?"

"Wonderful," said Ellison Frost, "wonderful."

"We thought they were pretty good. Of course, with the market like it is, we could afford to cut limbs like that and spare peaches by the bushel. We could have given away whole crates of 'em for souvenirs," Henry Middleton laughed loudly, "but we thought we had enough just like this."

"Yes, yes, I think so, too."

"I'm glad you like it." Middleton's little round squirrel-like face would have looked pleased if it had been capable of showing any expression at all. The eyes behind his glasses were constantly bright, observant, and unchanging.

The waltz was over and everyone began talking. Mrs. Frost's neighbor looked back over her shoulder and said, "Janie Lee—"

"Hello, Margaret, how are you?"

"I'm not so well, Janie Lee, I never am in summer. I started to call you this afternoon but something came up, I don't remember now what it was. I've had a letter from the people in Marietta about putting up that Confederate marker for us. They want three hundred and fifty dollars just for the stone, and the engraving will be extra."

"Well," said Janie Lee, "that isn't too much for a man like the General. Besides, it would be an ornament to the Court House Square."

"But they decided not to put it on the square," cried Margaret Turner; "weren't you at the last meeting? No, I remember now, it was the day your missionary circle met. Listen, Janie Lee, they want to put it out in the country where the General was born!"

"Why, they can't do that, it's simply disgraceful! His father was my grandfather's own first cousin and papa would simply turn over in his grave if he knew the U.D.C. were showing so little respect to the most distinguished man the County ever had."

"Of course," said Mrs. Turner, "he left here when he was only seven years old—"

"I don't care if he did," snapped Mrs. Frost. "He was born here. And he came back and spoke once when he was running for governor. Papa carried us to hear him; I remember it was just after mama died, and papa said he would like to ask him to our house for dinner, but he wasn't sure of our cooking. I don't remember what the General talked about, but papa introduced us to him and he kissed us."

"Did he have on his uniform?"

"No. He really looked a great deal like papa, you could scarcely tell them apart, the same high forehead and lofty brow—"

"Hello, Mother; hello, Father! How are you, Mrs. Turner? Have you met Mr. Page?" Claire and Sabina had come up with their escort but it was Claire who was doing all the talking. "Oh, and Mr. Middleton, how are you? This is Mr. Page, Mr. Middleton. Are you having a good time? Don't you want some punch?"

"What kind of punch?" asked Ellison Frost cautiously.

"I'll get the ladies some," said Henry Middleton; "you wouldn't care for it, Mr. Frost."

"Oh, there's the music—"

Barrett Page had just enough time to get in his "Delighted to know you's" before Claire said, "This is ours, isn't it, Barrett?"

There was a bleak look about Sabina's mouth and Ellison Frost pushed his chair back. "Sabina, would you dance this one with your poor old father?"

She smiled at him. "Thank you for the rescue. I really had this one with Barrett, but Claire is no respecter of programs."

As they moved off she said, "Are you sure you don't want to hear the rest of the story about the General?"

He laughed. "We know it by heart, don't we? 'Papa' took them all to the hotel for dinner and they had baked pompano—"

"From Florida. And afterward they all drove down to the river near where the General was born and he said something about how much smaller it was than it used to be."

" 'The hills do not seem nearly so high nor the river so wide,' " Ellison Frost quoted.

They were laughing together and he was thinking how pretty Sabina looked with that dash of malice animating her face when someone touched him on the shoulder. "May I cut in, Mr. Frost?"

"I beg your pardon—"

"I said could I cut in?"

"It's being done, Father," Sabina explained; "girls aren't popular if they dance an entire number with the same partner. You know Tom Hewitt, don't you?"

"How do you do, Hewitt? Thank you, Sabina."

"Are you going to cut in on someone else?" she asked.

"No, I think I'll go back and see what has happened to the monument."

Confound the child, she was downright attractive tonight. He had actually enjoyed dancing with her, perhaps because she had talked to him as an equal not as a mere parent. When he got back to his seat he found Mrs. Nixon, the church organist, in his chair beside Janie Lee. "Oh, Mr. Frost, I'm so sorry—"

"That's quite all right, Mrs. Nixon, here's another chair—"

She turned back to his wife. "Janie Lee, did you say that you leave the skin on when you make your fig preserves?"

"Yes, I do. I put a little alum in the water, or is it ammonia, I never can remember, to take the roughness off, and they keep their shape so much better."

"Well, I declare, I never heard of that. Of course, Henrietta's always made mine, but this summer—" she leaned over and whispered in Mrs. Frost's ear.

"Again?" said Mrs. Frost, lifting an eyebrow.

Mrs. Nixon nodded. "And you know it hadn't been any time since—"

"I know—just last fall, wasn't it?" asked Mrs. Frost.

"Yes, yes it was. That first cold spell that killed my dahlias."

"Well, I don't see—" began Mrs. Frost in an undertone; "this is July, isn't it? Yes, I suppose it's possible—October, November, December, January, yes, it's possible—why doesn't she leave him?"

"Oh, she does, every once in a while, they both take up with somebody else; then the next thing you know they're back together—"

"It must be love," commented Ellison Frost.

Mrs. Nixon clapped her hand down on Mrs. Frost's knee. "Isn't he a caution?" Her outraged laughter rose shrilly. "I declare, Janie Lee, he's a sight. I didn't know he was listening to a word we said."

"Don't pay any attention to Mr. Frost," remarked his wife, "he'd know what we talked about even if we talked about something else."

Ellison Frost laughed then. "Janie Lee, that's the funniest thing you ever said in your life. I'll leave you two to your vital statistics. Can I fetch you some punch?"

"Do you want any more punch, Susie?"

"No. Do you?"

"No. It's sort of tasteless tonight, I think, too much of something and too little of something else. I never put that orange crush stuff in mine, do you?"

"No. Just the pineapple and ginger ale and grape juice—"

"Do you use the sliced pineapple or the crushed?"

"I always use the sliced. It comes a little higher, but then you can usually economize on your sandwiches—nobody is going to lift up the bread to see what is inside it. Where did Mr. Frost go?"

Mrs. Frost put her hand to her mouth and whispered but Mrs. Nixon shook her head. "No, he went out the front door. You don't suppose he is going to take a drink, do you? I understand all the men take pocket flasks to the dances. Who's the handsome boy Clarissa is dancing with?"

"Mr. Page, I suppose. No, it isn't either. I don't know who it is. It looks like—no, it couldn't be."

"Couldn't be who?" demanded Mrs. Nixon.

"Why, I was going to say it looked like that new young man at the filling station, but surely—"

"That's who it is, all right. Honestly, now—"

"Isn't it the truth," echoed Mrs. Frost sadly. "I'm surprised at Clarissa, but then you know she thinks it is smart and modern to do things like that. But you'll never catch Sabina doing such a thing—"

"Have you seen the Murrays' new house, Janie Lee? You haven't? You ought to go see it before they get the floors done and lock it—the living room, dining room and breakfast room are across the front, and just back of the living room is Mrs. Murray's bedroom. Or is it back of the dining room? Let me see, yes, it's back of the living room and there are two great big closets in there. They've got central heating but Mr. Murray insisted on having a fireplace in his room; he said he wanted to see the fire burn. They've got three bedrooms; they didn't need but two, but Mrs. Murray said she wanted an extra room so when the children came home—Janie Lee, are you listening?"

"Yes. I'm listening. Are they going to get new furniture?"

"Well, yes and no. That is, they are going to have new rugs and draperies and get a few pieces of furniture at a time. Of course, they didn't ask me about it, but if I was going to put all that money in a house, I wouldn't have put the dining room in the front of the house; and why do they need two rooms to eat in? And I'd have had a sun parlor and left off the breakfast room and bought new furniture. I don't think anything looks worse than old furniture in a new house. You and Mr. Frost ought to walk down there Sunday afternoon."

As Ellison Frost had left the room he had encountered Claire briefly. "Are Cox and his son here? I haven't seen them."

"No, Father. I meant to tell you that we asked them and neither accepted. Perhaps they didn't have the proper clothes."

Outside, the air felt wonderfully fresh and clean, and he decided to smoke a cigarette as an excuse for staying out. His wife, who had not wanted to come, was having a much better time than he was. But then Janie Lee loved to talk about food, and food was the great common denominator. The poor talked about getting it, the middle classes about preparing it, and the rich about digesting it.

If the conversation of all the elder people was like the bits he had heard—and he had reason to believe it was— what could be expected of the young ones? Shades of Calhoun, Pinckney and Matthew Fontaine Maury! Wha had become of the South's statesmen and scientists? And what had become of the literature, of the Laniers and Poes and even the Thomas Nelson Pages?

It suddenly occurred to him that Sabina, so far as he knew, had never seen an author and that he must try to find one to show her before the species was totally extinct. It was not because they were worth looking at, but precisely because they were not that he felt this compulsion. Sabina loved books so much that she might get the idea writers were something rare and beautiful like the snowy egret, whereas the specimens he remembered seeing had looked as grubby as oysters giving no indications of the pearls they concealed within. Perhaps it was the instinct of protective coloration that induced this outward negligence, or it might be that they believed eccentricity in dress was a hallmark of genius.

Ellison Frost strolled over to a group of pines through whose boughs the moon filtered in fantastic, spidery patterns. He was not, he told himself, a prig or a pedant who wanted Browning read at picnics or dancing partners who quoted Dante. It was not the triviality of the conversation in Frost Haven that he rebelled against, it was the emptiness, the euphemism, the denial and avoidance of fundamental issues. Small wonder that he found more real meat in the simple words of a tramp; the tramp had at least come to grips with reality. And yet, there were times when he hungered for something more. In despising the academic fop, the present-day South was probably justified; but there was no excuse for despising the philomath as well. They had swung to the opposite extreme and perfected a state of demagoguery where if a man had any learning he was socially bound to conceal it. As a reaction from the oratory of Calhoun and Alexander H. Stephens, they now demanded of their politicians (there were no longer any statesmen, the breed had disappeared) the speech of farmhands, illiterate and ungrammatical. This toadying to the lowest was unendurable to Ellison Frost and he was damned if he would ever yield to it, ever lower his standards for the sake of conformity or cheap popularity. Where once people had pretended to know more than they did, they now pretended to know less, and he was convinced that of the two the latter was the more dangerous. "Homespun philosophers," "folksey books," best-sellers that could be read by maids and gardeners—this was democracy. But the final and complete democracy was death. Let the democratic intellectuals remember that.

When the music ceased he went back into the ballroom, to the little potted artificial peach trees, the sprays and boughs of peach limbs whose leaves were beginning to wilt, and the silly words and catch phrases that eddied about the room.

"Oh, Mr. Frost, you haven't had any refreshments, have you?" A young girl came up to him and proudly handed him a plate. "We ordered these from Atlanta."

"Thank you, my dear." For a moment he thought it was a peach, but when he touched it with his fork he found that it was ice cream, tinted and leaved. The small iced cakes were embossed with twining green leaves.

"Very pretty, isn't it?" asked the bank president.

"Quite, quite," said Ellison Frost.

"I always say that occasions like this do more toward bringing people together than—than anything else."

"Next to a political rally, perhaps."

"Oh, yes, you are right, Mr. Frost." The president slapped him on the back and looked over his ice cream at a young girl standing by the door.

"Next year," suggested Ellison Frost, "if prices are like what they are now, I think we should convert the entire crop into peach brandy and just let everybody get drunk off it."

"Lord, ain't it the truth? Excuse me, Mr. Frost, I think my wife wants to see me." The banker went over to the young girl, and Ellison Frost heard him say, "I'm John Hartford and I'm sure I know you, but you'll have to tell me your name."

Yes, there was nothing like an occasion of this sort for bringing people together. Mr. Frost wished that he could think of it in the proper spirit, as a thank offering to Demeter for the rich yield of the fruit, as a sort of midsummer festival typifying the bounty of these Georgia acres. But as Henry Middleton had pointed out, the prodigality of the boughs and fruit only meant that the crop was too large and the price too low.

Perhaps he had better go back and see what Janie Lee was discussing with her friends. As he passed the doorway that opened out onto the tile piazza he caught a brief sight of two figures close in each other's arms. It was so dark that he couldn't be sure, but they looked remarkably like Claire and Barrett Page. At the window near them he paused and then he was sure he heard Claire's voice.

"I'm worn out with it, Barrett; it's intolerable. Let's go back North."

"You know I hate it as much as you do, Claire."

"I don't know whether you do or not. Sometimes I wonder."

"Claire, you are being unreasonable."

Then Mrs. Frost came up. "Oh, here you are, Mr. Frost; I simply couldn't imagine what had become of you. I suppose you've been having a very good time."

"No, I'm sorry I came, sorry I asked you to come. Shall we go?"

"Go? Now? Why—we can't leave Sabina."

"Sabina will be all right. Where is your shawl?"

"Mr. Frost, I do believe you are angry about something, and I know you won't tell me what it is."

He lighted a cigarette and was furious to note that his hand was shaking. "Where is your shawl? I'll get it. You can wait for me at the door."

"It's on the back of the chair where I was sitting—"

Stupidly she gazed after him wondering what on earth could have upset him so.

When they were nearly home he said, "If I should miss seeing Claire at breakfast, will you ask her not to make an engagement for the evening. I want to see her in the library after supper." And that was the last word she was able to get out of him.

CHAPTER VI

THE NEXT DAY WAS HOT AND SULTRY; THERE WAS NO freshness even in the early morning air. Dust which had been accumulating for many days and nights (for it had no opportunity to settle then, from being constantly disturbed) hung so thickly in the air as to make it almost opaque. It formed a heavy film over the roadside shrubbery, fences, grass and rocks; and pine needles nearest the road were coated with it.

Lila May and Mrs. Frost tried to keep the windows in the house pulled down and the shutters closed, but someone, most probably Claire, was constantly opening them. In the morning after the dance Ellison Frost came down earlier than usual for his breakfast and left before the others had got up. Mrs. Frost came next, saying she wasn't hungry but she would try to drink her tea; by the time she had finished her bacon and eggs she was able to eat some salt-rising bread and strawberry jam which she needed to keep up her strength. She was going with friends to a district conference of the church in an adjoining county, a long, hot, dusty ride, but as secretary of the association her presence was imperative. She was gone, in her navy blue washable voile and last year's hat, cheered somewhat by the prospect of the basket dinner which would be spread under the trees—huge platters of fried chicken, boiled ham, chicken pies, salmon salad, potato salad, deviled eggs, peach pickles, watermelon-rind preserves, apple fritters, peach puffs, "rights and lefts," layer cakes, pound cakes, lemon pies, and huckleberry pies with enough juice to run down one's chin.

When Sabina came down an hour later she found Claire in her riding clothes already at the table, looking as fresh as if she had gone to bed at eight o'clock the night before.

"How can you do it?" Sabina complained; "dance all night and get up and go riding the next morning?"

"I sleep so much harder than you do," said Claire; "I don't just lie in the bed in a semi-conscious state of repose. I give it my all. I don't woo sleep, I whip it into submission. And then, of course, I have a clear conscience that makes a difference."

"Meaning—?" said Sabina.

"Nothing. I just have a clear conscience, that's all."

"Have you?" asked Sabina. "Who is going riding with you?"

"I am going alone. Barrett is not going with me, if that's what you want to know. And I started this inquisition. Who brought you home last night?"

"Why, Barrett did; you saw us leave. You said Mr. and Mrs. Hartford were going to bring you."

"Are you sure you came straight home?" demanded Claire, pouring a second cup of coffee.

"Of course we did," answered Sabina indignantly. "I never did anything but come straight home in my life. If you think I ever sat in a car with a man by the side of the road and let him put his arms around me—"

"There, there now," soothed Claire, "mustn't get its little feelings hurt. Might do you good to come home late once in a while, though I don't advise staying out with Barrett Page."

"Why not?"

Claire shrugged. "Well, you have to go at these things gradually. Better begin with someone less experienced and less dangerous than Barrett and sort of work up to him."

"How do you know he's dangerous?"

"My dear child," said Claire benignly.

"I suppose you think you could handle him."

"Yes." Claire's tone was as sweet as the fig preserves.

"It's a pity," said Sabina, "that you never have a chance to try. It might interest you to know that he is a gentleman, and a gentleman with a very good mind. He is interested in music and drawing and literature—of course you wouldn't understand that."

Claire rang the bell for the cook. "Lila May, bring us some toast."

"Ain't no mo', Miss Clarissa. Miz Frost—"

"All right, never mind." Claire put her napkin on the table and rose. "Bye, honey chile, and don't forget what mama told you."

"About what?"

Claire spread her hands despairingly. "There, you see? You've forgotten already. About staying away from the big bad Yankees. And remember, it hasn't been so very long since you informed me he was *not* a gentleman! You shouldn't change your mind so often, you'll wear it out."

"You are just about as subtle, Clarissa, as a traveling salesman's jokes."

Claire lighted a cigarette. "You and your subtleties! Some day you are going to wake up and find you are nothing but a five-foot shelf of classics. Now do you want to know who brought me home last night?"

"No. I suppose it was the boy from the filling station."

"It was Barrett Page. If you don't believe me, ask him."

"I knew it all the time. I just wanted to see what you were going to say," declared Sabina.

"Like fun you did!"

Claire went out through the kitchen to the stables and Sabina sat looking morosely at her coffee. Somehow she felt that Claire had told the truth about Barrett bringing her home, and of course she, Sabina, had lied about knowing it. She should have known better than to attempt competition with Claire. Of course Claire would get him whether she wanted him or not; he was the best that Frost Haven offered; he had shown a decided preference for Sabina. Therefore, Claire had to have him.

The surprising thing to Sabina was that he had ever preferred her at all. It had been quite a shock and she had been so grateful for it that she had lapped it up as food and drink, and had now come to depend on it.

The half-hearted attentions of college boys and the few young men she knew had never meant anything to her because she had felt that Claire would have despised them. But Claire had said from the first that Barrett Page was attractive. And Barrett Page had preferred Sabina— to all outward appearances.

That knowledge, or rather that belief, had given Sabina faith in herself, had enabled her to believe herself attractive, to laugh with her father as Claire did, to express her own opinions as if they were worth expressing. In thinking of herself as a charming girl and companion she had not had to console herself so much with the superiority of her mind. Barrett Page had bestowed a priceless gift upon her, self-confidence, and she had loved the gift, been immeasurably grateful for it. Because of his admiration for her rather than for Claire, she had concluded that he had unusual perspicacity, discrimination and intelligence. Now Claire had rudely jerked the props from under her, leaving her more defenceless and uncertain than before.

She did not greatly blame Barrett for finding Claire more attractive, everyone always had. But she censured him for not seeing that Claire was using him to keep her hand in. Or was Claire seriously interested in him, was she in love with him? Even if she was, Barrett should be allowed some say-so in the matter, he should not permit Claire to make up his mind for him. Did he know that Claire was weaving her web around him? It was difficult somehow to think of Barrett as a helpless fly; in fact, the whole thing seemed rather odd. Had Claire made the story up, as a "Hands off" sign for Sabina? Had Claire's wishes anticipated the actuality?

This not only seemed probable, but it was vastly comforting. Sabina decided that she *would* ask Barrett Page, in a devious way, of course—something like this, "It was pretty late when you and Claire got in from the dance, wasn't it?" No, that was too obvious, it would never do at all. It would be better to say, "Claire must have gone home with the Hartfords, she was so late getting in." Then, if he *hadn't* brought her home he would wish he had, if she were so fascinating the Hartfords took her home with them. And he would wonder why Sabina hadn't asked Claire about it instead of him. No, that wouldn't do either.

"You finished, Miss Sabina?" asked Lila May coming into the room.

"Yes, Lila May. Am I keeping you from the dishes?"

"Yes'm. That sho musta been some party y'all had last night, way everybody's acting this morning."

"It was a very nice party, Lila May, nobody got tight."

"Needn't tell me," said Lila May. "Didn't I hear them white folks ridin' up and down the road singin' at the top o' they voices? One car come up in my yard and park' and turn' off the lights—they think I just a iggerant nigger and hit don't matter. They git out a bottle—they's two couples of 'em—and I tell you, Miss Sabina, I ain't never see such scandalous goin's on in all my bawn days."

"What did they do?" Sabina asked interestedly.

"They didn't git a chanct to do nothin' much," said Lila May with satisfaction. "I got my old man's shotgun and I went to the window. 'You'se white folks,' I sez, 'and I'se just a plain black nigger, but this here's my land, and I don't want no such doin's on it. If you don't git offen hit before I count ten, I gwi shoot,' I sez, and I put one bullet 'plunk' right in the chinaberry tree."

"Did they leave?"

"Did they leave! Miss Sabina, they couldn't turn

'round quick enough. They lit outer there like bats outer hell. I meant what I tole 'em, too, I ain't never been so scandalize' in my life. Me just home from church and have to put up with such as that!"

"You forgot the coffee cups," said Sabina. "What were you doing having church on Friday night, Lila May?"

"Candlelight Service for the Ten Virgins," replied Lila May briefly.

"I never heard of that. What church do you belong to, Lila May?"

"The Colosie and Universal Overcoming Church of God."

"What does that mean?"

"I don't know'm."

"Tell me about the candlelight service."

"Ain't you never see it?"

"No."

Lila May set the stacked plates on the table. "Well, they gits 'em ten colored virgins—"

"Where do they find them?" asked Sabina. It seemed to her like the recipe for rabbit stew. "First catch a rabbit—"

"They just goes out and gits 'em. And they has the service on the third Friday right after the full of the moon. The preacher he talk a while and then the gals come up and stand befo' de altar and he gives 'em all a candle and they stand there holdin' hit and sometimes they giggle and look sorter silly like. Then somebody put out de lights and ain't nobody make a sound. Then the preacher start prayin', kinder easy like at first and he roll off de Scripture jes like he done wrote it he-self. He tell about David dancin' befo de Ark, and Solomon's wives, and de Chillun of Israel and Sodom and Tomorrow, and he rip through that Book from coverlid to coverlid. Then he git to goin' stronger and stronger, and talk about puttin' yo' light in a bushel and lettin' it shine befo' men. And the folks all say, 'Amen, brother, Amen, brother.' Then he talk faster and louder and pretty soon he most shoutin'. And the brothers and the sisters say, 'Lawd God, Jesus ain't it so.' Sorter drag out the 'Lawd,' you know."

"And then what do they do?"

"Then they says it faster and faster, 'Lawd God, Jesus ain't it so.'" Lila May patted her foot in accompaniment to the rhythm of the words. "'Lawd God, Jesus ain't it so,' and they keep on sayin' hit jes like that till you wants to get up and throw your arms in the air and march around the heavenly throne. And the preacher says, 'Praise God, bless His Holy Name,' and the folks a-shoutin' gits louder and louder, and *ALL* of sudden jes like a clap o' thunder they's silent. Ain't nobody say nothin'. And you hear the folks a-breathin' and you smell 'em a-sweatin'. And you sets real still a-holdin' onto de bench and you caint see nothin'a-tall."

Lila May breathed heavily and wiped her face with her apron. "Then they's a little teency weency speck o' light down at de altar where de preacher done lit one of dem candles. Pretty soon he lights another one and passes on down de line till he done lit all ten of 'em. And de gals stand there holdin' de tall white candles and the light make a sorter yaller glow about they faces. Then somebody start playin' de organ and the gals march down the aisle outer de church goin' real slow so the candles won't go out. We all stands up then and starts singin', and first thing you know hits all over and everybody throw they arms around everybody else and come away feelin' joyful. Is you ever see anything like that, Miss Sabina?"

"No. I really haven't, Lila May. What *is* a virgin, Lila May?"

"Why, Miss Sabina, hits gals with immacerlate perceptions, like the Virgin Mary and the Infant Jesus."

"Oh, I see. Young girls with babies, and they aren't married."

"Yassum. We don't have no trouble findin' 'em. We has ten new ones every third Friday after the full of the moon."

"Well, thank you, Lila May, for telling me."

"Aw, that ain't nothin', Miss Sabina. Hits my duty to spread the gospel wherever it's needed."

Lila May took the dishes to the kitchen and Sabina wandered into the living room thinking how strange it was that there were so many kinds of religion and everybody thought his kind was the best. She recalled hearing of a new cult in the county called snake-worshippers whose members actually fondled live reptiles of the most deadly species, and urged their children to do so. There was competition among the mothers, she had heard, as to whose offspring could handle them better. Frequently someone was bitten and his survival was regarded as proof of holiness.

She wanted to tell somebody about the candlelight service for the ten dusky virgins, but it was too risqué; you couldn't go around talking about virgins even when they were colored. Of course, Claire could, Claire would make a grand story out of it and have everybody in stitches. She would stand in the middle of the room, taking three quick little puffs at her cigarette as if one were not enough, her nostrils would quiver sensuously at the intake; then she would blow the smoke out reluctantly; she would make you see the virgins holding the candles before the altar, and the sweating darkies working themselves up into a frenzy just before that silence that was like a "clap o' thunder." And she'd save the definition of a virgin for the very last so that everybody would be weak with laughter, and say, "Claire, you're simply a scream. I wish I could tell a story like you do. You can tell one as well as a man." But Sabina was not going to tell this one to Claire.

Claire loved an audience, the larger the better, and hated to be alone. Sabina's idea of a plethora of people was one other besides herself. Claire had never been in a hostile or uninterested group because she set the key for it. While Sabina, in no matter what group she found herself, always felt alien to it. If it consisted of conservatives, as it always did in Frost Haven, her attitude was rebellious, she was convinced that she was a liberal, a radical. But when, on the rare occasions she was away from home, she chanced to be among liberals, she became the most hidebound reactionary. She never differed openly with them in conversation but secretly nursed her variation, withdrawing in spirit from them and into herself.

Now she moved idly about the living room in search of a book or magazine she had not read. She wanted to forget Claire, the dance, the sultry day. Here was a facsimile edition of John Donne's *Biathanatos* with its ordered, perfect prose, making self-homicide seem not only logical but eminently desirable. It was just the thing for a winter's night before the fire with some of the reverend gentleman's acid love poems to act as an antidote.

But Sabina was too outdone this morning with Claire to settle down to metaphysics; she went over to the piano and began playing the "Revolutionary" Étude in C minor of Chopin. In an old girandole mirror on the opposite wall she could see the reflection of her head and shoulders as well as the tall vase of pink gladioli on the piano. It was quite a nice picture, especially for color: the pink flowers made her eyes appear bluer and her dark hair was an excellent foil for both. As her fingers stumbled over the intricate left-hand "runs," she thought that it was a pity somebody did not paint her like that, "Girl in a Mirror." The picture, of course, would not show the wrong notes she was playing. Some day when she had plenty of time she was going to sit down and learn to play those notes accurately, even though such drudgery meant losing for a while the feeling and sweep of the piece; but she never seemed to have that much time.

The sound of the doorbell pealed through the house and when she looked up she saw Barrett Page standing in the entrance. "May I come in?" he asked.

"Of course, Barrett. How are you?"

"Are you here all alone?"

"Yes—temporarily."

"Would you like to go downtown with me for a Coca-Cola?"

"Yes, I'd love it."

"Where's Claire?"

"Riding." Sabina hesitated. "She should be back soon if you want to wait for her."

"Perhaps we'll see her at the drugstore." He walked over to the piano. "What was that you were playing?"

"The 'Revolutionary' Étude."

"I thought so but I couldn't be sure."

"Was it that bad?"

"Yes. You ought to be ashamed of yourself."

"I wasn't watching the notes," she said defensively.

"What were you watching?" He looked around then and saw the mirror. "Ah, Sabina, when are you going to quit living in a mirror? Come along, child. I'm hot and I'm thirsty."

"You are not very nice this morning."

"No. I'm my natural self. Sabina," he demanded suddenly, "have you ever been kissed?"

"Why?"

"Have you?"

"In a way, yes."

"I thought so. Sabina, would you kiss me just once?" She walked over to the sofa and sat down. "I might sometime."

He followed her. "Now," he said.

"Barrett! In the broad open daylight? Now? Why?"

"I want to know something." Before she could answer he was seated beside her and his hard arms were around her. "This doesn't mean a thing," he told her; "it is purely in the spirit of scientific investigation."

"No, please don't, Barrett. I'm not a guinea pig." She tried to pull away from him but he held her. "That is undignified, Sabina, and very childish. Are you going to kiss me, or aren't you?"

"Yes." That was for Claire who had said he was dangerous.

"Are you sure you want to?"

"Yes."

"Then why don't you go ahead and do it?"

"Why, I thought—*you* were going to kiss *me*."

"And you were going to sit back and suffer yourself to be kissed. No, thank you." He stood up, annoyed. "Come on and let's go get the drink."

Sabina, too, was irritated. She had wanted him to beg her, or force her. "I don't believe I want a drink," she said coldly.

He laughed and took her hand. "What a child you are. When you grow up, drop me a postcard, and if I'm not dead of old age, I'll come take a look at you. Sabina," he held the car door open for her, "when you were younger, did your mother ever take you out into the garden and tell you about the birds and the bees?"

"No," she answered sullenly.

"I believe you."

He got in and started the car, and she saw that his face was serious. She wished she knew what he was thinking, was it about Claire? She felt like an idiot just riding along and saying nothing. "Barrett, do you like the South?" she asked in her best conversational tone.

"I'm crazy about it; nobody ever does anything here. Why? Is this is a proposal?"

Sabina flushed. "I was only making conversation."

"Oh. Then the next question is, 'Have you seen our water works?' Sabina, what do you think about?"

"Why, I scarcely know—nothing very definite, just sort of vague, half-formed ideas."

"Why don't you clarify them, Sabina, find out what it is you want and where you are going? Are you afraid?"

"Afraid?" she repeated indignantly; "of course I'm not. What have I to be afraid of?"

"I don't know, but you are, of something. If I didn't like you so much and think you had possibilities, I should be tempted to let you go on with your sleepwalking. You are terribly exasperating, and yet challenging, too."

"Thank you," she said quickly and wondered why she was not displeased. At least he was thinking about her and not about Claire, and she was glad he had added the word "challenging."

"It wasn't intended as a compliment," he told her. He was driving very slowly and now he turned and looked at her. "There are many things abut you I don't approve of—but confound it, you are appealing. You make me want to rescue you from your ivory tower. You are a statue, a Galatea, and I want to play Pygmalion. You are a sleeping beauty, and I want to wake you up, see what I can make of you."

"Why don't you?" she asked impudently.

"Well, it would be quite an undertaking, and I am not at liberty to do it." He turned his attention once more to driving. "I was about to begin your education a short while ago when I asked you to kiss me. I'm sorry about that; I shouldn't have asked you."

"It doesn't matter," she said slowly. What had he mean by not being at liberty? Was it Claire? It was alway Claire who interfered, who stole the spotlight.

His next words seemed to prove that theory. "Whe did Claire get in last night?"

"Why, don't you know? She said you brought he

home." Now she would find out whether Claire had told the truth or lied.

"She said that?"

"Yes, she told me at breakfast."

"That's strange. I wonder why she did that. She knows better."

Ah! so Claire had lied! Sabina felt immeasurably better; she pushed the hair out of her eyes and smoothed the tucks in her green linen dress. It was a pretty dress, with a small scalloped collar and pockets and very fine pearl buttons. She smiled at Barrett Page because he had not brought Claire home. "Barrett, I have a new short story; would you like to read it?"

"Of course I would. What's it about?"

"Well, it's about two old maids, sisters, who live in the same house but haven't spoken to each other for twenty years—"

"And one morning," he interrupted, "they find a baby on the doorstep."

"No."

"A puppy, then."

"No."

"A man under the bed."

"No."

"Well, what do they find?"

"Nothing. They lose something. One of them wakes up and finds she has lost her voice; she *can't* speak to her sister, and that makes her want to," Sabina explained.

"And so their young niece comes to live with them and reconciles them," he said, "and marries the butcher's son and everybody lives happily ever afterward."

"No."

"All right. But why write about old maids? Nothing could possibly happen to them that would be interesting. Sabina, why don't you write about young love?"

"Oh, it's so monogamous."

"You're a strange girl. You are witty, but you have no humor. You are clever, but you have the emotions of a twelve-year-old child. And you're as lovely as the dawn."

"Why, Mister Page!"

"Well, you already knew it. Besides, I wish you weren't."

"Why?"

"Use your imagination."

Sabina used it freely and found it very pleasant.

CHAPTER VII

At the packing house the sultry day seemed hotter than elsewhere, for the fur from the peaches was thick in the air, it mingled with the dust brought in by the wagons and by trucks and clung to the sweating bodies of the workers. Their faces, arms and hands were stinging, their tempers short. By noon two cars had been packed and dispatched and by mid-afternoon another was sealed, ready for departure. The fourth, unfilled as yet, stood on the siding, dripping ice water, and small boys had crawled under it to catch the precious drops. Black boys and white boys, they lay side by side between the rails fighting amicably for access to the cooling stream. Their black mothers were in the orchards, the white ones under the shed, too busy to bother with racial distinctions. Twice during the day sisters of the boys had brought the babies of the family to the shed where their mothers could suckle them. The tired sweating women had sat down briefly, unbuttoned their blouses and known the relief of lightened breasts.

Older boys were putting crates together, fitting them with baskets, passing on to others who pasted on the colored labels. They were constantly interrupted by cries of "Crate" and ran to take a box to the packer who had just finished. The one just completed must be covered with a pink paper "cushion" and have a top nailed down over it.

The fruit rolled endlessly out of the buckets into the bins; there had never been so many peaches in all the world. The packers' weary fingers fumbled for "two's," or "two's-and-a-half" to place on the top layers, and accepted one-and-three-quarter inch ones for fillers. In each basket of each crate the bottom layer must rest stem down, point up, and the top layer just the opposite. At each packer's feet was a bucket for "culls," fruit too ripe, too green, with split-seed, or wormy—these would be taken home and canned or preserved. When the packer called "Crate" she was given a card with her number on it; each card meant that she had earned four cents. By nightfall she would have a hundred perhaps, or more if she were an exceptionally good packer. They had begun at daylight and the bins had not been empty since then. One wagon with its rows and tiers of buckets deposited its load and drove off, to be followed swiftly by another. Often a load would be condemned by the packers. "They're pulling it too green—tell the pickers it's too green"; but the superintendent would say, "Use it anyhow, the Yankees will never know the difference." But the chief complaints came when the superintendent brought orders for "special" or fancy crates which meant delay and care in choosing only the finest fruit.

A government inspector came along, lifted a peach out of a crate that was being packed, cut it open with his knife and grunted with disappointment when he found it perfect. He was only happy when the fruit was overripe or oversize, or plucked too green, had dryrot at the center, or was too small. Then he could condemn an entire car and if the owner insisted on shipping it subsequently, he would not clear enough to pay for the freight.

Matthew Cox had irritably counted the number of crates in each car; he knew that there should be four hundred and seventy-two, yet each time he counted, there were either more or less. In disgust he went back to his small office and began sorting the cards by number so that he could make out the pay roll. Sam Cummings was running around, as one of the packers said, "like a chicken with it's head cut off." "Got to work tonight," he told them; "if you go home for your supper it just means you'll be that much later getting through. We got to git four cars today or know the reason why."

The cries of "Crate," "Crate," rang out almost constantly and with each hour the heat, dust and flying fur became more unendurable. Some of the less experienced packers had scratched their stinging arms until the skin was torn from them; the men's shirts that had been white early in the morning were now reddish yellow and so wet with perspiration that they clung like constricting bands around chest and shoulders. The women had unfastened their shoes and stood on them rather than wore them. Some of the crate-makers were young boys from town and their tender hands were swollen, blistered, peeling. One of them brushed the tears from his eyes when no one was looking and went doggedly on driving nails. When his eyes got too full, he missed the nail and hit his fingers.

Ellison Frost saw the child's determination and smiled. "Come into the office a moment, Carey," he called. The boy came quickly but his manner was apprehensive. "Mr. Frost, I've turned out as many as anybody."

"I know you have, Carey, you're doing fine."

A sob broke from the boy's throat. "My hands kinder hurt, though."

"I'm going to swap jobs with you for a few minutes. You drink this Coca-Cola and I'll nail crates for a while."

"Aw, Mr. Frost, I couldn't let you do that."

"I'd like to very much. You keep the office for me; if anyone comes in and asks you anything, just tell him 'No.'"

"Yes, sir. Is that all you do, Mr. Frost?"

"Just about."

Ellison Frost wondered what he was going to do about tomorrow's being Sunday. There were more peaches in the orchards ready for shipping than could be disposed of tonight; the ox was obviously in the ditch. Peaches did not observe the Sabbath; they went right ahead and ripened.

He took up Carey's hammer and set to work beside a tough little country boy.

"Carey quit?" asked the moppet.

"No."

"Sick, huh? The sissy—"

"No, he's doing a job for me."

"Humph!" There was skepticism and disgust in the boy's tone.

Ellison Frost was happy to be doing something with his hands. All day when he should have been at the exchange getting market prices and giving orders for the destination or disposal of cars he had been thinking of Claire and what he should say to her. He had not been able to sleep or to put his mind on anything. He was still unable to decide whether to "pack" tomorrow or not. He had heard Sam Cummings telling the packers not to go home for supper but he thought he should have to change that even though one of the refrigerated cars was left standing unfilled on the tracks.

He tossed aside a finished crate and began to assemble another. It was a great relief to think of himself as Carey Thomas, working for seventy-five cents a day with none of the responsibilities of an owner on his young shoulders, none of the long history of a peach in his mind as he made a box to carry it off. And the person in New York, Chicago or Cincinnati who ate the peach would never know the labor that had gone into its production: it was a year-round operation, not merely a matter of getting it gathered in the orchard and put into a basket.

As soon as one season ended, the next began; the trees had to be pruned, trimmed (the fruit grew on new shoots, not on the old branches), diseased trees had to be dug up and replaced by saplings. The rows between them must be plowed and sown with winter grain or peas to provide food for the soil. Then there were sprayings— a spray of lime and sulphur to prevent scale; frequently the earth had to be removed from the base of the trees and treated, the trees themselves had to be whitewashed to prevent borers. After the buds began to form there was the constant danger of a freeze and the necessity of building smudge fires.

"You finished two more crates?" the boy beside him asked admiringly.

"Yes. I like it, don't you?"

"It ain't so bad. I've done two myself."

"Good boy."

"I help my papa at home; he lets me fix all the fences that need mending, and sometimes he lets me help him work on the barn and outhouses."

The calls of "Crate," "Crate," "Crate," went through the shed. Another wagon pulled up to the side and buckets of fruit were noisily unloaded on the platform.

Ellison Frost felt the perspiration trickling down his back but he did not object to it. He was thinking how, each year, the sight of the orchards in bloom seemed to him worth all the worry and money they had cost him. There had been money for the spraying materials and machinery, money for the "hands" the year round. They had to be "carried" through the winter, provisions bought for them, and if they were ill, their doctors' bills paid. There was always money needed for payrolls, for plows, for trucks, for water tanks.

But when he walked through the blossoming orchards in spring, all that was forgotten. He had frequently wanted to take off his shoes and walk barefoot through the furrows. It was then, not at harvest time, that he felt the poetry of orchards, thought of Demeter and the richness of the soil. There was the first small red blossom of the Elbertas which were paradoxically the last to ripen; then the pale, almost lavender bloom of Carmen and Early Rose; the Hileys next; but of them all the Georgia

Belle had the largest, thickest, most beautiful blossoms. They seemed actually to look unreal, artificial, as if they had been made of paper by the deft hands of Japanese.

Then the blossoms fell, and the hard little peaches began to form. That was when the trees had to be "bumped" so that the fruit infected with curculio would fall, be caught on canvas stretchers and burned. And if there were still too many of the hard green fruit on the branches, they had to be thinned by crews working from dawn until sunset. There was a final spraying of lime, sulphur and arsenate of lead, and after that prayers for sunshine and just the right amount of rain.

Ellison Frost's hands went on working, the blows from his hammer falling simultaneously with those of the lad beside him. Subconsciously he fitted the pieces of pulpy wood together; the nails seemed to drive themselves in deftly and the finished box moved off without any apparent assistance from his mind.

He was thinking that the weather was remarkably indifferent to the fate of peach crops. Frequently the blossoms would begin opening in late February or early March and there would be heavy rains followed by a freeze. In each blossom would be a small lump of ice just large enough to kill the embryonic fruit and make the blackened petals drop off. Almost every year, it seemed, the orchard owners predicted that ninety per cent of the new crop had been killed—and there seemed always to be ninety per cent left.

Only rarely did the trees bloom under ideal conditions and then they were a sight to behold. Even when the blossoms had begun to fall, to be replaced with dark green leaves, the blown petals falling like snow and scattering over the hillsides seemed as insubstantial as a dream. A man, conscious of their evanescent beauty, saw in the process something at once poetic, historic and universal.

And how could a feeling like that be explained to Sam Cummings who saw only so many crates to a tree, so many or so few dollars to go into the pockets of his faded overalls? To Sam, a rabbit was something to be shot and sold, a tree represented stove wood which he would cut and carry into town on his queer little "cart"—a wagon body set on the chassis of an old truck and pulled by a mule whose hair was thick and matted with cockleburrs. Sometimes the whole family rode in the cart. Kitchen chairs were placed in it, and Daisy, Tippy, Cummings' wife and his mother would sit there, the three women in calico dresses and sunbonnets, holding buckets of huckleberries which they would peddle from door to door. The old mother always reminded Ellison Frost of a character in *Tale of Two Cities*, the one who knitted while the French Revolution boiled around her. Old Granny Cummings would never be a schemer, she hadn't enough sense; but one got the impression that she was absolutely ruthless, absolutely amoral. She dipped snuff, and spat, and uttered her dicta. Her choice of words sometimes made Ellison Frost ill; at other times he thought they came straight out of Shakespeare and Chaucer: strong old Anglo-Saxon phrases that had probably come fresh from the mountains of North Carolina; coarse words, associated with animals, with life in its crudest and most elemental forms. In winter she wore high-laced men's shoes, woolen stockings, and over her homespun frock a man's khaki army overcoat. Her hat was a sergeant's khaki cap. She had got these from Daisy's elder brother, her grandson, who had been in the army and was now living in Alabama, probably for very good reasons.

The old woman nodded a great deal, had to be kept awake with very strong tea (over which there was generally a greasy scum); and when she opened her eyes you saw beneath the visor of her cap that one of them was useless from having been pecked in the iris by a chicken many years ago. The pupil was now askew, and far up under the wrinkled eyelid. Her fierce, pointed nose was hawklike; and there was no doubt that Granny ruled the Cummings family "from a to izzard." She was an old woman to command distrust, possibly fear, but also a certain reluctant respect. She had what Claire affectedly called, and what she herself naturally called, "guts."

The thought of Claire brought him up sharply. Why was he wasting time making crates when her future happiness was at stake? He was suddenly conscious of the wet garments clinging to his aching back, of the weary muscles in his forearms and hands. Where was Cummings? Was little Carey Thomas going to sit in the office all day drinking that Coca-Cola? Was Matthew Cox never going to finish counting the slips and making out the pay roll? He had been putting bills and silver into envelopes and sealing them ever since lunch; the boy seemed of late to have had something on his mind besides peaches. And at Matthew's age that could mean only one thing.

Ellison Frost started across the platform to look for the boy but he was intercepted by the overseer. "Mr.

Frost, looks like we're goin' to have to hold things up long enough for 'em to go home and git some supper. They say they won't work less'n we do let 'em go."

"Of course they need supper, Cummings. We couldn't ask them to work without it. What time is it?" He pulled out the thin gold watch that had belonged to his father. "It's five-thirty now. Suppose we let them have the next hour off. I'm sure they'll work better afterward."

"They better," said Cummings grimly; "seems like half of 'em been layin' down on the job."

"Young Cox isn't in his office. Have you seen him?"

"Reckon he's hangin' around my place; seems like him or his pa's there half the time."

"Your place? Do you mean your house? What are they doing there?"

Cummings smiled and Ellison Frost thought he had not known that a smile could be so nasty. "I got a daughter, you know," Cummings said, "same as you have."

"What did Matthew do about the pay roll?"

"He done paid 'em off. Wouldn't surprise me none if he was gone for the day."

"That's quite all right," Ellison Frost lied, "I recall now that I told him he could go." But it was not all right. Not for the world would he have Matthew Cox involved with the Cummings family. The next thing anyone knew there would be a shotgun wedding and Matthew would find his brave young ambitions lying shattered in the dust.

"Where is his father?"

"Over at the Hilltown orchard."

"See if you can get him on the phone, I want to speak to him."

Ellison Frost was glad to see that Carey Thomas had returned to work and his own office was empty. He sat down in the cane-bottomed chair before his desk and put his head on his arms. What was he going to say to Claire? What did he honestly think about the whole matter? To suspect was one thing; to believe was another. He could suspect Claire of being Page's mistress, but he could not believe it. And yet, could there be any doubt of it? The words he had heard had been too clear, too convincing to permit of any other interpretation. Suppose now that when he questioned Claire tonight she should lie again—what should he do? Call young Page out and challenge him to a duel or have a shotgun wedding in his own family? Should he say, Sir, never darken my doorstep again; you have betrayed my hospitality, to say nothing of my daughter?

He hadn't the faintest idea what fathers did about these things in this modern world—yet obviously they occurred just as they had a half-century and more ago. He had heard of locking girls up in their rooms and feeding them on bread and water; but if he knew Claire, she would slip out the window. But he did not want her to marry Page, not under these circumstances or any other, if he was the kind of man he seemed to be.

The telephone rang and Ellison Frost said, "Yes?"

"Cox is on his way over here now," reported Cummings.

"When he arrives, send him in here immediately."

Mr. Frost rose, lighted a cigarette and began walking about the room. The thing that made him angriest was the fact that he had liked Barrett Page. He had thought him sound, intelligent, and far above the average in every respect. It was not pardonable but it was understandable that Page should have had Claire for his mistress in New York. Ellison Frost could see that. Claire had been alone, unattached, friendly with those Bohemians in Greenwich Village—and she was as guilty as Page up to that point. But it was Page's duplicity, his coming to Frost Haven, posing as an admirer of Sabina, abusing the hospitality of the Frost home that seemed the most outrageous act of all—a thing difficult to reconcile with his straightforward, almost stern demeanor.

The ashes from his cigarette dropped unheeded on the floor as Mr. Frost stopped short; he was trying to exonerate Page and giving Claire the benefit of no doubts whatsoever. Now why was that? No father had ever loved his daughter more or had more faith in her. Why should he accept her guilt as a matter of course and be amazed at the man's? Was it because a father knowing his own weaknesses was not surprised to find them reproduced in his own child, but expected the children of other men to be stronger, invulnerable?

He answered, "Come in," to a knock at the door; then said, "Ah, Henry, I want to see you. Have a seat over there."

"I'm rather busy, Mr. Frost," said Henry Cox taking off his hat and fanning himself with it.

Ellison Frost closed the office door. "Henry, there are some things more important than peaches. I want to talk to you about a very personal matter and I hope you won't think it is none of my business." A fine way to begin, with such pat, platitudinous phrases! They must have been invented for just such trite situations!

"Why, no, Mr. Frost."

"You know how much I think of you and Matt, always have since the first year you worked for me. I feel as if I had helped raise Matt—how old was he when I first saw him?"

"Let's see," said Henry Cox, "he's twenty-one now, and that was seven years ago. He would have been fourteen, sir. Has Matt been doing something he shouldn't?"

"Well, I don't know about that. Sit down, Henry, sit down." The big man reached back for the chair and pulled it under him but his body did not relax; there was nothing limp about him except his blue shirt and dungaree pants. His blue eyes were alert and his crisp reddish mustache seemed to bristle.

"I feel that I am partially responsible," Ellison Frost went on, "because the Cummings family are in my employ and living on my land. Henry, Sam Cummings tells me that Matt has been hanging around that daughter of his, Daisy, and may be over there now. He has paid off the workers and gone without asking anyone."

Henry Cox started to speak but Ellison Frost waved his hand. "No, I'm not mad about that. If Daisy were a nice girl I shouldn't say a word to you, I'd just let Matt know he couldn't do things like that without getting permission. But here's the point, Henry: that family is the scum of the earth, God knows I ought to know, and Matt's too fine a boy to be mixed up with them."

"You know how boys are, Mr. Frost," Henry Cox said slowly and apologetically, "when there's a little slut around so handy that all you have to do is whistle and she comes running. I ain't excusing Matt, you understand, but it seems there ain't much for him to do when he gets off from work. The other college boys and girls in town think they're too good to have anything to do with him."

"I know, Henry, I know." He was a fine one to be talking to a father about his child's morals, and how much easier it was to settle their problems than one's own! "It's not so much Matt's morals I'm worried about as—something else. Henry, I don't trust that Cummings family, they're not just poor, they're po-white trash and you don't know how low-down they can be. Cummings has a prison record. His son is living in Alabama and mixed up with that revolting snake cult. The grandmother is an obscene, ruthless old hag. They are not only degenerate, they are depraved. They wouldn't stop at anything, any sort of low trickery, blackmail—I wouldn't put anything past them."

There was a question in Henry Cox's face and Ellison Frost answered it. "Why do I keep them here? I'm sorry but I can't tell you that, Henry. I would if I could."

"I know for a fact," said the other man, "that Matt don't care anything about the girl, he couldn't. He's got too much sense—the fact is, Mr. Frost, I think he's in love with somebody that won't look at him and it makes him mean, makes him want to hurt somebody because he's hurt himself." He rose slowly. "I'll speak to him about Daisy. I can't promise it'll do any good—he thinks he's his own man, but I'll tell him what you said."

"Thank you, Henry."

"Thank *you*, Mr. Frost."

Ellison Frost was rather proud of the way he had handled that. If it was true, as Cummings had said, that Henry Cox as well as Matthew had been hanging around

Daisy, the warning would apply to him also, and the father, at least, would have enough common sense to abide by it.

"I'm going home now, Henry; can I offer you a ride?"

"I'll ride as far as the highway with you. Feels like it might rain tonight or tomorrow."

"Yes, it's very sultry."

Although the majority of the workers had gone to supper, the heat under the shed was still intense and the air still thick with fur and dust. Darkies lounged about on the platform, some of them drinking soda-pops, others dancing to the music of a jew's-harp which a pickaninny was playing. One lanky youth was humming,

> "Oh, I've got a gal and a bull dog, too,
> Gal don't love me, but de bull dog do—"

and shouting, "Hey, Silly-bub, step on dat music, dat's too solemncholy. Faster, nigger, a heap faster'n dat!"

Some of the pickers from the orchards had broken open a watermelon and had their faces buried in sections of it. Two half-grown colored boys had a checkerboard that had been made from a corrugated box-top. For "men" they were using bottle tops and one of them shouted to his cautious opponent who kept his "men" back from the center, "Hey, you, come on down to de Mason and Dixon line!"

Flies were swarming about the discarded bottles, hovering over the watermelon rinds and crawling across rotten fruit. There was the strong acid odor of putrefaction from cull dumps and from the outdoor latrines.

"Henry, I want you to order some slack lime Monday morning and see that it is distributed in the proper places," said Ellison Frost.

"Yes, sir. Mr. Frost, aren't some of those darkies pickers?"

"I don't know, they may be."

"Hey, you," called Cox as he was getting into the machine, "are any of you boys pickers?"

"Yassuh, I is." "I is," came half-a-dozen answers.

"Well, great jumping Jehosaphat! What in hell do you think you are doing here?"

"We'se takin a hour off for supper—"

"The devil you are! I suppose you think you can pick peaches by moonlight. Get back to the orchards this minute—" Henry Cox turned. "Mr. Frost, I guess I'd better stay here. Niggers won't work unless somebody's standing over them every minute." He got out and closed the car door. "Thank you just the same, Mr. Frost. And I won't forget what you said."

"Can I send you some supper? Some sandwiches, and milk?"

"No, thank you, Mr. Frost. I'll be all right."

"So long, Henry."

As he left the packing house and turned to go through the Elberta orchard Ellison Frost wished that he had asked Cox about packing tomorrow. Of course, if it should rain tonight and tomorrow was cool, the packing could wait. But if it did not, and the sunshine and heat were as intense as today—

The road made a sharp curve that led directly in front of the Cummings house and standing before that house was someone—yes, it was Matthew Cox. The boy was evidently talking to the girl on the porch and he seemed quite angry, he was making abrupt and awkward gestures which changed suddenly into pleading ones.

The girl's words became audible as Ellison Frost came nearer. "I won't, I tell you. You got no right to tell me what I'll do and what I won't. Now go on away, Matt, I'm sick of you—"

Then the boy's answer, "And I tell you you can't treat me this way. You went out with father last night, you know you did, and you're going with me tonight. Who do you think you are, you miserable little—"

She went into the house and Mr. Frost hoped that was the last of it. But the boy called to her, "Daisy, come back—I haven't finished with you yet—"

In a moment she returned and there was a rifle in her hand. "Well, I've finished with you, and if you don't get the hell away from here—"

The setting sun was brilliant on the boy's angry face; it glinted on the rifle barrel. The girl's grandmother came out on the porch. "Daisy, put that thing down; ain't nothin' to git so mad about—"

Daisy pushed her away with her elbow. "Lemme alone, I'll tend to this."

Ellison Frost stopped the car and came up beside Matt. "Daisy, I think your grandmother is right, you'd best put the rifle up."

Matt laughed. "You needn't worry, Mr. Frost; she's just trying to scare me; the little fool thinks she can bluff me with that .22—"

"Hush, Matt," commanded Mr. Frost. "Daisy, give that gun to your grandmother—"

"You stay outer this," she said; "it ain't no business of your'n—"

"Daisy—" He started up on the porch and she cried shrilly, "You stay where you are—"

Matt Cox was almost bending double with laughter. "I'll swear, Daisy, anybody'd think you meant it." He looked at Ellison Frost and explained, "She's defending her honor, Mr. Frost. Isn't it a beautiful sight?"

"You stop that laffin'," screamed Daisy; "stop it—" And then there was the deafening explosion. The air smelled like gunpowder and Daisy was lowering the rifle. Ellison Frost's ears were useless and the sunlight in his eyes was blinding.

Something touched his legs and when he stooped down he saw Matt lying face down on the ground with one arm outstretched.

"Matt, Matt—"

Ellison Frost tried to lift the boy up but could not. He realized then that the boy was unconscious and that blood was fast discoloring his shirt. He wasn't dead—yet —there was still a faint pulse. Should he be moved?

He heard the sharp impact of flesh on flesh and looked up to see old Granny Cummings slapping the girl's face. "Now you see what you done," she was crying shrilly; "looks like you done hurt 'im, he ain't a movin' none—"

"I meant to kill 'im," said Daisy.

Granny's bony hands flew to the girl's cheeks again. "You simlin-headed idiot, you bloody, silly little fool!" She knocked the rifle to the floor. "Go see what ails 'im, he ain't gittin' up—"

Ellison Frost wanted to scream also. Why didn't some-one come? He was afraid to leave Matt, afraid Daisy would shoot him again. He wished that he had the gun in his own hands; but he seemed to be unable to move. His feet were fixed to the soft red dust, he could not walk as far as the front steps or even so far as the bright cosmos and sun-baked wilted zinnias growing in the yard.

"Get Dr. Mannering on the phone," he commanded; "ask him to come here at once. If you can't locate him, get any doctor you can but get one immediately. Then come here and help me carry this boy into the house. Send for his father down at the packing shed." His voice rose uncontrollably. "Get somebody and get him quickly."

Neither of the women moved for a moment. "She couldn't 'a' hurt 'im," said the old crone; "he's just playin' possum!" She came cautiously down the front steps then, and shook her finger in Ellison Frost's face. "And you, Mr. Frost, don't you go tryin' to get Daisy in trouble for this. She was just mad, that's all—"

"For God's sake, Mrs. Cummings, this boy may be dying! Will you *do* something?"

She drew back slowly and repeated, "Dying?" Then she began screaming again, "He ain't! She didn't do it, do you hear? Daisy, you git in the house like I told you—"

Ellison Frost brushed past her and started into the house. "Where's your phone?"

"Don't you tech Daisy!" shrilled the old woman; "don't you lay a hand on 'er!"

He found the phone in the hall and by a miracle got the doctor at once. When he came back to the front yard there were darkies who had come up from the orchard. Sam Cummings was there and his wife, but Daisy was gone. One of the darkies said, "You want us to take 'im in the house, Mr. Frost?"

"No. The doctor will be here in just a few moments; he says not to move him. One of you boys go down to the shed and tell Mr. Cox."

"Alec done gone."

Ellison Frost wished that he did not have to be there when Henry Cox saw his son.

He looked down at the still body of Matthew Cox. The boy's dark hair was rumpled, his face almost buried in the dust and his right arm outflung as when he had fallen. He wanted terribly to lift the boy's head out of the dirt but he was afraid. It made him angry to think of the boy so defenseless, so exposed to the gaze of the curious and the hostile—it was almost as if he were dead. And death was such a democratic institution: anyone could come and look at you, anyone might bury you, and afterward your dust became mingled with the dust of all the world's thieves and kings and cutthroats and housewives and harlots.

When he looked at Sam Cummings and his wife he saw that there was nothing in their faces except sullenness and a certain crafty watchfulness.

The sunset just over the worn brown hills was a riot of splendid color—too brilliant, too gaudy.

He saw Henry Cox coming up the road then, and the sight of the man's face made Ellison Frost want to thank God that he had never had a son.

At six o'clock that afternoon Mrs. Frost returned from her district meeting. The minister and his wife helped her into the house and she collapsed on the living-room sofa.

"Take my hat, Lila May," she commanded weakly, "and get me the slop jar."

"Bring it in here?" asked the colored woman.

"You'll have to, I can't get upstairs. Hurry, Lila May, I never was so nauseated in all my life."

"Yes'm."

A few moments later Mrs. Frost lay back in exhaustion. "I fell better now. I was so afraid I was going to have to ask Mr. Wilhoit to stop the car and let me get relief. I suppose it was the heat. Take that out, Lila May, and bring me some crushed ice."

"You want a doctor?"

"No. I'll be all right now. Where is Miss Sabina? And Miss Clarissa? Has Mr. Frost come home?"

"If I didn't know how you felt about drinking, Miz Frost, I'd sho say you was drunk. Yo' eyes is as red as beets and you spit up enough—"

"That will do, Lila May," interrupted Mrs. Frost. "I am not intoxicated. It always makes me sick to ride in a car when I have to sit on the back seat. I'm sure Mr. Wilhoit is a very good driver, but the way he whipped around those curves—I thought I'd never live to get home. If we have to go one more mile, I thought—"

When Lila May returned with the crushed ice she was still talking. "I tried to whisper to Mrs. Wilhoit to ask him not to go quite so fast but she was comparing recipes for Lady Baltimore cake with Mrs. Nixon—"

"Hello, Mother," said Claire coming into the room; "drunk again?"

"Miss Clarissa," reproved Lila May, "you hadn't oughter talk to her like that when she's so sick."

"She always is after one of those sprees. What did you have for dinner, Mother?"

"I never saw so much food in all my life, Clarissa, you would have enjoyed it. I do wish you and Sabina would take more interest in church work, it is the greatest sorrow of my life that you don't. Many a night I have lain awake worrying about it, but some day you'll see it as I do. If I didn't believe that, I wouldn't have strength to go on."

Claire sat down on the piano bench. "What did you have to eat?"

"Well, there were long tables under the pine trees out in the grove, *you* know, right next to the cemetery, and we were all so tired and hungry by that time that we ate like pigs. They had great platters of fried chicken—just the good pieces, of course; the scraps were made into pies, the neck and gizzard and wings and back and liver— nobody ate the pies. Then there were great dishes of baked country ham, the best ham I ever put in my mouth, and big old-fashioned country biscuits, peach pickles, watermelon-rind preserves, sliced tomatoes, potato salad —it was good, too; I think it had pimientos in it, or maybe it was red pepper—then there were deviled eggs, cucumber pickles, salt-rising bread, rights-and-lefts, and every kind of cake and pie under high heaven. There was a pineapple upside-down cake that I wish I had the recipe for, and pound cakes—great slices *that* thick— caramel layer cake; those country people certainly know how to cook! But I honestly believe that huckleberry pie was the best thing they had; I tried to buy one of them to bring home with me but there weren't any left."

"Who presided?" asked Claire.

"A returned missionary, and he gave one of the best talks I ever heard in my life."

"What about?"

"I've forgotten now, but it was a perfectly splendid talk—he'd been in one of those foreign countries, somewhere in Asia or Africa—oh, I do remember now, he told us all about the marriage customs of the savages."

"All?" Claire repeated.

"He told it beautifully, of course, there wasn't anything objectionable in it. Just how they bought their wives for so many cattle or sheep. He said the fatter the women were, the higher price they brought. We all smiled a little at that."

"Discreetly," said Claire.

"Yes, discreetly, of course."

"Sabina," called Claire, "come on down and hear about the sexual life of the savages."

"I wonder—" began Mrs. Frost.

"You wonder what?"

"I wonder if I should have eaten that last piece of huckleberry pie. Clarissa, will you ask Lila May to bring the slop jar back?"

"Oh, my Lord," said Claire.

The telephone was ringing in the back hall and Sabina answered it. "Yes, Father. What? When? Why, how perfectly awful, yes, I'll tell her. Good-bye, Father."

She came slowly into the living room. "Matthew Cox is dead."

"Who is Matthew Cox?" asked Mrs. Frost. "Oh, I know, the superintendent's son."

"He was shot," continued Sabina.

"How perfectly terrible," said Claire. "Do they know who did it?"

"Is Lila May coming?" asked Mrs. Frost.

"Yes, here she is now."

"Mother, father said tell you he wouldn't be home for some time yet."

"I declare," said Mrs. Frost, "I don't think Mr. Frost ought to worry me this way when I'm sick. Sabina, get me some more crushed ice. You can put it down that the boy had been doing something he shouldn't or he wouldn't have gotten shot. I declare, my head is killing me."

"Do you want some aspirin, Mother?"

"No, I don't think I could retain it." Mrs. Frost closed her eyes and in a few moments was asleep.

Claire and Sabina went out into the hall. "Do they know who shot him?" whispered Claire.

"Father didn't say."

"I wonder if it was anybody we know."

"Of course not, Clarissa."

"Where was father telephoning from?"

"He didn't say. Why didn't *you* answer the phone?"

"You got there first. Well, there's one good thing about it," said Claire cheerfully, "Father won't want to see me in the library tonight. But I'm sorry about Matthew; I only saw him once but I thought he was a very handsome boy—a sort of peasant Hamlet."

Sabina strolled out into the garden to watch the birds sipping water at the edge of the pool and Claire followed her. "Hasn't it been hot today," she complained, holding out her organdie skirt to catch the ghost of a long-dead breeze.

CHAPTER VIII

❈

SABINA WAS SORRY THAT MATTHEW WAS DEAD. SHE HAD frequently suspected that he admired her very much, was perhaps in love with her—from the proper distance, of course. He had never said anything to her, but she had noticed that he was nervous and ill at ease in her presence, that he gazed at her with gratifying admiration. It had made her feel as beautiful and inaccessible as a star, and she would miss his silent homage. Her admirers were not too numerous.

But how on earth could he have looked twice at Daisy Cummings? If he had admired Sabina Frost, how could he have endured the presence of Daisy?

Sabina hoped that the girl would be publicly hanged from the big oak tree by the cemetery, with a black cloth over her face, and her head subsequently stuck up on a pike on the court-house square. The electric chair was much too good for her. Daisy was out now on bail and evidently as unconcerned as if she had only shot a rabbit in the snow. She could be seen walking to the crossroads store in her pink dress and sunbonnet with Tippy trotting at her heels; she would be chewing gum and Tippy sucking at a long stick of peppermint candy, his big head lolling loosely from side to side. Among the Cummings family no one seemed the least bit worried except Granny whose shrieks and moans sometimes reached the Frost house on a clear night. They were more like the cries of an animal in pain than of a sorrowing human being.

Mr. Frost, so far as Sabina knew, had never had that talk with Claire in the library. When he was not busy in the orchards he was making trips to Macon to confer with the prosecuting attorney. The trial was set for August and was only a few days distant.

But as the days wore on Sabina frequently forgot that Matthew was dead. It had happened so suddenly, was over so quickly, and it had not been an actual experience to her. It was very difficult always for her to remember just who was alive and who was dead. When she had got in the habit of inquiring of someone about an invalid relative, and associated the sight of him with that particular inquiry, she was quite likely to say, "Mr. Waller, how is your father today?" long after the old man had been laid to his final rest. It was not that she had cared how the old man was, or listened to the reply, or would have indeed have known him if she had seen him, but it was something to say. Nowadays she always asked Miss Lucy Taylor about her mother. Old Mrs. Taylor had been having rheumatism or strokes ever since Sabina was a child, and it was as natural as saying, "Good-morning," to add, "How is your mother today?" She knew that if the old lady were to die tomorrow, her inquiries would continue for perhaps a year or two.

And then the obverse was equally true: she would see someone walking along the street and would start at the sight. Why, he's dead, she would think; I know he is, I read it in the paper or someone told me—

And when she asked her mother if Mr. Neil Allen wasn't dead she would say, "Why, no, Sabina, where did you get such an idea as that?"

Nearly always she would find the answer in one of the stories she had written; she had written a story about Mr. Neil Allen or someone else; he had died in the story, and therefore he was dead. He had no right to be walking the streets like his own ghost.

Another thing which bothered Sabina considerably at intervals was Time. It was more variable and unstable than the weather; sometimes great slices of it were like a tiny moment; at others, a moment stretched to infinity. She would be playing bridge and thinking very hard about something abstract and involved; she would put down cards subconsciously. And when she realized suddenly where she was, she would have no idea how many hands had been played, who had taken the tricks, whether the game had just begun or if it was time to go home. The players' talk would be floating confusedly around her: "The Tilbury house is vacant, but I hear it has been rented for thirty-five dollars a month." "I simply can't stand that blue dress she wears; I didn't like it the first year she had it. She's got plenty of money, but she simply will not pay enough for a dress to get one with sufficient material in it—her shoulders always look drawn up and her chest slumped in." "Why, that's where they spent their vacation last summer and they simply swore they'd never go back again." "I think she looks awful, and it isn't surprising when he treats her like that. Don't you think so, Sabina?"

"Yes, I certainly do." What and whom were they talking about, she would wonder.

But more frequently Time folded up like a kaleidoscope when nothing happened, when the days were so much alike that it was impossible to tell Tuesdays from Fridays. This was particularly true in winter, but she had also known it to happen in summer; she would find herself doing something at a certain time, picking up a story she had left off weeks before at ten o'clock on Wednesday, and it would seem to her that no time at all had elapsed since then.

She could have told you when Hannibal crossed the Alps, and when Antony first saw Cleopatra, or Dr. Johnson first went to dinner at Mrs. Thrale's. But these facts were things associated with books, and in no way connected with calendars or clocks. They were all part of the vague past; Washington's inauguration as President of the United States was as remote as the building of Solomon's temple. And now the shooting of Matthew Cox by Daisy Cummings was also part of the past—one week, two weeks or a century ago—it was done.

But Barrett Page remained in Frost Haven, and Sabina had a general impression that he had been there for some time. Her mother was always mentioning it. Sabina had become so accustomed to his presence that she had difficulty in recalling what her life had been before his arrival. She had something to get up for in the morning, and something to think about, in the most nebulous forms, at night. She saw herself pouring tea at the old Page home in Boston, taking the children for a walk in the snow—the children were either adopted or borrowed from another member of the Page family—she saw Barrett and herself attending concerts and making a pilgrimage to the home of Emily Dickinson in Amherst.

In the meantime she found the *status quo* equally pleasant. It made no demands on her, it gave her prestige over Claire, and formed a sort of magic carpet on which she floated in a realm of unreality through the haze hanging over the Southern hills to the snow-burdened air of Boston.

She ate, slept, dressed and undressed without being conscious of any of the details concerning the transaction. She repeated to herself the charming things Barrett Page had said to her and found their counterpart in volumes of poetry. When her father was absent from home she took books to the dining table with her, propped them against a water glass and read as she ate. Someone had told her of seeing and hearing Edna St. Vincent Millay read some of her poems; had said that the poet wore a sea-green velvet gown, and Sabina came to believe that she herself had been present. She felt that she had heard the poet reading the lines about the sea, had beheld the velvet gown. It was what she herself would do some day, one day in the infinite future.

And yet, whenever she was alone with Claire she became conscious of the awful immediacy of the present and of reality. For Claire, Time was laid out in neat little parcels, a half hour for this, a quarter of an hour for that; and Sabina became cognizant of the passage not of days or hours, but of just so many very definite minutes that could never be recaptured. It was depressing to Sabina, she felt as if she were being cheated of something, was being kept from doing something very important. But when she was by herself, the urgent things escaped her, she could not recall what it was that had seemed so imperative or why it had seemed so. With Sabina, things never *were*, they always *seemed* to be.

One night, a week before the date set for Daisy Cummings' trial, Claire came into Sabina's room to discuss the possibility of Daisy's being found guilty. In Claire's hand was a silver-backed nail buffer and she was polishing her nails vigorously. "Ten to one," said Claire, "Daisy will go free."

"How can you say that, Clarissa?" Sabina removed the hair from her comb and brush, and dropped it into the receiver hanging on the side of her dresser.

Claire shrugged her shoulders. "Well, for one thing she is a female. For another, this is the South, and Matthew was a damn Yankee."

"What's that got to do with it?"

"You'll see. Southern womanhood must be protected at all costs; it is the most beautiful thing that ever came out of the old South. Watch Reconstruction rear its ugly head again."

"But Clarissa"—Sabina slipped a pale blue kimono about her shoulders; she felt naked in her camisole and knickers—"she killed him in cold blood. Murder is murder."

"Not when a women does it. It's either a *'crime passionel'* or 'the unwritten law,' or she's protecting her virtue. I wonder," Claire said as she inspected her nails critically, "if she loved him."

Sabina sat down in the only rocking chair and watched Claire dangling gracefully on the side of the bed. "Love him?" she echoed. "How can you say that? You don't know what love is."

Claire looked up. "I beg your pardon? Would you mind saying that again?"

"I said you don't know what love is," Sabina repeated stiffly.

"My great-grandmother's cow! Well, tell me, Sabina, what *is* love?"

"After all," said Sabina stubbornly, "you know he wasn't going to marry her."

"Nobody said anything about marriage. We were talking about love. Do you think they are synonymous?"

"They should be."

"Oh, my gosh! Frankly, Sabina, I'm surprised at you. I thought you would say that love was moonlight in a garden, the first kiss, that sort of thing." Claire threw the buffer aside and ignored her fingernails.

"That's the old Romeo and Juliet tradition, Clarissa. Of course nobody believes in that now; such recklessness, such intensity, 'all for love and the world well lost.' Love is finding a man with plenty of background and money so that you won't be marrying beneath you— and then going to dinner parties and concerts with him."

"Very nice," said Claire. "Very pretty. You haven't by any chance found one, have you?"

"I don't know, I might have."

Claire was sitting up very straight now. "It wouldn't be Barrett Page, would it?"

Sabina said nothing.

"Has he asked you to marry him?" Claire demanded.

"N—no. But he will."

"Oh, my everlasting aunt." Claire threw back her head and laughed until the tears rolled down her cheeks. Then she fell back on the bed and laughed still more. "The saints in heaven preserve us!" She turned over on her stomach and her muffled groans continued. "Honestly, I'm going to die if I don't stop laughing—say something, Sabina—talk about the weather—"

"What's so funny about it? I don't see anything at all funny—" Her cheeks were burning and her throat hurt. Was it so funny as all that that she had said Barrett Page was going to ask her to marry him? Damn Claire! What right had she to laugh that way?

Claire was sitting up weakly and wiping her eyes. "It wouldn't be so funny," she said between gasps, "it might even be tragic, if you hadn't just given me that definition of love! Oh, Sabina Frost, you adolescent!" Claire rose and stretched her arms. Her robe slipped back exposing the soft silk underthings that clung to her body. Sabina was conscious of her own embroidered handkerchief-linen ones with ribbon run through them—the bow tied around her chest was suddenly too tight. They were old-fashioned, tacky, like the room and all its furniture, the tester bed with its canopy of dotted swiss, the high mahogany dresser, the wainscoting and wallpaper.

"Listen, Sabina," said Claire, "Barrett Page is not going to ask you to marry him; he isn't going to ask anyone. I advise you to forget that you ever saw him. Perhaps it isn't as funny as I thought it was."

"Barrett Page is in love with me," Sabina said stubbornly.

Claire reached down to pick up the nail buffer. "What do you mean?"

"What does anyone mean by love?" Sabina asked.

"I don't know. What does the dictionary say?" When Sabina did not answer Claire went on, "What does the dictionary say about marriage? Does it mention dinner parties and concerts? Background? Position? Breeding? If it mentions breeding it will refer to procreation and not to table manners or family trees." Claire was not cool and amused any more; her brown eyes blazed. "I knew you were not going to fall in love because you weren't sufficiently alive, you couldn't forget yourself long enough. But I at least thought you would have romantic and sentimental ideas about it. I certainly didn't expect you to be worldly and scheming about marriage! That is the last thing in the world I should have dreamed of!" She drew a deep breath and went on, "So you want to marry Barrett Page because he has money and position! I'd love to *see* you married! You want to sit on a satin cushion while your housekeeper sews your fine seams. You want to go to concerts and have your picture in the society news! Don't forget that after concerts husbands and wives go home—together. Or not together, and you sit there by yourself wondering where he is and whom he is with. Don't forget that you are expected to know the price of lard and baking soda, and to keep the laundry bills down, that men wear pajamas more frequently than they do dress suits. You couldn't sit with your nose in a book all the time; no man wants to marry a a revolving bookcase. There are plenty of libraries in the United States—"

Sabina had risen and was standing facing her. "All right. You've said enough. Nobody will ever want to marry me. I'm not alive. You are. I have all the imperfections in the world and you have none. Well, I'm sick of it, do you hear? Get out of my room and stay out. Don't ever come into it again—" She was shaking all over with anger, with self-pity. She wanted Claire to leave so that she could throw herself on the bed and sob with humiliation. But Claire was looking at her strangely. All the anger was gone from her face, it only looked sunburned and a bit drawn.

"Sabina, I'm sorry. It's quite true that I have no right to talk to you as I did. I suppose I got tired of having the girl who loves books always the heroine of the story, and perhaps whoever made us did, too. We aren't even true to type; perhaps father was right when he said that you and I got mixed up in the making. If you are going to be the ingénue, the innocent, you can't be worldly about marriage. And here am I, the sophisticate, advocating true love. It doesn't make sense. I suppose the truth of the business is, I'm jealous."

"Jealous? Do you mean envious? People are jealous of what they have and envious of what they have not—"

"Oh, my God!" said Claire, and she closed the door behind her.

Sabina sat down on the bed and looked at her trembling hands and legs. She had not felt like this since the day she and Claire went horseback riding and Barrett Page first came to the Frost house. She had tried then to defy her mother and Claire and been figuratively spanked and put to bed as she had tonight by Claire alone. What had all those words of Claire's meant? What had Claire's anger meant? How did she know that Barrett Page was not going to ask anyone to marry him? Of whom was Claire jealous? What was there about her, Sabina, that made everyone treat her as a child? Her intelligence was at least normal, if not higher than the average. But she was lacking in something—what was it? Claire's words made her feel desolate, sick with a cold, miserable emptiness. And yet, paradoxically, for the first time in her life she felt that she had won a victory over Claire. How? How could she do it again?

When Claire announced the next day that she was leaving for New York Sabina was surprised and even more delighted. She was confident now of her victory, but still at a loss to explain it. "Isn't this rather sudden?" she asked politely.

"No, I've been thinking about it for some time."

Mrs. Frost did not protest too much. "You'll wait until your father returns from Macon—"

"No, I have to go today. Tell Father I'll explain later."

"I'm afraid he won't like it, Clarissa," Sabina felt bound to say; "there was something very important he wanted to talk with you about—"

"Perhaps he'll get back before I leave. If he doesn't"— Claire looked up for a moment from her packing—"tell him—tell him it will all come out in the wash."

"Clarissa!" The ejaculation came from Mrs. Frost.

Sabina smiled. This precipitate departure of Claire's had all the earmarks of flight. She was convinced that it was the direct outcome of their conversation the night before. Claire had lost the battle—for what? For Barrett Page? Now Sabina would have him to herself.

But her triumph was short-lived. Only a few hours

after Claire left, Barrett Page came around to say good-bye. He had suddenly been called back North; he wanted to thank Mrs. Frost for her hospitality and ask if he might come again next summer. This time Sabina did not smile. She sat frozen and silent, all the life within her stopped.

"It was nothing," Mrs. Frost said of her hospitality. "I am sure the girls have enjoyed your little visit. Strangely enough, Clarissa left just a few hours ago."

"She did? Has she gone back to New York?"

"I believe so."

"Well, I must be getting along. Tell Claire I'm sorry I missed her. Good-bye, Mrs. Frost." He bent down and kissed the astonished lady on the forehead. "Good-bye, Sabina; I'll see you again."

Sabina held out a cold hand and tried not to look at him. "Good-bye, Barrett." There was something in his eyes that said, I know you hate me for this. It really isn't my fault. Let's get it over.

He closed the front door as he went out, and Mrs. Frost said, "I don't trust that young man. I certainly don't like the way he has acted; his behavior has not been that of a gentleman. Where are you going, Sabina?"

"Upstairs. I left the water running in the bathtub."

"And I don't believe it is a coincidence that after all these weeks he and Clarissa are suddenly leaving on the same day. That puts an entirely new construction on the affair, and the more I think about it, the madder I get. She didn't telephone him, did she?"

"No. I think they communicate with drums."

"With what?"

"Tom-toms. *You* know."

"I don't know what you are talking about. I wish Mr.

Frost was at home. I never was so mortified in all my life—"

When Sabina reached her room she closed the door softly, then turned the key in the lock. "Mortified!" she repeated bitterly. "I never was so mortified in all my life—" she said, mimicking her mother's tone. "His behavior has not been that of a gentleman!"

In the mirror she caught sight of her stricken white face and she wished that she had something with which to break the mirror. Her fists—

She walked over to the south window and pushed back the ruffled curtains. There was the road, quite empty—his car had already vanished from sight. The orchards, now bare of their fruit, stretched endlessly over the hillsides; but they were green (verdantly green, she thought, relishing the redundancy), and jay birds screamed at the sparrows in the oak trees. It reminded her of something from Burns, some lines about "Ye flowery banks o' bonie Doon, How can ye blume sae fair?" and "Thou'll break my heart, thou bonie bird—"

Burns was not one of her favorite authors. He, also, had not been a gentleman.

CHAPTER IX

Mrs. Frost met her husband at the door when he came in that evening from Macon. "Oh, Mr. Frost, the most dreadful thing has happened, Clarissa has gone back to New York; she just left at noon, without any sort of explanation whatsoever."

"I'm not surprised; I've been expecting that."

"But why? Do you know why she did it?"

"I think so."

"Well?" She was waiting, hoping that he would tell her, but afraid from long experience that he would not.

"Well, let her go."

The look on her face was both amusing and pathetic; it was one of bafflement, frustrated curiosity and suppressed chagrin. For a moment his conscience smote him, he should have pretended more surprise; he'd been cruel to take the edge off her news with his callous nonchalance. He took off his coat and hung it on the hall tree. When he looked at his wife again he saw that her expression had changed, she was rallying for a second attack, a much stronger one; already her manner bespoke the confidence of a vindictive triumph.

He pulled up a rocking chair and sank wearily into it. "Yes, my dear?" He was exhausted with the day's strain, with the long hot drive and the far more fatiguing hours in the lawyer's office. He had come home, he reflected ironically, to rest.

Janie Lee leaned back in her chair and began building up slowly to her new climax. "I thought you wanted to see Clarissa; there was something you'd intended saying to her ever since the night of the dance."

The bait she was dangling before him was too obvious; he could see the hook concealed in it. "No, I changed my mind. I have nothing to say to Claire."

Irritably she smoothed the pleats in her figured voile dress and he watched her plump, ringed hands with amusement. How restless a woman's hands were, never still, always eloquent of her inward disturbance. The motion of a man's hands was outward as if he were pushing something away from him, but a woman's was inward as if she were trying to draw something to her.

She was so visibly upset that he decided to help her at once. She would feel better when she had told him. "Where is Sabina?"

"She has been in her room all afternoon."

"Now don't tell me she is grieving over Claire's departure!"

"Not over Claire's."

Ah! She had spoken the words slowly and in capital letters. Since Sabina was not grieving over Claire's departure there was but one interpretation. "So Barrett Page has gone, too."

"Yes."

"They did not leave together?"

"Not exactly. She went by train at noon and he came by a few hours later to say that he was driving back. I don't think it looks at all nice."

"No." He was appalled at the flagrancy of that; such lack of finesse and subtlety was unlike Claire. "Uh! Claire must be slipping," he said in one of her own phrases.

"If you ask me," Mrs. Frost retorted, "I should say that she has already slipped."

"Janie Lee!"

"I have nothing to retract," she cried hotly; "it is disgraceful and you know it! It's all very well for her to be modern and smart, you've encouraged her in it. But I won't have my house disgraced—"

"Hush, Janie Lee. I'm sure it is only a coincidence—"

"A coincidence! How can you be so blind, Mr. Frost? You think Clarissa can do no wrong." Her voice rose and broke. "You've always spoiled and pampered her. I've said nothing because she was your daughter. But it has hurt me." Tears ran down her full cheeks and she pushed them away with her hands. "It has hurt me more than you'll ever know to see how partial you were to her—in preference to my child. You act sometimes as if Sabina did not belong to you at all—"

He stood up abruptly. "Sabina never seemed to want to belong to me. Claire did."

"Oh, yes, she made up to you all right, twisted you around her little finger, got anything she wanted out of you."

He was silent, remembering that he had once said that if Claire wanted to jump over the moon he would hold it for her while she jumped. It seemed now that exactly that had happened.

"Sabina never asked you for anything in her life," Mrs. Frost went on passionately.

"She was too proud. She thought she would be humbling herself. But she would have got it if she had asked for anything."

"You can say that now. But how do you think she feels, up there in her room? That man has made a fool of her—with Clarissa's connivance—"

He hadn't thought of that. "Oh, come now, Janie Lee, it isn't so bad as all that. I don't think Sabina was in love with him—"

"But think of her pride! Think what people will say!"

"Oh, the devil, Janie Lee! As if *that* mattered! The Frosts have always done as they pleased and let people say what they pleased. As for Sabina's wounded pride, that is of no importance. If pride is all a girl has, then I say she deserves to lose it. But if she really has anything to be proud of, any basis for honest pride, she will come through all right. I'm not worried about Sabina, she'll never die of a broken heart."

"Why do you say that? How do you know?"

"Why? Because she—never mind. Never mind that now. My dear, I am very tired; I think I shall go wash up. And I need hardly add that it will be best not to mention this subject again.

"Not mention it? Why, Mr. Frost, what are you going to do about Clarissa?"

He turned in the doorway. "Do? Do you think I

should go after her, catch her by the hair and drag her back? Do you think I should call Mr. Page out and challenge him to a duel? I shall do nothing at all. If Claire has lain in her bed, as you so delicately suggested, then let her make it up again. If not, there is no cause for any excitement, or for any action. Is supper about ready?"

"I don't understand you, Mr. Frost, I declare upon my word of honor I don't. Sometimes I think I don't know you at all." She sighed as she rubbed her eyes with her handkerchief. "Yes, supper is nearly ready; Lila May is putting it on the table now."

At the foot of the stairs he encountered Sabina. "Oh, hello, Sabina, how are you?"

"Fine, thank you, Father. Did you have a successful trip?"

"Er—I really don't know, child. I can't tell until I have washed some of this dust off—"

He looked back at her in amazement, struck by her perfectly composed face, her smooth hair, her careful grooming. Possibly, he reflected, the girl had no heart (as he had almost told her mother a few moments ago). If she had, he thought with a glow of pride, it had either not been affected, or she was concealing it beautifully. It wasn't every girl, even if she was heartless, who could have come down to supper like that. How had she achieved it? She was behaving as if nothing at all had occurred—supper as usual. That was it, he thought exultantly: Sabina had spent the afternoon convincing herself that nothing had happened. And evidently she had succeeded. The summer had been misspent; it had ended disastrously, therefore it did not exist. It had never been. And so, doubtless, with Barrett Page. If you mentioned him to Sabina now, she would probably raise her eyebrow and say, "Who? I don't believe I know him."

What a triumph of self-deceit, Ellison Frost thought chuckling to himself. But what of Claire? He could not adopt Sabina's method and say that Claire did not exist. It was true that he had felt he did not want to see her, that he had nothing to say to her—but that was because he was too hurt, because he was too torn between the certainty of his mind and the incredulity of his heart. And he had felt, too, that the murder of Matthew Cox so closely paralleled events in his own family (if there was not indeed an analogy) that he had not permitted himself to think of Claire and Barrett Page. The two problems had arisen almost simultaneously; the chief difference as he saw it was that the Frosts and Pages had put aside firearms several generations back (excepting, of course, during times of national and intersectional emergency) while the Cummingses still used them. His chief concern now was to see to it that Daisy Cummings never used a gun again.

Two days before the trial began, Daisy's half brother, Bud, came home from Alabama, and if Ellison Frost disliked him on sight, he found that he liked him less on each subsequent occasion that he saw him. Bud Cummings had, like his father, a sort of native shrewdness, or rather a low cunning; a family that had for generations been unable or unwilling to achieve survival by honest methods, yet had somehow survived, for God knew what purpose, defective and diseased in mind as in body; this was the Cummings family; this was every Southern po-white.

The man was considerably older than Daisy, tall and lank; he had a mangled arm that had been cut off at the elbow, the result, someone said, of a sort of exhibitionism. At a harvest festival once in Alabama, feeling inferior and shut out, unable to attract attention in another way, he had suddenly in a frenzy of anger thrust his arm into a threshing machine.

His most noticeable feature was an exaggeratedly long, pointed, projecting chin—a caricature of a chin—but it was his eyes that told the man's story: they were the color of buckeyes or horse chestnuts that grew wild in the woods, and they smouldered with resentment, with fanaticism of some strange, unexplained sort. He was the type of man who hated everything and everybody: the new representatives of worldly success as well as the old impoverished aristocrats; yet he seemed also to hate his own class because it did not make itself the equal of the others. He distrusted everything that was foreign and at the same time reviled his own country and its government. During the World War he had been drafted, as a private of course, and here too he had found himself in the role of an inferior. Society was his enemy; every man's hand was against him and he found his consolation in religion, in the Holy Word where all men were equal in the sight of God.

"You believe that," Ellison Frost said to him at their first meeting.

"Of course I believe it. I know it," Bud Cummings declared with conviction.

Ellison Frost went on to bait him. "Then you admit that the darkies are your equal, that the members of the black race are your brothers under the skin."

"Niggers? Listen, mister, I hate a nigger worse'n pizen."

Ellison Frost laughed. "I believe 'worse than a rattle-snake' is the term generally used."

The man looked at him suspiciously; then after a few moments answered, "Yeah, I hate 'em a heap worse'n rattlesnakes."

It was obvious from the beginning that Bud considered his sister not merely justified, but innocent of any crime whatsoever. He declared himself amazed that there should be any necessity for a trial. But it was he who engaged the lawyer, who later spent hours eliminating men chosen as jurors and managed in the end to have a jury composed, in the best legal and constitutional tradi-tion, of Daisy's peers. It was not especially difficult in middle Georgia to find twelve men of Daisy's mental and moral caliber; men who did not need the paltry stipend were always unwilling to serve, but moonshiners from the back hill country, derelicts and renegades were abundant.

Daisy, chewing the inevitable gum, wearing the in-evitable pink chambray dress and sunbonnet, sat between her father and her lawyer. Watching her as the trial got under way Ellison Frost was reminded that in his youth he had been unable to distinguish between two famous paintings; there had been one called *Simplicity* and one *Innocence*, he could never tell which was which. The two had seemed interchangeable then. As he looked now at Daisy he knew that Simplicity could have two mean-ings, one synonymous with innocence, the other with stupidity, meanings as different from each other as night and day, as death and life.

From the beginning the courtroom was crowded; peach season was over; cotton had been chopped and was not yet ripe for the picking; the revival meetings at the churches had been held in July; it was too early for sugar-cane grinding. The trial was as great a godsend as any other free circus would have been. And it was obvious from the start that the sympathy of the crowd was with Daisy. Was she not one of them? It was immaterial that they did not know her as an individual; it was sufficient that she belonged to the oppressed class of the underprivileged. Was she not a woman and a Southern woman at that? The man she had killed had been a Yankee; Granny Cummings had said so in her testimony; "a varmint," she had called him, "a sneakin', thievin' varmint, tryin' to get round my Daisy with his fine words, tryin' to take advantage of her innocence, and her as pure a girl as ever drew the breath of life—"

Daisy's lawyer, Colonel Warren, had taken his cue from Granny. He had heard the thunderous approval her words elicited and he based his case on them. Matthew had been a damn Yankee, a university student using his superior knowledge to attempt to seduce the pure, simple girl of the people. If she had not understood his words, her woman's intuition had warned her of their meaning; warned her that her honor, the purity of her womanhood were at stake.

"She's as good as free," announced the prosecuting attorney to Ellison Frost at the end of the second day. "What can anyone do? It's a case of class prejudice, and she's got them all lined up solidly with her. And then there is the old sectional hatred revived; I shouldn't be a bit surprised to see the Ku Klux Klan ride into the courtroom at any moment dragging a bunch of carpetbaggers by the heels. It's a perfect setup. All we need now is a lynching; they'll probably lynch Henry Cox for letting his son look lecherously at Daisy. Daisy! She even had to have a name like that, the Jezebel! the bitch! They think because she walks upright that she is a human being, not an animal. Why, the cat meowing in the parsley bed is a consecrated saint compared with that girl!"

"There ought to be a law against it," said Ellison Frost sourly as he poured out drinks.

"Law!" cried Colonel Thibaut. "Who makes the laws, Ellison? People like Sam Cummings and Bud; there are twenty or a hundred of them to every one that is even averagely decent. They ought not to be allowed to vote. Voters ought to be made to pass tests, intelligence tests, information tests, before they are given the franchise."

Ellison Frost raised his glass. "To democracy, Michael, 'that government of the people, by the people, for the people, shall not perish from the earth.' "

"To the peepul!" Michael Thibaut replied solemnly, "and that great epitome of American demagoguery, Abraham Lincoln."

"With liberty and justice for all! We'd better hush, the Daughters of the Confederacy might be listening, and they wouldn't know what demagoguery means. I wonder," Ellison Frost went on, "if Daisy is eligible for membership in the U.D.C."

"Probably. Her grandpappy probably toted a gun alongside of Lee at old Bull Run," the attorney chanted.

"I'm not sure that Lee was at the battle of Bull Run."

"It is no matter, the principle remains the same. Killing Yankees is certainly an old Cummings custom."

"You are irreverent—but not immaterial. Michael, Henry Cox's testimony on the sluttishness of Daisy would be ruled out, wouldn't it?"

"Quite. Prejudiced, you know. Couldn't testify yourself, could you?"

Ellison Frost walked over to the window of the small hotel room. "No, I'm sorry. There is a certain fastidiousness about the Frost traditions."

Michael Thibaut put down his glass and leaned forward intently. "Ellison, we have *got* to have a witness who will swear that he knows from personal experience that Daisy is—what she is. Try once more—surely you can think of someone—"

"Do you think I haven't lain awake nights trying to do that very thing? After all, Michael, I know the girl only slightly—"

The attorney spread out his thin hands. "Then how are you so sure? Perhaps we are on the wrong track, perhaps she *is* a virgin of purest ray serene—"

"Oh, no," said Ellison Frost quickly.

"You are certain."

"Beyond the slightest doubt."

"You'll swear it."

"Yes."

"Good so far. But we need to prove it."

Ellison Frost came back to his chair opposite the attorney. "There has been living proof of it in the courtroom every day since the trial began. I may as well tell you now, Michael, and put your mind at rest. We've got proof but I didn't want to have to use it. The foolish child, Tippy, who comes every day with the Cum mingses isn't Daisy's little brother as everyone thinks; he is her son."

The lawyer sprang up from his chair. "Ellison, are you sure?"

"Of course I'm sure. He was born on the night they moved into my overseer's house. I went over there to see Sam on business and his *wife* came to the door; she thought I was the doctor."

"Yes?"

"She said, 'Doctor, I just want to tell you hit ain't me havin' the baby like Sam told you; hits my daughter. And if a word of this ever gits out, Sam'll kill you. That's all. You can come on in now.'"

"What did you do?"

"I said, 'Mrs. Cummings, I'm hard of hearing and I didn't understand what you were saying. Will you please tell Sam that Mr. Frost wants to see him?' She said, 'He ain't home' and looked at me suspiciously. I begged her pardon. She shouted, 'He ain't home' and I said I'd see Sam in the morning. Of course he told her later that I wasn't deaf at all."

"Of course. And they've never shot you?"

"Not yet. For one thing, I never let it 'git out' as the Cummings *Frau* put it. For another, those were lean years and I got into debt to Sam; when I couldn't pay him his salary I gave him stock in the orchards—"

"You idiot, Ellison! Why didn't you give him personal notes?"

"It doesn't matter. I've got the money now to pay him off; it will take all the cash from this year's crop, but I had rather owe anybody on God's green earth than Sam

Cummings. I'm going to get rid of that family, lock, stock and barrel. I've got the certified check in my pocket. Sam wouldn't accept one that wasn't certified. Where are you going, Michael?"

Colonel Thibaut had picked up his hat. "I'm going with you to Sam Cummings's house. Come along. And in the morning, Ellison Frost, you go on the witness stand."

When they reached the overseer's house they found him 'resting' on the front porch, his shoes off, his straight chair tilted back against the wall. He rose slowly and unwillingly as they approached the steps. "Howdy, Mr. Frost. Howdy, Colonel."

"How do you do, Sam. Colonel Thibaut and I want to see you on a little business."

"It ain't about the trial? The lawyer feller said for me not to talk none about that."

"No. It isn't about the trial."

"Set down," Sam said ungraciously. "I reckon won't nobody bother us here. It's sho been hot today, ain't it."

"Yes, it has been very warm. Are all those your dogs, Mr. Cummings?" Colonel Thibaut asked about the hounds that had come from around the house and under it, barking noisily at the strangers.

"Yessuh, they sho are. I dunno how many I got, seems like they just accumulate. My wife, she says they eat too damn much, but we don't bother to no great extent about feedin' 'em; just sort of let 'em shift for theyselves."

They looked it, thought Ellison Frost. He was eager to get this job over with; he had not been near the Cummings' house since the afternoon Matt was shot, and he felt somewhat like a traitor to Matt, sitting here talking amenities with Sam. Just inside the door was the room in which the boy had died. Ellison Frost was painfully conscious of it. Through the open window he could see the high old oak bed where Matt had lain and around which Henry Cox, the doctor, and he himself had sat—all helpless. Old Granny Cummings had hovered around the doorway listening and watching as she was no doubt doing now. There were the crude calendars on the wall, the glittering "God Bless Our Home" over the mantel and the cedar boughs on the whitewashed hearth; then too, as now, there had been the odor of frying ham and strong black coffee. But this time there was no smell of medicines from Dr. Mannering's black bag, no moans from a boy who was dying on the bed.

Frightened chickens came running out, squawking, from the barnyard and behind them Tippy, shooing them with his single garment, his head rolling as if it might drop off on either side.

"You have a nice view of the countryside here," Colonel Thibaut was saying to Sam.

"Yessuh, I reckon so."

"I suppose you'll be sorry to leave it."

"Leave it?" Sam looked up. "I ain't got no intention of leavin'. Hits part mine; you can ast Mr. Frost there."

"That's what we came to see you about," Ellison Frost spoke rapidly. "I'm ready to take up those papers, Sam."

"What if I ain't ready to give 'em up?" the man said truculently. "Maybe I done decided I'd ruther have the land."

"It doesn't make any difference what you've decided, Mr. Cummings," Michael Thibaut told him. "I'm here as Mr. Frost's attorney and he is waiting to take up the papers. So, if you don't mind, bring them out and you will be given a certified check for the full amount."

The overseer stood up. "Hit ain't legal; you can't take my land away from me!" Ellison Frost wanted to laugh at the sight of Sam Cummings, ignorant, barefoot, telling a Federal prosecuting attorney what was and was not legal. "Will you fetch the papers, Sam?"

"They ain't here; they're at the bank."

"Sam, bring the papers out."

The man went slowly into the house and began whispering with one of the women. Ellison Frost looked at his counselor and spoke softly, "It looks as if we were going to have trouble. I hope you don't mind being shot in the back, Michael."

"Not at all. It always gives me a good appetite for supper. Nice people, the Cummingses."

"*We* think so."

"That Sam is an Old Man of the Sea if ever I saw one, Ellison, becoming heavier on your shoulders all the time."

"Perhaps he is Christ in disguise."

"Umph! the disguise is perfect, I should never have guessed. Confound you, you've got the craziest mind, Ellison."

"But you like it."

"Of course I do, reminds me of my own. Tell you what—let Cummings have the orchards, sell out to him, and you come practice law with me."

"Sound idea. There—you've got me talking like you. Do you think we'd make any money?"

"No. But we'd have a lot of fun. Oh, here's your man." As the overseer came out with a heavy green box, the attorney addressed him, "Mr. Cummings, how would you like to keep those papers and buy the remainder of the orchards?"

Sam set the box on his chair and bent over to unlock it. "You caint git round me that way. If Mr. Frost wants that land back hits good land and he aint gwi sell it. If hit ain't no good, I don't want hit at no price."

"You've been working on it for four years," Ellison Frost told him, "you ought to know by now whether it's any good or not."

Sam pulled out the papers and looked at them. The two men watching him could see the thought passing through his mind: if the orchards had been a money-making enterprise, Ellison Frost would never have had to give the equity to his overseer in the first place. "I done decided I'll take the cash and buy me a place summers else. This ain't no life for a man—"

"Just as you say, Mr. Cummings, it is entirely up to you. If that is your decision, here is your check and I want you to sign this release."

The man read it over slowly, went into the house again and finally came back out. "Bud says hits all right. But I ain't got no pen—"

Colonel Thibaut drew a fountain pen from his pocket and extended it. Cummings wet the point with his tongue, leaned laboriously over the box, and eventually handed over the paper. He stared at the floor a few moments, spat into the cosmos bushes, then spoke slowly, "Mr. Frost, you ain't goin' on the witness stand, are you?"

"I suppose I shall, Sam. I was present when the shooting occurred."

"I ain't sayin' nothin' bout the shootin'. Everybody

knows she done that and she had a right to do it. If I was you, Mr. Frost, I'd stick to the shootin' and not say anythin' else."

Michael Thibaut shot a warning glance at Mr. Frost. "Well, good-afternoon, Mr. Cummings, we'll see you tomorrow."

"Just a minute, mister, not so fast. I just want to tell Mr. Frost that he's got a daughter same as I have and I reckon he wants to pertect her good name. If he don't want it known about Miss Claire and that Mr. Page bein' seen in Atlanta together at a hotel about a month ago, he'd better not say anythin' about my Daisy."

"I don't know what you are talking about, Sam," Ellison Frost said coldly. "Come, Michael, let's go." His legs felt like worn-out leather straps; he wasn't sure they would get him to the car.

"You ain't foolin' me none; you know well enough what I'm talkin' about, and you'd better think it over, mister. I'm warnin' you," Cummings called after him.

Ellison Frost did not answer the man. "Would you mind driving, Michael?" he said to his friend.

"Not at all. Where do you want to go—home?"

"No. Drive to the telegraph office, please."

"Something up?"

"Yes. I've got to wire Claire."

"Ellison! You aren't going to take seriously anything that low-down, conniving, blackmailing blackguard said—"

Ellison Frost leaned back wearily against the seat. "But it may be true; I've been worrying about it for some time. . .

"Ellison, you *know* it isn't true! I know Miss Claire

well enough to know that, and if I didn't, I'd still know it wasn't true because she is your daughter."

"Very pretty, Michael. Thank you. But just the same I've got to wire her to come home and straighten this thing out. I should have done it weeks ago but I just wouldn't face it." Then he smiled wanly. "If I were my other daughter I would now go look in a mirror to see how much I have aged in the last ten minutes."

"There's good reason why Miss Sabina should like mirrors. There's no excuse at all for you."

It was dark when they reached the outskirts of town. Inside the banker's house there were lights showing the family grouped around a radio; there were earpieces fastened on their heads and an alert intentness in their bodies. "You couldn't give me one of those things," Colonel Thibaut remarked; "I don't care if they do cost a fortune. But the *nouveaux riches* will buy any new-fangled thing that comes along, just so it's expensive enough."

Farther up the street college boys and girls were gathered on front-porch steps, twanging banjos and uku-leles. Their songs hung on the lazy air. "I've got the alco-holic blu-u-ues," moaned one doorstep, and "Mar-quita, I need you, I do," wailed another.

Petunias were ghostly against the velvety darkness of the lawns and from somewhere came the faint fragrance of late-blooming roses. Younger boys and girls stood on the sidewalks with garden hose watering the dusty streets and occasionally each other; nursemaids walked home-ward with the glow of cigarettes lighting their dusky faces. "It's a strange new world we live in, Michael," Ellison Frost said, "and a rather terrible new world. I don't think I particularly like it. Noise and crudity and the inevitable rise to power of vulgar people. Frankly, I am bewildered by it, lost—"

"It isn't you who are lost, it is they. And the tragedy is, they don't want to find themselves. It is undoubtedly the result of the war."

"Yes, we can blame everything on the war. But I thought it was rather a good war, in the best St. George-and-the-Dragon tradition. They are only using it as an excuse for doing things they've always wanted to do and never before dared. Well, here we are. We'll soon know about the younger generation. Michael, you'll have to drag that trial out somehow until Claire gets home."

Two nights later Claire and Barrett Page stood in the library at Frost Haven and Ellison Frost was walking distractedly about the room. "Why didn't you tell me, Claire? It wasn't fair of you not to—"

"But I thought you *knew*, father! You acted as if you did. After all, you're pretty smart, and I couldn't believe that you didn't know." Claire's red curls gleamed in the light, and her father thought her expression was much happier. She, too, must be glad to have this thing cleared up.

"You've been awfully decent, sir," said Barrett Page. "We both appreciate it."

"Oh, I haven't forgiven you," Ellison Frost interrupted; "so far, I'm only relieved. You don't know what a strain I've been under."

"You suspected the worst," accused Claire. "My, my, what a lovely, clean mind you have, Father, and what a compliment you paid Barrett and me."

"Perhaps I did suspect the worst as you say, Claire, but I don't think I ever believed it."

"Oh, let's sit down. Father, compose yourself. Sit over there in your leather chair. I'll take a straight-backed one because I'm doing penance and Barrett can have its twin. He's as guilty as I am. It was *his* aunt who caused all the trouble."

"I'm in no mood to sit down," declared Ellison Frost; "there's too much to be done."

"Yes," Claire put in, "you haven't even said, 'Bless you, my children.' You haven't even offered us a drink."

"I feel much more like taking you out to the woodshed. I don't approve of it, it isn't the way to do things. It's a cheap trick and I say to hell with the money."

"But you can't say that, Father," Claire cried; "it's three hundred thousand dollars!"

"I think he's right, Claire," said Barrett Page; "it wouldn't be fair to take it now. We thought it was smart at the time but I don't think so any longer. Of course, on the other hand, it wasn't exactly fair of Aunt Alice to do that in the first place, the money should have come to me anyhow. The old lady is a misanthrope and a misogamist— Cigarette, Claire?"

"Thank you. It's like this, Father." Claire pulled her chair over and took his hand. "If we keep it a secret until Barrett's birthday next January we'll get the money; he'll be thirty-two then; and that is the age Aunt Alice stipulated. But if we announce it now it's three hundred thousand dollars gone down the gutter."

Ellison Frost withdrew his hand. "I can't give my approval, Claire. It's dishonest."

Claire stood up; her eyes flashed. "So it's worth three

hundred thousand to you to be able to testify against Daisy Cummings—"

"No. It isn't that at all, Claire!"

"Claire," said Barrett Page, "we broke the terms of the agreement. And I think your father is absolutely right. After all, we'll have enough to live on comfortably, quite comfortably—"

Ellison Frost went over to the window and pulled back the heavy red draperies. It was too hot in the small room with the doors closed, but this was not a thing that could be settled on the front porch. The room somehow oppressed him with the sense of his own failure. There were his law books in the old secretary, yellowed and dusty, the unanswered letters in the pigeonholes of his desk. Perhaps he had had too little regard for money. Perhaps Claire had been right when she said he only wanted to have his way in order to insure Daisy's conviction. No— it was *not* that. It was an old-fashioned, quixotic sense of honor that probably had no place in this new world. Perhaps Claire was wiser, more of a realist—it was their life, hers and Barrett's; he had no right to interfere with it. He turned then and spoke, "I'll say no more about it. It seems to me, Barrett, that the decision must be yours."

He could hear the small insects that had been attracted by the lights beating against the window screens. He could almost hear the old gentlemen in the oil portraits on the wall holding their breath. The library of Frost Haven had seen so many things come and go, new brides, new heirs, old ways, old people, wars, Sherman's army, desolation—was it now to see the last of honor fled?

Barrett Page was looking at Claire. "I'm sorry if you don't agree with me, Claire, but I'm tired of living a lie.

I couldn't enjoy the money if I got it that way. I say, Thank God for a man like your father, and to hell with the money." Then he added, "You would have married me without it."

"Yes, Barrett, I would."

"Then let's forget about it."

" 'I could not love thee, dear, so much, Lov'd I not honour more,' " quoted Claire. "Unaccustomed as I am to being noble in public, I suggest that we all have a drink. It isn't every day that father acquires a son-in-law and his daughter turns up her nose at a quarter of a million dollars."

"Claire, if you aren't satisfied about this—" began her father.

She waved her hand in a lavish gesture. "Oh, don't mind me; I'm subject to the will of my lords and masters—"

"You're a mercenary wretch—"

"And you're a sentimental idealist," she told him, "but somehow I like you. Kiss me and I'll promise not to say another word about it. Say, 'All is forgiven, my erring daughter.' "

"I'm afraid," he said slowly, "that this is what is known as a solemn moment. Claire, I hope you will be very happy, and Barrett, I am very proud to welcome you into the Frost family—such as it is. It isn't, actually, what it used to be."

"Don't apologize too much, Father."

"Thank you, Mr. Frost. The honor is mine."

"Now shall I call in Janie Lee and Sabina? And we must get this to the newspapers, too."

Claire ran her hand through her hair. "It won't be

necessary to confide in the newspapers if we tell mother. Open the door gently, Father; she's probably listening at the keyhole."

"Somehow," said Barrett Page, "I wish I didn't have to see Sabina—"

"I should think you do!" Claire cried.

"Oh, Sabina will be all right," Ellison Frost assured them.

"Do you mean that she wasn't—hurt—at the way I left so unceremoniously after all those weeks of—"

"Of what?" asked Claire.

"Oh, children, children! Sabina has been quite her usual self."

"I knew it," said Claire.

"Well, I'll be damned," said Barrett Page. And he looked a bit piqued.

"You thought she'd mope and pine, didn't you, sweet?"

"Not at all. I merely thought that she might have thought—"

"Well, never mind, dear. Better luck next time." Claire opened the doors and went into the living room. "Mother —Sabina—where are you? Come on down—" She turned on the lights in the hall, the kitchen, on the stairs, then came back to the dining room and began looking in the sideboard. "Everybody come into the dining room," she called.

"What's the matter?" demanded Mrs. Frost. "What is all this?"

"Mother, may I present your son-in-law, Mr. Barrett Page?"

"How nice," she said flatly. "When is it to be?"

"It isn't to be, it has been. Last March."

"Last March? Claire, you aren't—"

"Aren't what, Mother?"

"You mean you were secretly married and you are just now announcing it—oh, how dreadful, Clarissa! You know what people always think—"

"No, I'm sorry, Mother, I don't. What do they think?"

"Oh, dear—Mr. Frost—she isn't—?"

"Why, not that I know of. Are you, Claire?"

"If you mean, am I going to have a baby, the answer is no. Lord, what minds you people have. No wonder you apologized for the family, Father. Barrett, I apologize, too—good Lord, it makes me sick. Perhaps there is something to be said for Sabina after all; I'm beginning to understand why she is like she is. Sabina," she called, "where are you?"

"Oh, don't disturb Sabina, dear. She's gone to bed with a dreadful headache."

Ellison Frost rubbed his chin thoughtfully. "And she can't take aspirin because it is bad for her heart. Well, we have no champagne, but we have bourbon, Scotch, Irish whisky, sherry, port, sauterne, brandy—what will you have, Janie Lee?"

"Just a moment, I have to use the telephone. Mr. Page, will you come with me? I shall have to ask you some questions."

"Certainly, Mrs. Frost."

She sat down carefully in the telephone chair. "One-nine-two-three, please. Mrs. Alden? This is Janie Lee Frost. I have some news I want you to telephone in to the morning papers, Atlanta and Macon. Yes, we'll pay for the calls—"

Ellison Frost looked at Claire. Ten minutes later they

were still waiting for Mrs. Frost. Her voice came clearly, "On the paternal side she is a descendant of John Herrington Frost of Meadowbrook, Cumberwold, Hilltown on the Wye, Herefordshire, England, one of the founders of Lullwater College and an original settler of Albemarle County, Virginia. His wife, Patricia Keyne, was descended from the fourth earl of—"

Ten minutes later she had got around to the Pages. "His great-grandmother on the distaff side was the third daughter of the Quaker governor of New Jersey—what's that, Barrett? Well, just say, the daughter of Governor Hamilton Todd Carmichael—"

"Claire," said Ellison Frost, "you look so lovely tonight. Are you happy?"

"Beautifully happy, Father. Are you?"

"It follows, my child. It follows."

Sabina lay on her canopied bed exhausted and spent with weeping. The tears were all gone, but occasional gasps shook her body, her eyes were so puffed and swollen that she thought she would never again be able to open them. But why should she? There was nothing she wanted to see.

The sound of her mother's voice speaking over the telephone to Mrs. Alden was unbearable. She had known, of course, the moment Claire and Barrett drove up together with Mr. Frost that they were married. She had been practically certain of it ever since the day of their departure. But to be practically certain of something was a far cry from having to read about it in the morning papers. It was Claire's photograph that would appear in the Sunday society section, not hers; Claire, not she, who had married one of the Boston Pages.

Sabina could see the item already in print, recalling to an indifferent public the Frost grandfather who had not quite succeeded in saving the Confederacy, the grandmother whose father had founded some jerk-water college and published a book on the Shakespearean heroines; there would be the Frost ancestors from Runnymede to Trafalgar, Warburton ancestors from the time of the Crusades to the Quaker persecutions; the Hilliards would be dug out of their mouldering tombs, the Carleton-Maces would be credited with establishing and ruling the social, intellectual and political life of the South from the time of Lord Baltimore to the present. The indifferent public would be left with the impression that Europe would not have survived without Claire's ancestors and that the continent had been in a sorry plight since their removal to America. Of recent exploits by the family there would be little; of Claire herself, only that she was a graduate of Mrs. Castleberry's finishing school on the Hudson and a member of an expensive sorority.

Sabina wondered suddenly how much of all the high-sounding genealogical data was true, and if it was, what of it? If Claire had forty-nine bars for membership in the Colonial Dames would it make her less hedonistic, less domineering, willful and self-satisfied? Had Barrett Page married her because one of her forefathers had been Lord Mayor of London or because she had a fine, healthy body, a vivacious air and a sort of bright, burning beauty?

For the first time in her life Sabina realized that if your kitchen needed a new roof you couldn't cover it with bronze plates off your ancestors' graves. This ancestor worship was ridiculous—and yet—knowing that you came from people like that was something to lean upon when you needed support; when you felt that you yourself were in no way remarkable and had accomplished nothing that was at all noteworthy. A broken reed to lean upon was better than no reed at all, particularly when it had been one of the finer varieties of reed, grown in the private gardens of the nobility along the banks of an exclusive stream.

There was no longer the sound of Mrs. Frost's gracious "telephone voice," but now there was noise and laughter from the dining room. Sabina did not have to be there to see them: her mother sitting at the Hepplewhite table sipping sherry as if it were hemlock, her father moving around lightly, refilling glasses, looking at Claire as if she had hung the moon (in the best possible place) and brought down a nice collection of stars with her as souvenirs of the trip. The great crystal chandelier would be a-gleam and a-glitter, lighting the new Frost bride who would herself probably be shining like a tinsel star on a Christmas tree. Barrett's eyes, too, would be on Claire, a "look-what-I've-got" expression on his face, finding new beauty in a gift newly bestowed.

Or would he? Sabina turned over in bed and smoothed her rumpled nightgown. Would he be remembering that he had said, "Sabina, you are as lovely as the dawn . . . you are a statue and I want to bring you to life . . . sleeping beauty and I want to awaken you. . . ."

Had that been a necessary part of the campaign to hide his relationship with Claire? Had he not rather overplayed the part, or had she in her conceit, her hunger fo adulation, found a meaning in his words that was not inherently there?

There was one solace for her pride: he had been married to Claire before he ever saw Sabina; but the fact remained that he had made a fool of her. How was she going to punish him? There was suicide and there was fame. In only a few moments she could be dead but it might take years to become famous—months, at any rate. Suicide was much more dramatic. In the morning they would find her cold, still body, more beautiful in death than in life; and a front-page story not to be stuck off in the society section. But she did not quite know how to go about it; it was a messy business. A bullet through her brain or her heart—no, that sounded like a showgirl, and she did not have a pistol in the first place, had never touched one in the second place. There were bottles in the medicine cabinet with *POISON* on them: iodine, which might stain her lips brown, wood alcohol, household ammonia—the idea of killing yourself with anything so domestic as household ammonia! No, only a housemaid would do that! How did ladies kill themselves? They carried poison in a finger ring, or dissolved their pearls in wine—somebody did, perhaps it was spies. Now that she thought of it she could recall no lady who had done any of those things. Anna Karenina had thrown herself in front of a train—and made a nice mess, to be sure.

Perhaps after all fame would be better, a slow subtle poison eating deeper into Claire and Barrett every year, corroding their hearts and lives. Her first book of verse, *TWILIGHT BELLS*, "a brilliant new talent on the literary horizon," "the finest thing since *Endymion*," ". . . straight from the heart of one who has transmuted suffering into the stuff of genius . . . poems of imperishable beauty in tones of immortal irony. . . ."—it would be bound in blue and silver, handsomely printed on hand-made rag paper. The publisher would spare no expense, ". . . rarely in the history of this house have we had the honor of introducing to the world such an important new talent. The South has awakened from its long liter-ary slumber, has come to flower again, the richer for its Lanier, more poignant for its Poe, but surpassing them all—"

She would wear orchids on her shoulder when she stepped off the train in New York, and the reporters would ask, "How could a young girl have written such a mature, such a beautiful book?" And where would Bar-rett and Claire be? She would invite them to dinner at her hotel one night—if she had time.

The book wasn't actually written yet, but she would begin in the morning. She would take her red leather notebook and silver pencil and go down into the woods where the cattails pushed up their heads in the pond like—like something—and she would lie down at the foot of a tree drinking in the perfume of the strong rich earth. Perhaps she had best take some sofa pillows to lie on, and a parasol to keep herself from freckling. Tomorrow—Friday, August the sixth. August the sixth—there was something about the date that sounded important but she could not recall what it was. Possibly it had something to do with Daisy Cummings's trial.

CHAPTER X

"Think it over, Henry," said Ellison Frost as he walked to the door with his guest on the following night. "I'll give you a better house to live in than Cummings had, or you can stay in town if you prefer. But I'd rather have you on the place where you can look after the mules, the machines, the spray materials. And you can decide whether you had rather have a straight salary or run the orchards on shares. Frankly, I'd recommend the former."

Henry Cox lingered on the doorstep. "Either way will suit me, Mr. Frost. You've been mighty good to me. Somehow, it makes it easier not to have to go back to Ohio without— Matt. He was all I had, Mr. Frost, and I'd rather stay down here where I can—sort of be close to him. I suppose you think I am talking like a fool—"

"Indeed I don't, Henry. I understand. Cigarette?"

"Thank you, Mr. Frost—" The man's hand shook as he reached it out and he made an effort to steady himself. "Cooler tonight, isn't it?"

"Yes, it's fine." Ellison Frost hated to see him go away alone and lonely. "I'd like to walk up the road a piece with you if you don't mind, it's too nice to stay in the house. Henry, if I were you, I wouldn't count too much on Daisy's being convicted even after my testimony this morning. I personally thought it was going to turn the trick, I didn't see how it could fail to, but now I'm not so sure. Could you see that it had any effect?"

The big man walking beside him was silent for a moment. Then he said, "Mr. Frost, I don't believe anything anybody could say would have any effect. They had their minds made up before the trial began. You see, it isn't a case of the state versus Daisy Cummings, it's Daisy versus—well, versus society. Because Matt had an education they've sort of elevated him to your class, Mr. Frost. He couldn't be in your class while he was living," Cox said bitterly; "that's why he turned to Daisy. I never have told you this before, Mr. Frost, but I don't see any harm in it now. Matt's books were full of papers, poems, that he had written to Miss Sabina."

"To Sabina! For God's sake, Henry! Did he ever tell Sabina that he liked her?"

"He didn't like her, he was in love with her, just like a man could be with the stars, or the sea—something he could never own, but that would always haunt him. It wasn't Miss Sabina's fault, she didn't know anything about it."

"Henry, I wish I had known that—"

"You would have made her be nice to him," said Henry Cox, "invite him to your house. That wouldn't have done any good, it would have just turned Miss Sabina against him."

"Yes, yes, I suppose you are right, Henry, she's a stubborn little cuss. But I'm frightfully sorry. It upsets me—"

There was an old car lumbering up the road and the two men moved to one side. When it came closer it slowed down and a voice said, "Mr. Frost?"

"Yes. What do you want?"

"This is Bud Cummings, Mr. Frost. Granny's been took sick, bad off sick, and she wants to see you."

"Don't you go, Mr. Frost," said Henry Cox, "don't you go."

"Isn't this rather sudden, Bud? She was at the trial today."

"Do you think I am lying, Mr. Frost?"

"That is a delicate question, Bud. I shouldn't put it so bluntly."

"There's something important she wants to say to you, and Pa told me to bring you."

"I'll go with you, Mr. Frost," said Henry Cox.

"No. I couldn't let you do that, Henry, though I'm very grateful to you for the offer." He'd seen Henry's son killed there and he wasn't going to see the father killed also.

"Very well, Bud, I'll walk on over."

"Hits a right long way; I'm going straight there—"

"Thank you very much but I prefer to walk. Good night, Henry. Let me know your decision about the orchards as soon as you can. I'll see you in the morning." He was convinced, as he stood there, that he would never see Henry again, but there was no use in being melodramatic about it.

"Good-night, sir. I wish you'd let me go with you."

"No. Thank you, Henry."

Henry turned reluctantly into the path that led up to the dormitory and Bud Cummings took off his emergency brake and started on up the road looking, probably, for a place to turn around. Ellison Frost was alone now in the night and walking—he was certain of this—to his death. He could run after Henry Cox, clutch him by the arm, say, 'Go with me, Henry, I'm afraid, go with me.' Or he could hide in the orchards, creeping in the shadow of the trees back to the safety of his home. At least, some other man could; Ellison Frost could not.

The knowledge of impending death had come to him not so much from Bud Cummings's sinister face as from some inward source; something cold and final had turned the blood in his veins to ice, had said to him simply, This is it.

He walked slowly because he had not got over the shock. The end of the road was ahead—and he did not want to come to it too soon. It was too late to do anything now but there were a great many things about which he wished to think. The dark slumbering hills upon which he had looked for so many years—no, it seemed now that it had been only a few years—would never give up their secret to him, never tell him what lay beyond. And why should they? They would go on as they always had, fulfilling their function as hills—and what was that function? Providing men with a sense of mystery, and with dreams?

The young moon over them had a tender, virginal quality; a shy, immensely appealing young moon that seemed to be half afraid you would not like it, and tucked its head behind a cloud or a treetop while you made up your mind, begged it at last to come out.

Was this what a man thought about when he had only a few minutes to live? He should be reviewing his life, saying, I made a mistake there, or, This thing was well done. But the events of his life seemed unimportant; he had done the best he knew as he went along—and it now seemed amazingly insignificant, unworthy of even a brief review.

A breeze stirred in the orchards; he pulled his linen coat about him and buttoned it. Far up the road was the faint sound of a car, Bud Cummings had evidently found a place to turn around. That was where Bud had the advantage of him; he could not, when he got to a certain point, turn around and go back. There was something that he needed to think about very quickly and it kept eluding him; it was connected in some way with what he had been saying to Henry Cox. In a sort of panic, he tried to force the thought into the forefront of his consciousness; it *had* to come, but it did not. The car was only a half mile behind him, guided by Bud Cummings's left hand with the assistance of that stump which had been his right.

For a man who knew so many quotations from the philosophers he was doing very badly now; he should be repeating the lofty sentiments of the early Greeks and Romans instead of thinking how cold he was and how his feet kept trying to turn off the road into the shadows of those trees. He wasn't going to let them do it, of course; he wasn't going to hide like a common chicken thief.

When he looked back he could see his lighted house on the hilltop. Janie Lee was probably rummaging in the icebox for a snack before going upstairs—good old Janie

Lee, she had always known that the stomach was more important than the head. She would get along all right while she continued to put her faith in the church and her mind on the dining-room table. Claire, fortunately, had her Barrett Page; he hoped she would always have him; he was a fine, decent man—but there were reservations back of his serious gray eyes.

And Sabina! That was it, it was Sabina he had wanted to think about; he was appalled to realize how little he had ever thought about her. He'd been so busy worshiping Claire that he hadn't understood that it was Sabina who needed his help; he had gone along saying, Sabina will be all right. Now he saw quite clearly that the child was bewildered, confused. If she went on imagining the kind of life she wanted, comparing it with the reality and seeing the disparity between the two, something would happen.

It was a fine time to be coming to that conclusion when Bud's car was driving up and stopping. Its body shook as Bud pulled up the brake; it was panting like a dog after a hard run. "Listen, Cummings," said Ellison Frost before the other could speak, "if I am going to be shot, would you mind doing it now? I have an aversion to your father's house; I had rather not go there."

There was a glint in the man's eyes. "Ain't nobody goin' shoot you, Mr. Frost."

"Two negatives. Look here, Bud—"

"You might as well git in, Mr. Frost; you are goin' with me whether you like it or not." Bud patted the revolver that was strapped around his waist. "Don't think because I got just one arm that I cain't use this when I'm a mind to—but ain't nobody got any plans for shootin' you."

Ellison Frost got into the palpitating machine and slammed the door hard several times before it caught.

"Your grandmother isn't really sick," he said.

"That old woman? Ain't nothin' on God's green earth that would kill 'er; she'll live to be as old as Methuselah and even then I don't reckon she'll die. She'll just be translated."

"I hope," Ellison Frost said caustically, "that she'll be translated into better English than your family now use."

"Looka here, Mr. Frost, we cain't help it that we ain't got the education you have, we ain't had the chanct. And whose fault is it? It's yourn and people like you, but our day's comin', mark my word. The Bible says the poor shall inherit the earth—"

"I beg your pardon; it says the meek, not the poor."

"Oh, so you know the Bible, too, do you?"

"I have a small acquaintance with some of the finer books of several nations."

"Look, Mr. Frost, if you want to live to git where you're goin', you better shut up, because I ain't gonna take much more o' yo' lip. My family's done taken all off of you that they're goin' to—"

"Bud," said Mr. Frost, "what did you do in Alabama, what was your occupation?"

"I was a preacher," the man replied sullenly. "Why?"

"A preacher?"

"Yessuh, a preacher. You got anything to say about it?"

"No. Not a word."

The episode was taking on the unreality of a nightmare; only a part of his mind was working and that part was concerned now entirely, illogically with curiosity about Bud Cummings. He was trying to piece together all the things he knew about the man and make a pattern, a human being, but all he got was a scarecrow that had suddenly become animated and given the awful power of life and death. It doesn't make sense, he thought; what have I to do with this creature, and he with me?

Bud made an abrupt right-hand turn and Ellison Frost said, "This isn't the way to your father's house."

The man did not answer. The breeze whipped through the car, blowing their hair in their eyes and Ellison Frost's tie across his face. They were on a rise between two cornfields for a moment, then the road on each side became wooded; there was an open branch through which the car splashed without pausing. Far over on a hill Mr. Frost saw lights—were they fireflies? It must be Hill Dennis's place, he figured, but Hill had moved off a year ago to Florida and no one had occupied the house since. Bud turned again on the crest of the next slope into a rutted, grass-grown road that was little more than a cow path. He was having to go more slowly now and Ellison Frost wondered why he didn't try to get away, open the door cautiously, try to get behind one of the pine trees on the right before Bud could shoot him. Of course, the Cummingses were pretty handy with guns, but he might be able to make it—and then what? He was too close now to those lights; he would be found, tracked down like an animal. Whoever those men were with lights, they had dogs also whose barking was clearly audible.

The road came to an end at a barbed-wire fence and Bud brought the car to a stop. "Here's where we git out," he said; "we walk from here."

Should he make a run for it now? He opened the car door and when he stepped out two men came up from behind him and caught his arms. "All right, boys," Bud Cummings said, "we got 'im. Let's go."

"Ain't you go' turn off your lights?" asked one of the men.

"Sure. Sure. I forgot 'em."

Bud stepped in front of the car to go around, and in the light Ellison Frost noticed something he had not seen before: Bud's left sleeve was rolled up, showing innumerable marks on it like tattooing, only they did not form a design. What were they—the perforations of a needle? Did Bud take dope?

They set off into the woods, Bud leading the way, the other two men following Mr. Frost to see that his hands remained bound. "He's mighty quiet, your prisoner is, Bud," one of them said; and Bud answered, "Yeah, his words ain't go' do him no good now. We'll do the talkin' from now on."

Those marks—what did they mean? What kind of preacher was Bud Cummings? The barking of the dogs became louder, voices were audible, and suddenly the woods were almost as light as day. Ellison Frost saw them then: a circle of motley men, women, dogs and a few children staring intently at the ground. Some of them held kerosene torches, others burning pine knots, and the smaller children were clinging, whimpering, to their mothers' skirts.

"I'm glad to know, Mr. Frost," said Bud, "that you're a stu-dent of the Bible. Maybe you'll take part in our service we're having tonight."

There was the Cummings family, of course: Sam in his overalls that had the pockets ripped off and hanging down; Granny in her soiled "sea-island" dress, high shoes and army cap; Cummings's wife in a shapeless black and white calico print dress, with Tippy clasping one of her legs. There were one or two other men whose faces were familiar; the remainder were strangers. None of them spoke to him and he was glad. The dogs—he recognized them now as Sam Cummings's—were constantly trying to get to the center of the circle. And then, suddenly, he saw what was in the center: a worn croker sack, tied together at the open end, and inside it an object was turning and writhing. It could be only one thing, a snake. So this was the kind of "service" they were going to have —the ritual of the snake cult.

Such a sensation of revulsion and nausea swept over him that he staggered back. The men behind him jerked his arms and one of his feet slipped in the pine straw. "Hold 'im, Andrew," commanded Bud. Ellison Frost could not take his eyes off the object writhing in the gunny sack in the center of the circle.

One of the women handed Bud Cummings a Bible and with the stump of his arm he found the place for which he was searching. "The sixteenth chapter of Mark," he said, "verses seventeen and eighteen. That's our text, folks, the word of the Great Jehovah himself laid down for us to follow. But I've got something I want to say to you good people first—"

Ellison Frost looked again at the perforations on Bud's

arm. This time he knew what had caused them, and he knew what kind of preacher Bud was. He wished that the light was less bright, that he could not see the patches on that man's worn trousers, the greasy spots on a woman's apron and a girl's snuff-stained teeth. God, God! He closed his eyes. Why did it have to be this?

Two women behind him were whispering. "My Jane," said one, "you oughter see 'er, she can handle 'em just like they was butterflies. She ain't never been bit but onct, and she warn't swole up so awful bad then."

"My Alice," said the other, "she nearly died, but she ain't scairt of God or devil now. She says she could handle two at a time—"

"God!" cried Ellison Frost. "God!"

"First," said Bud Cummings, "we want to thank God for the new converts He has sent us. Tonight, brethren and sistren, we have some young people who want to take part in the ceremony for the first time. They have confessed that they want to be punished for their sins if they have sinned; if they are pure, they want to prove it in the sight of God. Remember, we have God's own word: 'And these signs shall follow them that believe: In my name shall they cast out devils; they shall speak with new tongues;

" 'They shall take up serpents; and if they drink any deadly thing, it shall not hurt them; they shall lay hands on the sick, and they shall recover.' "

He raised his hand skyward. "Now let us repeat the creed; say it after me: 'I believe in the power of God to keep and preserve His loved ones—'

" 'I believe in the power of God to keep and preserve His loved ones—' "

" 'I believe that he has evolved this means for testing the faith of His disciples—' "

The group repeated his words dully, some of them mumbling and making gibberish of the lines, others interpolating, "Amen, brother," and giving shrill cries of, "Aye, Lord; so be it, Lord."

The little moon came out boldly, suspended above the treetops, and hung there as if its curiosity had got the better of its shyness. More than ever the scene became unreal: the torch flames were brighter than in actual life; the baying of the hounds was louder and more mournful; the people forming the circle looked like something out of *Pilgrim's Progress* etched by Goya; or rather it was a new Imaginary Prison by Piranesi. On the face of Bud Cummings there was a wild gleam of fanaticism; his eyes burned like live coals, his long chin was pointed upward.

It was difficult to determine where the creed ended and his prayer began, for the words seemed the same: "God, these are your children who are gathered before you to prove their faith in your Word. We believe in it, God, just like we believe all them miracles in the Old Testament. Hits put down there for us to follow, and we're a-comin', Lord, a-comin' to sit on the right hand of the throne; with the children that you rescued from the fiery furnace, with Daniel that you rescued from the lion's den, comin' to sit with the saints in heaven. There ain't no separation and distinctions there, we go' all walk on the same golden streets and play the same golden harps, the high and the low go' all stand equal before Thy throne, oh God, just so we prove ourselves worthy to go there. Help us, oh Lord, to prove ourselves worthy, we ask it in His name, for Jesus' sake, Amen."

He walked slowly, as in a dream, to the center of the circle and knelt before the bag. The crowd looked on motionless, and even the dogs were quieter, panting softly and watching. Bud drew out the dark gray serpent (a timber rattler, Ellison Frost decided) and looked steadily into its eyes. After a time he began rubbing its rough back with his hand. Then he stood up. "I want to ask the new converts to come forward: Sarah Ann McDonough, Sammy Allen, Maria Tilden and Horace Calloway."

The boys approached boldly, and one of the women, but a child was looking at Bud with terror in her face. "Come forward, Sarah. Remember, it's God's word: 'And these signs shall follow them that believe: In my name—' "

The child walked slowly. She was a slender thing, about twelve years of age, blue-eyed and flaxen-haired. "I—I don't want to now," she cried. "I said I would, I know I said it, but I can't— I can't—"

"Stop it!" Ellison Frost shouted. "You can't do this to the child; it's inhuman, it is so evil that no God in heaven will permit it." He tried to break loose from the men but they held him silently. No one seemed to have heard him.

"Come on, Sarah Ann," crooned old Granny Cummings, "you been't afeered."

"Look at me, Sarah Ann, look into my eyes; just walk toward me and listen to what I say." Bud Cummings was speaking to the girl as if no one else were there. The pine knots filled the air with resinous smoke, and the odor of cheap corn whisky mingled with that of human sweat. "The serpent is your lover, Sarah Ann; it does not harm the pure in heart. Take it up in your hands, caress it, fondle it; say, 'This is my lover, Jesus Christ,' and his love will enter your soul."

The child's mother raised her scornful voice, "My Sarah Ann ain't scairt—she's proud to do it—go on, Sarah Ann—"

But the child screamed and flung herself down moaning into the soft earth. "No, no, I can't do it—" Her mother kicked at her prostrate body. "You fool, you silly little fool; I'm ashamed of you, that's what I am—you're a coward—"

The others looked on fascinated and began to chant something that had no intelligible words, no obvious meaning.

Ellison Frost shut his eyes and would have swayed if he had not been so tightly held. He thought they must have begun passing the snake from one person to another for he could hear the contact of its rough body against hard calloused hands, and in the meantime the monotonous chant went on.

When he looked up, in spite of himself, he saw that the other woman whose name had been called was reaching out her hand. Bud Cummings was speaking to her as he had to the little girl, his face alight as the evil body twined itself about the woman's arm. On her face, too, was a sort of obscene exaltation as with her left hand she caressed the scaly thing on her right and the serpent was winding itself tighter and tighter. She was whispering to herself; her body was taut, every muscle in her arm stood out, and the veins seemed about to burst in her neck.

Masochism and sadism, thought Ellison Frost, watching, and at the same time hating himself for watching. It was impossible to look elsewhere than at the woman's transfigured face, white, burning—and expectant. Her breasts were heaving, her breath coming rapidly as she awaited the sharp, destructive blow. Her head was tilted back now, her eyes closed almost as if she would swoon, and the serpent's head was raised. There was a sharp hiss, and Ellison Frost tried to turn away, staring at the ground.

The snake evidently fell then, for the dogs rushed forward, eager to drag it away with them to the woods, but they were held firmly on leash.

Ellison Frost scarcely heard what followed, his mind and senses were paralyzed. He was aware that the snake was being passed again, and then the ropes were loosed from about his hands. The serpent's body was extended toward him and he took it without a word.

He knew vaguely sometime afterward that the lights and the people were gone; he was conscious for only a few moments; and he thought that he ought to do something about his daughter Sabina, but he was unable to move.

When they found him several hours after daybreak he had been dead for some time. Clarissa, who had come with the searching party, clung to her husband and sobbed; it was Michael Thibaut who spoke his friend's epitaph, "He always wanted to know what came next. I think he knows now."

CHAPTER XI

THE LONG HOURS BEFORE THE FUNERAL ON SUNDAY AFTER-noon turned Frost Haven into a sort of restrained house party, Sabina thought; it was at least "open house" to the townspeople and all the relatives who lived near enough to come. On Saturday night she and Barrett Page had gone to the telegraph office for a moment and on their return she was amazed to see that the house was lighted as for a ball. She had, actually, never seen it like that, lights in every room from garret to basement, and even the ground floor that had once been used as a business office, later as a playroom and a study, was glowing. The result was that the house seemed almost the "mansion" it had once been, brilliant from portico to portico, its white columns gleaming, the lovely wrought-iron steps ascending from the ground at each side to the center doorway on the second floor. You expected to hear waltz music inside, and through the long windows to see figures in costumes, wide satin skirts, powdered wigs, knee breeches and buckled slippers moving gaily and sensuously about the floor. You took it for granted that you would be met at the door by powdered lackeys and that you would sip steaming hot punch that came from a huge cut-glass bowl.

"Isn't it awful, Barrett," Sabina had said as they drove past the front door so that they could slip in as inconspicuously as possible at the rear.

"It is, rather. Sometimes the refinements of civilization almost reach over backward to the state of savagery."

"Everybody in town who *is* anybody is here," she said bitterly; "you could call the social register and check them off one by one. And it doesn't stop there; the people who aren't invited anywhere always take advantage and go to funerals."

As they went into the house there were relatives in the kitchen, in the dining room; and the front rooms were filled with people. Sabina slipped upstairs and in her own room she found an aunt and a cousin going over the contents of her closet. "It's sinful," the aunt was saying, "it's nothing short of sinful with all the poverty there is in the world for one spoiled girl to have so many clothes!"

"Look, Mama," the cousin was saying as she held up a frock, "look at this. It's got a New York label in it, and I bet it cost seventy-five dollars if it cost a penny."

"And these shoes! Hilda, count 'em! I want to know just how many pairs of shoes there are on those racks! I declare, I never in all my born days—"

"Hello," said Sabina.

They looked around confused. The aunt said, "Hilda was just showing me some of your new frocks; I hope you don't mind. I stay at home so cosely I never get a chance to see pretty things like these. I can't imagine where you go to wear so many clothes, Sabina."

"I don't go anywhere; I just like to see them hanging up in the closet," she answered. "There are some more in the wardrobe in the hall, or have you already seen those?"

"You aren't displeased, are you, Sabina?" said the aunt in a pained voice. "Of course, if you don't *want* us to see your clothes—I didn't know we were doing anything wrong—"

Sabina wanted to say, "Oh, my God!" as Claire always did when she was too exasperated to think of anything else. Instead, she sat down wearily and answered, "Don't mind me. We are having open house."

Aunt Millie's face flushed. "I don't see how you can talk like that, Sabina, at a time like this, when your poor father is lying downstairs a corpse. And what do *you* care? You just resent the intrusion on your privacy. Instead of appreciating the effort people make to show their sympathy, you hide away from them as if they had no right to be here—"

"They haven't—"

"Sabina! What an unnatural girl you are! I assure you that if it had been left to me, I would never have come, but when my own sister is in trouble and asks me to come to her, I would put down everything—"

"Aunt Millie," said Sabina slowly, "do you realize that nobody in this house has been to sleep since Thursday night? Do you know that not one of us closed her eyes last night, and we haven't had a moment to be alone all day—not one—people bringing food, as if we were beggars! Cakes and pies and fruit and dressed chickens in fruit jars that looked as if they came off a biology laboratory shelf, angel food cakes, pound cakes; do they think we are getting ready for a funeral feast? And flowers! I never want to see a flower again—"

"Sabina, those people are your father's and your mother's friends and I know Janie Lee appreciated every one of them. She made me keep a list of who sent what."

Sabina went on, "People coming in, asking, 'Can I lend you a black dress to wear? What songs do you want sung? Are you going to ask just your own minister or all three ministers? Shall we have two songs or three? Will you have the funeral here or at the church? Just how old was your father, Sabina, I *said* he was fifty-five, but my husband said, No, he was sure he was older than that because they went to high school together—'" Sabina's voice became natural again as she continued, "They've asked everything except how much money he left and I know they've checked up on that somewhere else."

Hilda touched her mother's arm. "Come on, Mama, I reckon Sabina is worn out. And there are a lot of people downstairs you haven't spoken to—"

"Yes," said Aunt Millie. "I hear that your father's business affairs were rather in a mess, Sabina. I do hope it isn't true—Ellison was a fine man, don't misunderstand me, but he was so reserved. Janie Lee says he never mentioned his business to her. I'm afraid they were not as close as husbands and wives should be. But then I always said the Frosts were peculiar people, *very* peculiar, I never actually understood Ellison."

"We are proud of being peculiar," Sabina told her, "and we prefer not to be understood."

"Mama, are you coming?" asked Hilda. "I certainly wouldn't stand there and be insulted."

"Poor Janie Lee," said Aunt Millie, "to be left all

alone, with nobody but a daughter like that," and she closed the door behind her.

As they went down the hall Sabina could hear her cousin saying, "There were nineteen, Mama."

"Nineteen what, Hilda? Offerings?"

"No, Mama, nineteen pairs of shoes in Sabina's closet. I counted 'em."

By the next morning it was even worse. Cousin Tom and Cousin Ella arrived from Holly Grove up in Sussex County, Great-Uncle Peter Chisholm Wade came up from Danville, the Terrell cousins from Hilldale came by train and telephoned from the depot that they would like to have a car sent for them. They arrived with profuse apologies for not getting there earlier and immediately began looking at the flowers, complaining because the cards had been removed from the offerings.

Mrs. Frost was still in bed, still demanding if the dresses ordered from Atlanta had come. "Suppose they don't fit? Suppose they have to be altered? I nearly always have to have the seams let out—Sunday—I don't think we should have tried to have the funeral today."

"Somebody will fix it for you, Janie Lee, you mustn't worry about that," Cousin Kitty told her.

"But it's Sunday—I never thought I'd permit sewing in my house on Sunday," said Mrs. Frost beginning to sob again.

"The ox is in the ditch, Janie Lee; there, there, don't get yourself upset, it's only a few hours until time for the funeral. You must bear up."

At noon the darky from the post office brought the special-delivery packages and Mrs. Frost raised herself up in bed to examine the dresses. "That one is Sabina's, it's too old for the child, she'll look like she's a thousand in it, I declare I do hate for her to have to wear black. Ask her to come try it on, will you, Kitty? And take that into Clarissa's room; I suppose this is her hat, too. Crepe—with the veil, that's very nice."

"It seems a shame," said Cousin Kitty, "for Clarissa to have to wear mourning when she's a bride, I'm surprised that she's willing to do it."

"Kitty, you don't know Clarissa; she can make black look as if it were made especially for brides. Will you look in the third drawer of the dresser and hand me my corset, Kitty?"

Mrs. Frost lifted the folds of chiffon from the tissue paper in the box, then she lay back sobbing. "Kitty, I just can't stand it, I can't bear it—"

"You *can* bear it, Janie Lee, because you have got to. You *have* to for the girls' sake; you can't let them see you give way like this. If it was God's will that Mr. Frost should be taken that way—"

"I don't believe God had anything to do with it," Mrs. Frost declared rebelliously; and Cousin Kitty cried quickly, "Hush, Janie Lee, you mustn't talk that way, it's sinful. You are not yourself—"

There was a knock on the door and Cousin Ella asked, "May I come in? It's Ella—"

"Yes, come in, Ella, and close the door; I've got to try on my dress."

"Oh, you *ordered* a dress! The things that people with money can do! I don't see how you got it here so quickly."

"I called up the saleswoman who always waits on us and she was so nice; she said, 'Mrs. Frost, I'll attend to it myself and get it off this afternoon. And may I say how exceedingly sorry I am to hear about Mr. Frost. The state will miss him.' That's what she said, 'The state will miss him.' I thought it was very nice of her. He had a lot of friends. Everybody has been so kind, I declare when I think how little I have done for other people, it makes me so ashamed. I don't deserve all this kindness. Is that you, Sabina?" she said in answer to a knock at the door.

"Yes, do you want to see me, Mother?"

"Come in, Sabina, I want you to try on your dress."

"In here?"

"Of course. You don't mind Cousin Ella."

"You *have* been fortunate, Janie Lee," said Cousin Ella, looking at the chintz draperies, the thick rugs and fine old furniture. "God has been good to you. You've never known what it meant to have to worry about money. And when I think how we grew up, almost in poverty, you might say—"

"Nonsense, Ella, we weren't any poorer than everybody else; it was just Reconstruction period," interrupted Mrs. Frost.

But Cousin Ella went on reminiscently, "Walking four miles to school, barefooted, in the snow, eating sweet potatoes and corn bread and sorghum syrup for our lunch. I know papa and Uncle William did the best they could, and it didn't hurt us, but what a difference between that—and this. The rest of us weren't as lucky as you, Janie Lee. Understand, I'm not complaining, but you ought to get down on your knees every night and thank God—"

"Mother," Sabina broke in, "it's too long. I can't possibly wear it."

"You can hem it up, can't you?" asked Cousin Ella.

"Sabina never did study domestic science," apologized Mrs. Frost; "it wasn't offered at the college she attended. We preferred that she take the straight literary course, she's very literary."

"Do you mean to tell me," demanded Cousin Ella, "that Sabina Frost can't put a hem in a dress? Well, if that isn't a pretty come-off! Here, child, hand me some pins. Lord, but you're tiny, how many inches are you in the waist? Look at that waist, Janie Lee, it's a good thing it was Clarissa who got married instead of you, Sabina. You'd have a sweet time having babies, I must say—"

"Ella, please—" said Mrs. Frost.

"Pshaw! She might as well know it—"

"Thank you, Cousin Ella, but I'll get someone else to fix the dress," said Sabina.

"You needn't get in a huff, miss, and switch off. Anybody would think you'd never heard that women had babies. What is Janie Lee raising you for, anyhow, an old-maid schoolteacher?"

"Mother, I've got to go back downstairs. What shall I do about the dress?"

"Just take it off, dear, Ella will fix it."

"I had much rather she didn't."

"I know, dear, but the—the ox is in the ditch. Cousin Ella takes in sewing, she'll fix it nicely for you."

"Oh," said Sabina, relieved, "we can pay her."

"Pay me! Well, if that isn't the straw that broke the camel's back! Janie Lee, I've a good notion to walk out of this house and never put my foot in it again—"

"Ella," the sobs came back into Mrs. Frost's voice, "I didn't think you would do me this way at a time like this. Sabina didn't mean a thing, you forget that she's just a child—"

"A child! Well, it's high time she was growing up! Why, when my Alice was Sabina's age she'd been married five years and had two children. Step out of the dress, Sabina, and tell your Cousin Tom I want to talk to him before the funeral. Where is he?"

"I think he's sitting out on the back veranda with some of the other men."

"Don't let him get drunk before the funeral, keep your eye on him, Sabina. And I'm sorry I said what I did."

"Oh, that's all right, Cousin Ella. I think you're awfully sweet to fix the dress for me."

"Huhm!" said Cousin Ella as Sabina left the room, "she can be mighty nice when she tries!"

"Yes, Sabina has beautiful manners," Mrs. Frost agreed, "but she's very delicate and high-strung. This was an awful shock for her as it was for all of us."

"Do you know what she reminds me of?" asked Cousin Ella. "I don't mean any harm by this, but she reminds me of those three little monkeys, the see-no-evil, hear-no-evil, speak-no-evil, or the first two anyhow. She seems to go around with her eyes and ears closed. You'd actually think, from the way she's acting, that she didn't know her father was dead."

"Oh, but you don't know Sabina. That's her Frost pride. She'd die before she'd let anyone see her under the stress of emotion. Other people don't understand her as I do. Why, when she was a child, Ella, before the days of automobiles, when we'd go riding in the carriage she would cry because she thought the rocks hurt the horses' feet. I've seen her cry when Lila May killed chickens for dinner, or when one of her little pets was injured. You've never seen anybody as tender-hearted as she is. And once —I couldn't tell you this when she was in the room— once I took her calling with me to see Mrs. Nixon who had a right new baby. And do you know Sabina acted so strangely, she was sick in bed for three days after that. She was either too young to have been there and have seen it, or too old. I never knew which. But we never mention things like that before her. It nauseates her. You see, her soul is of such a delicate, beautiful simplicity—so pure and unsullied, Ella—I don't know quite how to explain it to you."

"Maybe you're right, Janie Lee," Cousin Ella's mouth was full of pins, "but it sounds like the most unmitigated tommy-rot to me. We never were able to afford any souls in our family. It was all we could do to provide for our bodies."

"You mark my words," Cousin Tom was saying on the back veranda, "every unattached female in the Frost and Regis families is going to try to move in on Janie Lee. They'll tell her it doesn't look nice for two lone women to live here unprotected. Of course, the truth is, they're afraid there won't be any more checks coming in now that Ellison is gone, and the idea of having to go to work will scare them out of ten years' growth. Yes sir, Janie Lee's going to have more devoted female relatives than you can shake a stick at. And Millie and Hilda will be the first to arrive."

Great-Uncle Peter Chisholm Wade crossed his legs carefully, setting the wooden one down as silently as possible. "Need a man," he said, "a woman's no protection. It took the whole Union army four years to shoot a leg out from under me and they wouldn't have done it then, sir, if it hadn't been for a woman."

"Uncle Peter," said Claire, "don't you think we could have just one more drink before the funeral? How about it, Cousin Tom?" She was lying down in the swing, her head propped on pillows. "With only one more drink the present would become part of the beautiful past, there'd be a veil over things—"

"Miss Claire," asked Colonel Thibaut, "where can I find your husband? I want to talk with him."

"Barrett is being a gentleman, he's host on this delightful occasion. You'll find him doing his duty in the living room, the library, or wherever he is most needed. We simply couldn't have made a success of this funeral without Barrett."

"A Sunday funeral is nearly always a success," Cousin Tom corrected her, "unless it rains. What were you saying about the woman, Uncle Peter?"

"Did you address me, sir?" Uncle Peter put his hand to his ear.

"Yes, sir, I asked what a woman had to do with your getting shot at—where was it, Petersburg?"

"Petersburg is correct, sir. I can see her just as if it was yesterday, big laughing brown eyes, chestnut hair, a complexion like apple blossoms, and the finest figger south of the Mason and Dixon line. I could span her waist with my two hands, sir, damme if I couldn't. We'd been marching for three days, eating cracked corn and acorns, our clothes in tatters, barefooted as the blackest nigger in the fields, sir, and nearly every man of us weak from dysentery—"

"Pardon me, sir," Barrett Page broke in, "but I should like to speak to my wife. Claire, won't you come into the living room? There are some people who want to see you."

She waved her hand impatiently. "I know. '*Dear* Clarissa, what an awful, awful thing! Do tell me exactly how it happened. I simply couldn't believe it when Mrs. Thingamabob called me. I had just gotten up from the breakfast table—we had some specially good apple rings with our bacon, did you ever try them together?—and I was trying to decide whether to order groceries first or to sew buttons on Bill's union suits. You really do look dreadful, Clarissa, and I hadn't gotten over the shock of your being married—to one of the Boston Pages, no less! My, my! Well, you certainly did make up for lost time when you *did* get married—' "

"Claire—"

" 'And my dear, I do hope it isn't true, but I hear that your father's affairs were in an awful mess—' Barrett, I want just one more drink."

"All right, come along with me. I'll take you upstairs and then bring the drink to you."

"No. Cousin Tom wants one, too, don't you, Cousin Tom?"

"You'd better go with your husband, Clarissa. We'll be all right," Cousin Tom answered uneasily.

Claire got to her feet unsteadily. "Barrett, I'm not going to the funeral. I *can't*."

"You'll have to, Claire."

"No," she said as they went toward the stairs, "I'm going to get drunk. I think that is what father would have done if I had—if I had died like that."

"No, you're wrong, Claire. He would have waited until afterward."

"Do you think so, Barrett?"

"Yes, I'm sure of it."

"Then that's what I'll do."

"You don't suppose," Cousin Tom said to Great-Uncle Peter, "that she is under the influence of liquor, do you?"

"Certainly not, sir. She's a beautiful woman, isn't she?"

"Yes."

"And a Southern lady?"

"Yes. But Uncle Peter, women are queer critters. When they were talking sometime ago about the girl who started this whole thing, Daisy, I think her name was, I got to thinking. Do you reckon she loved that boy she shot?"

"No, sir, I can't agree with you there, sir."

"Sometimes they take drastic measures. I knew a young lady, a very fine intelligent young woman, who didn't believe in war or violence or bloodshed. But when the war came along she had a sweetheart in the North—I refer, of course, to the Civil War, sir—and she dressed up like a nigger mammy, rode through the Confederate lines, on to those of the Yankees until she finally delivered a piece of important information to her sweetheart's regiment. She told me once that sometimes at night she'd wake up in a cold sweat thinking what she had done, but she couldn't have done otherwise, she said. 'A woman in love,' she said to me, 'is absolutely ruthless; she will sacrifice anything, anybody, for her beloved.'"

"Ought not to go around saying things like that," grumbled Uncle Peter, "it ain't ladylike. Now that little piece at Petersburg I was telling you about—oh, howdy, Colonel, draw up a chair."

"Thank you, Mr. Wade." Colonel Thibaut sat in the swing which Clarissa had just vacated.

"Pour yourself a drink, that boy Grover will get you some ice. Grover? Grover?"

"No, thank you, Mr. Wade. Not now."

"Colonel, I hear you've been mighty nice to Ellison's family and I want you to know that we appreciate it. Yes, sir, we are all deeply indebted to you."

"Not at all, sir. I wish I could do more. And I also wish this funeral were over, I dread it."

"It was a terrible thing, Ellison's going like that," Uncle Tom said.

"It was a terrible thing his going at all. I don't think I ever knew a man as fine, deep down in his soul, as Ellison Frost."

"Why sir, Ellison was all right, I never heard of him doing a mean thing in his life, but I never saw that he was anything remarkable," declared Uncle Tom. "Did you, Uncle Peter?"

Uncle Peter leaned his white head forward courteously. "Did you address me, sir?"

During the hours preceding the funeral there was an almost unending line of darkies filing into the library where the casket reposed. They came in through the kitchen and dining room, stood for a moment looking down into the flower-banked coffin, then moved on through the living room into the back of the house and out once more into the yard where they would stand until the service was over. The negro men held their hats in their hands and were silent, the women sobbed openly.

Every chair in the house was occupied at least a half hour before the service began; men stood on the wide front veranda discussing crops, the prospect of rain and the summer's average temperature. Occasionally some one told an anecdote of Ellison Frost's early life emphasizing his impracticality, his arrogance or his wit but always coming back in the end to the fact that they themselves had not understood him and the implication that his variation had not been in his favor. The death of the last male of the Frost line meant the direct end of something, but it was something which had had its day, a distinct anachronism that had in it some thing of reproach, of disapproval toward modern days and ways. And among the men standing on the veranda as well as among the men and women seated inside there seemed to be an atmosphere of relief; there would no longer be before them, living, an example, a standard which they could neither define nor attain. They might deny its superiority to their own standards, profess to disparage it and question its existence, but they had been conscious of it in some form, however shadowy or intangible.

At one end of the piazza someone was telling the anecdote about the hunchback who had been strapped in his coffin so that the lid might be fastened down, and how the watchers "sitting up" with the body had been startled into hysteria when the straps broke and the corpse of the hunchback sat bolt upright in his coffin.

"The way I heard it," one of the storyteller's companions said, "it was a nigger and they were having the funeral at the church. The preacher bolted over the pews and the crowd broke the doors down trying to get out."

In the living room Mrs. Nixon was whispering to the woman beside her, "When I strike a chord I want the quartet to rise. Do you think it is time to begin now?"

"The undertaker will give you the signal," murmured the soprano, who added, "Do you see those flowers on the stand by the mantlepiece? I just know Mrs. Conway fixed them, you can always tell. She had some in the church last Sunday and honestly, I would have been ashamed to send them to a dogfight; she won't pull her flowers with long enough stems and then she just jams them down tight into the first thing she sees."

"She does the best she knows how," Mrs. Nixon said reprovingly, "and that's all God asks of us. It's the thought, the motive that counts with Him."

"All the same," the soprano contended, "I know it hurts Him to see flowers treated that way. They have their feelings just the same as we have."

"Oh, really, Jane, don't you think there's such a thing as carrying things too far." She leaned forward then and whispered, "Doesn't Janie Lee look awful! She's been under a doctor's care ever since it happened. I don't think she should have tried to come to the funeral."

"She'll go to pieces when it's over," the soprano agreed. "I've seen women hold up wonderfully until it was all over and then they'd go to pieces—just like that."

"I wonder," said Mrs. Nixon contemplatively, "how much life insurance he had. I heard that he was carrying a hundred thousand dollars at one time, but he dropped most of it; in fact, *some*body said he'd let it lapse entirely."

"The undertaker is signaling you."

"Oh. Thank you." Mrs. Nixon took her seat at the piano, struck a chord in the key of G and the quartet rose.

In the dining room Sabina sat in the front row of chairs between her mother and Barrett Page. Back of her were all the relatives of the Frost and Regis families and immediately before her in the library were the three ministers and the casket. She closed her eyes and told herself that it was only a church service; the choir was singing, "There'll be no dark valley when Jesus comes," as she had heard them do on many Sunday mornings. And yet there was something different about the singing, it was slower, more subdued, and there had not been the heavy scent of so many flowers at church. But none of it had anything to do with her father; it was just something that had to be got through, as you would a wedding or a dull party you had not wanted to attend. And when it was over her father would come walking in, say, "Hello, Sabina, how are you? Is your mother upstairs?"

Of course, he was actually dead, and death meant something—she didn't yet know what—but it wasn't this. This was a thing that had occurred at a time when she already had more to think about than she could deal with. In a way, of course, it had been fortunate, it had taken her mind off Claire's and Barrett's marriage and had changed her overnight from the ridiculous state of a girl who has been jilted to a figure of sympathy: a bereaved daughter.

One of the ministers was praying now, and outside sparrows were twittering in the oak trees; she could even hear a dog splashing in the shallow pool and shaking the water from his body. She wished she knew what Barrett

Page was thinking as he sat there beside her. For her own part she was no more conscious of him as a man, as a personality, as the man she had hoped to marry than if he had been one of her own uncles. On her left, Mrs. Frost was breathing heavily, clenching and unclenching her hands, but she was, Sabina knew, listening to every word that was said with a sensation of fierce possessive jealousy, afraid that the speakers would not sufficiently praise her dead husband. She would remember every laudatory phrase, each commendatory adjective and mark the omission of any that were left unsaid. Her attitude was that they had come not to bury Caesar but to praise him.

On the row of seats back of her Sabina could hear the discreet sniffles of Aunt Millie, who had avowedly never understood Ellison Frost but had come because her own sister was in trouble and needed her. What had Aunt Millie done to mitigate Janie Lee Frost's trouble? She had only been one more of the ubiquitous relatives overrunning the house and Sabina reflected now that perhaps they had their use: their presence prevented the natural processes of thought. In protesting against their invasion she had at the same time been conscious that she did not want to be alone, to think. Being alone with your dead was barbarism, this was civilization; or vice versa. She did not know which was true, the premise, or its opposite. Perhaps neither.

Beside Aunt Millie sat Cousin Henry Allison who did not, surprisingly, have a buggy whip in his hand. Cousin Henry sold mules at large profits and had the reputation of being the most confirmed nigger-beater in the State of Georgia. Cousin Henry admitted that he'd rather whip a nigger than shoot one, but sometimes shooting was the only thing that would make one respectful, and no damned nigger was going to talk back to him. His wife, thin, sallow Cousin Katie, twitched nervously whenever he looked at her and it was easy to believe the story that she wept when meals were not ready on time for him. Cousin Katie had had a "major operation" many years ago and she could not endure children near her; they made her want to jump out of her skin.

Cousin Lucinda Terrell hiccoughed and tried to disguise the sound by blowing her nose. Cousin Lucinda had enjoyed her dinner as indeed she enjoyed all her dinners. Funerals seemed only to whet her appetite, making her feel alive, vigorous, perennial. Other people might grow old and die, she would remain fat and hedonistic, her conscience as clear as a baby's because she tolerated no weaknesses in herself, had no sins. The Lord himself had known that people had to eat, had he not performed the miracle of the loaves and fishes at Galilee, or was it the Mount of Olives? True, there had been no tartare sauce and French fried potatoes to eat with the fish, but with so many people to feed, you had to restrict your menu.

On Cousin Lucinda's right was her sister Cousin Nettie, who was (everybody said so), a fine woman. She had never done a lick of honest work in her life; she allowed her sisters to have the pleasure of her company according to their financial condition. When times were hard at one sister's house, she did not want to be a burden and moved on to a more prosperous home. But wherever she was, she was always a leader in the church, deciding on the new carpet for the Sunday-school rooms, appointing "circle leaders" in the missionary society and using every ounce of her frail body for the glory of God.

Clarissa once pointed out that she could not have been a leader anywhere else; that requirements in other spheres were higher and that every ounce of her frail brain would have been insufficient for leadership elsewhere, but Mrs. Frost only said, "Clarissa, you talk like a heathen."

Cousin Nettie was as thin as her sister Lucinda was stout and was very proud of "not eating enough to keep a bird alive." Her face consequently had a bleached look that some called spiritual and others said was puritanical; she had never been known to enjoy anything in either a mental or physical way and although she read constantly in the most innocuous magazines—*The Ladies' Home Journal, McCall's, The American*—the stories seemed to go in one eye and out the other. She had been reading the same story in all three magazines for the past twenty-five years and never once suspected that it was the same. Mrs. Frost had always held up Cousin Nettie as a model of female rectitude and Claire had frequently asked, "What has she ever done?"

"Well, she's a fine woman. Anybody will tell you that. She has behaved herself."

"Behaved herself? Did she ever have an opportunity to do otherwise?"

"Everybody respects Nettie, Clarissa."

"Why? Just because a rock sits on the same hill without moving for fifty years, does that make it respectable? Personally, I'd think a lot more of her if she had clerked behind a counter at the five and ten."

"Clarissa!"

It was one of those arguments that would never be settled but could always be dragged out and begun over again when things got dull. Mrs. Frost would defend

Cousin Nettie with her dying breath and Clarissa would go to her grave defending her own right to refuse to respect her.

Claire was sitting now with her eyes lowered and it was impossible to tell whether she was impersonating the mourning bride or whether her drowsiness was the result of keeping Cousin Tom company on the back porch. It seemed quite natural for Barrett to be sitting between the two of them, Claire and Sabina, as he had done so many times during the summer—and yet how changed everything was! Now Claire belongs to him, or he to Claire, and she, Sabina, was nothing. How they must have laughed during those weeks at her simplicity and her gullibility, at her conceit in thinking her company was desired when she had in reality been playing gooseberry. And how exasperated they must have been on occasions by her obtuseness. Yet even now it was impossible for her to believe that Barrett Page had spent one unwilling moment in her presence. Was he then such a consummate actor? Had he enjoyed seeing what he could do with the emotions and affections of an artless girl? How much of his admiration and pleasure had been genuine? What, after all, did she know about him? She had been interested only in the way he made her feel.

What did he think of the Frosts as a family and of the horrible way in which her father had died? Her hands were so hot against her lap that they made small creases in her georgette crepe dress. She moved them to the sides of her straight chair and tried not to think of the way in which Ellison Frost had met his death. It was too horrible —horrible and revolting and nauseating. There was humiliation even in contemplating it. He could so easily have been shot, through the heart or the temple—not in the intestines as the man was in *Hedda Gabler*—there was some human dignity in being shot, but this—

She wanted suddenly to put her hot right hand in Barrett Page's, say to him, Hold it tight—so tightly that I shall never think of that thing again. Not once. Ever. Help me not to. Help me to put it aside and never let it come back. I don't know who you are, but there isn't anyone else I can ask.

He stirred in his chair beside her, seemed conscious of her. Then he turned and, incredibly, he put his hand over hers and pressed it against the hard wood of the chair. Her own beat frighteningly against it for a moment and then she remembered that he was now her brother-in-law. It was the sort of gesture anyone might make toward a bereaved relative.

Just back of them and over the heads of the Terrell cousins a ghostly breeze from the garden set the great crystal chandelier to moving and the prisms tinkled emptily, a sound as anachronistic as the notes of a spinet. Throughout the rooms people stirred and looked around in wonder. Then they rose for the final hymn and Sabina laced her fingers together once more. In just a few moments they would go out to the old family burying ground by the edge of the apple orchard where the wrought-iron gate had already been unlocked and stood receptively ajar. The great key, someone had said, had been rusted in the lock and had broken off in protest when its removal was attempted.

CHAPTER XII

Mrs. Frost's health failed at eleven o'clock on Thursday morning immediately following an examination of her late husband's business affairs. That was, of course, a coincidence. Everyone said how brave she had been: she had held up during the funeral, through the discovery that the Cummings family was gone, lock, stock and barrel, and she had received with composure the news that Bud Cummings had got safely over the state line into Florida. What good would it have done to catch him? she asked. If Daisy could not be convicted when she'd shot Matthew Cox down in cold blood before witnesses, what hope was there of proving Bud guilty? The Lord would punish him, said Mrs. Frost, in His own time and in His own way.

Henry Cox had led the posse that pursued Bud and he was bitter over their failure. "We weren't going to fool with the courts this time, Mrs. Frost. I've had my fill of 'em. We were going to have the prettiest lynching you ever laid your two eyes on. I had a tree all picked out ready for him, but I guess it'll keep. We'll get 'im some day, I'm just as sure of that as I am of standing here."

"And let me know when you do, Mr. Cox," said Clarissa. "I want to be there. Promise me you'll let me know."

"She doesn't mean that seriously," Mrs. Frost told Henry Cox, "and I'm sure you don't, either. If you were a Southerner, Mr. Cox, you would know that there is only one justified provocation for lynching."

"I didn't know. What is it, Mrs. Frost?"

Mrs. Frost blushed and said, "I'd rather not go into that now. Good-night, Mr. Cox, and thank you so much for all you've done."

When he had gone Sabina looked questioningly at Claire and Claire answered, "She was talking about rape, my little innocent, specifically of a negro raping a white woman. It's the code of your hills. That reminds me, did you ever hear the story—"

"Claire," interrupted Barrett Page.

"Oh, sorry."

"You can tell me later," he added.

"All right, but Barrett, after all, Sabina is grown up and mother is a married woman."

"I don't agree with you at all, on either count."

"You don't agree with me that mother is a married woman?"

"No."

"How do you account for Sabina?"

"Parthenogenesis," he said laconically.

Claire laughed and Mrs. Frost looked confused. "Sabina, you had better go to bed, and I'm going, too. I'm

(DEVELOPMENT OF UNFERTILIZED EGG)

simply worn to a frazzle. We have a hard day ahead of us tomorrow: the cards of appreciation must be addressed and mailed, Colonel Thibaut is coming at ten to go over the papers, and there are sure to be callers. Good-night, Claire, good-night, Barrett."

"Good-night. Good-night, Sabina."

Damn, thought Sabina, as she followed her mother upstairs. Mrs. Frost paused at the door of her room. "Sabina, did you know what that word meant?"

"It sounded like one of the books of the Bible," Sabina suggested with malice aforethought. "Parthenogenesis, Exodus, Leviticus—"

"That doesn't sound right," her mother answered vaguely, "I don't think that is right at all—"

"I believe there was a Greek goddess named Parthenia—"

"I've told you before, and I tell you again, I don't want you reading heathen mythology. Good-night, Sabina." Mrs. Frost always accented the first two letters of mythology and made a syllable of them.

"Good-night, Mother."

Sabina got out her leather notebook and added "parthenogenesis" to the list of words she was going to look up some day. She left the book open on the night table so that she would be sure to see it on the morrow. But the next morning at eleven o'clock Mrs. Frost's health failed.

Colonel Thibaut had the papers spread out on the library table, the statement from the bank, canceled notes, bills, receipts, the safe-deposit box containing deeds and bonds, an orderly accounting of outstanding debts and assets, yellowed papers from the pigeonholes of Ellison

Frost's desk, innumerable papers that amounted to nothing except proof that the deceased man had been scrupulously honest in paying his debts. The Colonel sat for several moments looking at the papers, then he began collecting them and sorting them, putting the worthless ones on his right and occasionally one that might be of some value on his left.

"We'll have to have administrators, executors and all that sort of thing, won't we?" said Mrs. Frost.

"It scarcely seems necessary," answered Colonel Thibaut slowly.

"You mean I'm to do it? Why, Colonel, I don't know a thing in the world about business—"

Barrett Page looked at Claire and Claire looked back at him.

"I mean, Mrs. Frost," Michael Thibaut said hesitantly, "that there doesn't seem to be anything to administer. When a man dies without a will, his widow receives a child's share of the estate. What there is will be divided equally between the three of you. But you don't want to divide it, do you? You don't want to sell your home, your orchards—"

"But all those papers—"

"My dear lady, these papers can be thrown into the trash basket with no loss to anybody."

The color went out of Mrs. Frost's face. "All of them?" she asked.

"Not quite all of them. You want to keep your deeds, of course; I've put those back in the safe-deposit box. Then there's a little life insurance—"

"A little?"

"Enough to pay the expenses of the funeral, and, if

you're careful, perhaps enough to run the orchards until another crop comes in, though I'm not sure about that. I understand it's an expensive operation."

"No money," said Mrs. Frost. "No money—and I'd always thought we were weathly. We *were* wealthy, Colonel Thibaut," her voice rose suddenly, "we lived like rich people—"

"Mother," said Sabina, "please—"

"We *were* rich, we had everything! Why, Mr. Frost *gave* away money, he supported my relatives, he helped people who needed it—" She put her hand to her forehead and held it there. "I just can't think, I can't think at all—"

"Don't you see, Mrs. Frost," said Barrett Page, "that's exactly why you haven't got it now. People can't *have* their money and spend it, too."

"But he let me think we were rich," she cried. "Why didn't he tell me?"

"Mother, you are making a scene," said Sabina. "You don't know what you are saying."

Mrs. Frost put her head down on the desk. "My head —get me some water, Sabina—"

Claire jumped up. "She's sick, Barrett. Help me. Can you walk to the sofa, Mother?"

"Take me upstairs. I want to go upstairs."

"Can you walk?"

"Yes, yes. But hurry."

With Barrett Page on her left and Colonel Thibaut on her right she started slowly up the steps. Sabina ran to the telephone to call Dr. Mannering and as she went past the grandfather's clock in the living room she noticed that it was striking eleven. She thought it was strange that she, to whom time meant nothing, should have been conscious of it, and yet she knew, somehow, that she was going to remember it. There was an ominous and prophetic sound about it; she felt that this was no mere temporary indisposition of her mother's. Almost it was as if the clock were saying to her, It was at eleven in the morning that your mother became an invalid.

When Dr. Mannering came he declared that he had been expecting Mrs. Frost's collapse for several days; it was the most natural thing in the world. She would be quite all right after a few days in bed. He gave her a sedative, lowered the shades and turned the electric fan so that it would not blow directly on her. "If you should need me, call me," he said to Sabina and Claire as he was leaving, "but I don't think you will. She's as strong as a mule. The only thing you have to do is watch her diet, don't let her eat too much this hot weather, just liquids, fruits and vegetables."

"Well, that's a relief," said Claire when he was gone, "I was afraid she was sick and I hated to go back to New York and leave you alone with her."

"Mother's never sick," Sabina declared, for she was afraid Claire might stay. "As Dr. Mannering so delicately says, 'She's as strong as a mule.'"

"He certainly didn't examine her very thoroughly; I hope he knows what he is talking about."

"He does. I was ill last winter and I didn't know whether I had a streptococcic infection or cancer of the throat or pneumonia, or all three, but I knew I was going to die. He came in, told me to say, 'Ah,' took one look at my throat and said, 'Laryngitis.'"

"Was it?" asked Claire.

"Of course."

"You always were a hypochondriac. I'll bet you live to be ninety-seven and then die of something simple and childish like measles or mumps. I can see it in the newspapers, 'Miss Sabina Frost, one of the oldest inhabitants of Frost Haven, Georgia, died peacefully at her home last night. She was a young lady during the years of the World War and remembered seeing the doughboys sail from New York harbor. Miss Frost—' "

Sabina paused at the door of the dining room. "Claire, why do you say, 'Miss Frost of Frost Haven'? Do you think I'll be an old maid, live here all my life?"

"Uh-huh, with forty cats, while the roof falls in over your head. And you'll hide your money under the planks in the floor and in the wall behind the plastering."

"You might invite me to live with you."

"Law, chile," said Clarissa, "I'll be dead and buried behind the old church door long before then. Doesn't that fried chicken smell good! Where is Barrett?"

"I don't know."

"Lila May, do you know where Mr. Page is?"

"He out in the back yard talkin' with that Mr. Cox."

"Do you suppose we ought to ask Mr. Cox to stay to dinner?" Clarissa asked.

"Oh, Claire! Can you imagine Mr. Cox sitting at this table with those portraits looking at him, and under that chandelier?"

"Father would have asked him."

"Well, ask him, then, but he won't accept. He's at least got sense enough for that."

"I be dogged," said Lila May. "If he stay, I ain't. I bet

he act like he bawn and bred in de briar patch. I ain't waitin' on no po-whites, Miss Sabina."

"He won't stay, Lila May, and besides, he is not a po-white. His son went to college."

Lila May held the ice suspended above the tea glasses. "Did?" she asked.

"Yes."

"That make him quality?"

"No. But it proves he is not a po-white."

"I ain't so sho," said Lila May. "Seem like any old kind of trash go to college these days."

"Don't be a snob, Lila May," Clarissa admonished.

Barrett Page came in then. "I took the liberty of inviting Mr. Cox to dinner but he wouldn't stay."

"That isn't liberty," Sabina said for Claire's benefit, "that's fraternity."

Claire ignored the remark and Barrett only smiled slightly. "How is Mrs. Frost?" he asked.

"She's supposed to be asleep," Claire answered. "The doctor didn't seem to think there was much the matter with her; he says she'll be all right in a day or two."

"Good."

He pulled out Sabina's chair and then Claire's. "Sabina, I think we have the orchards fixed for the coming year if you and Mrs. Frost agree. Cox says he'll manage it on halves. You, of course, will have to pay the operating costs, furnish the materials, the supplies, the hands—"

"Halves? Isn't that rather high? After all, they are *our* orchards and we furnish everything."

"Do you honestly think that is too high? What do you ordinarily make on a crop?"

"There is no such thing as ordinarily. But sometimes owners make as much as ten thousand dollars a season."

"And at other times?"

"In two or three bad seasons they can lose that much," Sabina admitted.

"What do you think an overseer's salary should be?"

"Why, I don't know. What do you think, Claire, about fifty dollars a month?"

"Sabina," Barrett Page said, "day laborers make more money than that. I should say a hundred and fifty a month was a fair price, but you haven't got the cash to pay him. Besides, he's taking a chance, he may not make a penny out of his year's work. But he'll have more incentive this way than if he were working for a salary— and it's what your father offered him."

"How do you know?"

"He said so."

Sabina sipped her iced tea thoughtfully. It was so strange to be talking with Barrett Page about money, overseer's wages and peach crops; she had liked him better when he asked her for a kiss, talked about her writing, told her that she was beautiful. This was a bore.

"Will he live at the Cummings house?" she asked.

"No. He doesn't want to go there and I don't blame him. Sabina, that house ought to be locked if you can't rent it. I understand it is being used for immoral purposes."

"Do you mean that tramps go there and gamble?"

Clarissa sighed. "Sabina, you know there is only one kind of immoral purpose. This pose of innocence on your part is—well, frankly, I'm fed to the teeth with it. I never noticed it so much when father was living."

Clarissa pushed the bell for Lila May to come and remove the plates.

Sabina could feel the color rushing to her face. And I'm tired of hearing, 'You wouldn't do this if your father were living,' she thought. I'm tired of hearing, 'Your father wanted it this way.' I believe half the time they make it up just to get their own way. It has probably just begun; I'll hear it for years—

She pushed back her plate. "I don't want any dessert. It's too hot—and we're probably having huckleberry pie, anyhow."

"You must eat your dessert, Sabina," said Barrett; then he turned to his wife. "You shouldn't reprove or criticize Sabina for being innocent, Claire. I rather like it. It's refreshing to find a girl who doesn't know what immoral purposes are."

"Holy cats!" said Claire. "Did you fall for that? Sabina, I ought to take lessons from you. How fortunate it is for me that I haven't a jealous nature, and more fortunate still that we are leaving Saturday." Suddenly, she leaned forward and Sabina knew what was coming; she knew that Claire was going to make a noble gesture. Claire herself always ridiculed these generous impulses, said that her better nature got the worst of her, but she must have known that they were her most powerful weapon. "Sabina," she began, and Sabina said, "I'm sorry, I thought I heard mother calling me."

"You can go in just a moment. I want to tell you that this winter may be very hard for you. If it gets too bad, come up to New York to see us; we'll teach you how to have fun."

"Yes, promise us you will, Sabina," said Barrett Page.

"Really, Claire, you seem to have forgotten how little money there is. New York! Fun! And deprive the peach trees of fertilizer?"

"We'll send you a ticket—"

"I'm not an object of charity—yet—"

"Oh, very well! Stay at home and be a martyr if you prefer."

"I don't want your charity, or your pity—" Sabina rushed out of the room and as she went upstairs she could hear Claire saying, "Honestly, she's behaving like Sweet Alice Ben Bolt—"

"It was nice of you to ask her, Claire."

"I wasn't doing it to be nice; I think she needs to get away."

"Yes, I think so, too."

Upstairs in her room Sabina pulled furiously at the buttons on her black linen dress. Why didn't Claire and Barrett go on back to New York? Why must they wait until Saturday? Couldn't they see what a strain their presence was? If there was anything worse than having a honeymooning couple around the house she couldn't think what it was. Particularly when—oh, God, why didn't they go?

She threw the dress across a chair and lay down on the bed. "Yes, you are quite right, Claire." "It was nice of you to ask her." Poor Sabina. She needs to get away. The poor girl never has any fun, just an object of pity—

The heat seemed to roll up in visible clouds and sift intact through the screens into her room. She had made this room a place of refuge so frequently of late that it was beginning to take on the character of a convent cell. Whenever she ventured out of it there was a scene, and she came back gladly to it. But almost always it was she who made the scenes and she hated them, had no intention or desire to cause them. Why did she do it? Why had she behaved so childishly before Barrett? And why had she pretended to herself that she wanted them to leave when she knew she was going to miss them terribly?

It did not matter why. It was something she could not control. But one thing was certain: she was not going to New York like a poor country cousin. She would go in triumph or not at all. Claire and Barrett would leave on Saturday and she could begin writing her poems. Autumn was only a few weeks distant; already the sassafras bushes by the roadside were scarlet-leaved, and sugar maples were turning a honey gold. The sadness of autumn was such a poetic subject, and Sabina was so literary! Her mother had told Cousin Ella so. "Sabina is very literary—"

She laughed shortly and buried her face in the pillow. She couldn't write poetry, not good poetry. She could write it in her head and it sounded well enough, but not on paper. Sometimes the phrases would go singing across her mind, uplifting her, inducing a sort of ecstasy, an intoxicating sense of the mystery and unreality of beauty, and she would say, This is poetry. But when she sat down to write the phrases, they disappeared, the lines became awkward, stubborn, and broke down altogether, leaving her almost hysterical with frustration. And a publisher couldn't read or estimate the commercial value of verses that only sang in a writer's mind.

She alone knew that her mind was beautiful as only she knew the perfection of her body. She lifted her legs and studied their reflection in the mirror on the opposite side of the room. It was a nice body, like a miniature Aphrodite's—and what was she saving it for? She merely knew that she wanted to wrap it up and put it away as one would a precious bit of jade or an ivory figurine.

When Claire and Barrett left, Mrs. Frost was still in bed. She showed no inclination to get up and Sabina knew the rest would be good for her; at the same time she could not help but recall the feeling she had had on the morning of her mother's collapse, that she was going to be ill for a very long time. As the days passed Sabina began to worry and a week after Dr. Mannering's first visit, she summoned him again. The doctor seemed puzzled; this time he examined Mrs. Frost as thoroughly as he could and asked endless questions. He wrote out prescriptions and handed them to Sabina rather halfheartedly. Downstairs, later, he sat for a moment in the living room. "Frankly, Miss Sabina, I don't understand it. I can find nothing wrong with your mother. Her blood pressure is high, of course, it has been for years, but it is no worse. If she isn't better soon, you can ask someone else to see her. It could be the shock of Ellison's death but she isn't the kind of woman to take it that way, and besides, that would have happened sooner. She couldn't collapse from shock almost a week after the occurrence. I don't understand it."

"Do you think she should have company? People have been calling—"

"I'm damned if I know, Miss Sabina. We might try it and see. Not too many, of course."

"She wants me to stay with her all the time," said Sabina.

"Don't you do it. I won't allow it."

"But she frets when I am not there—"

"Let her fret."

"It won't make her worse?"

"No. That looks like selfishness on her part. If you give in to her now, there's no telling what she'll be demanding soon."

"You think then," said Sabina slowly, "that she'll be there for some time."

"It looks like it. You stay outdoors all you can, Miss Sabina; get yourself something to keep you busy."

Sabina got herself something to keep her busy, but it was not because the doctor suggested it, and it did not keep her out of doors. She got a job teaching English in the high school because there was not enough money otherwise to pay the servants, run the house, meet the doctor's and druggist's bills and keep the orchards going. One day early in September she said to Mrs. Frost, "Mother, I don't see how we can afford two servants; Lila May will have to go. We need Grover to keep the grounds, feed the horses, and he can clean up and cook fairly well."

"Have you lost your mind, Sabina?" Mrs. Frost demanded; "are you entirely out of your head? You know we can't let Grover come in the house now that your father is gone—"

"Why not? We've practically raised him—"

"That has nothing to do with it. Grover is a man and a colored man at that. Please don't mention it again."

"But Mother—"

"You weren't raised during Reconstruction period,

and I was. Please, Sabina—" Mrs. Frost turned her pink crepe de Chine back and sighed. "Will you lower the shades?"

"The shades are down, Mother."

"Well, perhaps it will be cooler if you let them up; it's terribly hot in here. Is the fan running?"

"Yes. Do you want some ice water? There's some in the thermos jug here—"

"It isn't fresh. Bring me some fresh water. And Sabina, these window sills need washing out; I want Lila May to do it tomorrow."

"They were just washed day before yesterday, Mother."

"They need it again. It's so dusty."

When Sabina returned with the water her mother asked, "Has Mrs. Nixon called today to inquire about me?"

"Yes, she called early this morning."

"What did you tell her?" Mrs. Frost raised herself up in bed to take the ice water.

"I told her you were about the same."

"But I'm not, Sabina. I don't feel as well today as I did yesterday. You should have asked me. I can't sleep at night. As night comes on I just lie here dreading it, knowing I shan't be able to sleep, wondering how I am going to get through the long hours—"

"When you sleep all day, how can you expect to sleep at night?" Sabina set the thermos jug and the empty glass on the table beside the bed; there was scarcely room for them among the bottles of medicine. Already the room smelled, in spite of the fresh air, the fan and the flowers, as if someone had been ill in it for a long time.

"How can you be so heartless, Sabina? I don't believe you have a bit of sympathy for me; you never come and sit with me. You act as if you can't wait to get out of the room. I want Dr. Mannering to give me something to make me sleep; is he coming this afternoon?"

"Why, no, Mother. You don't need him, do you? After all, it costs two dollars every time he comes—"

Mrs. Frost reached under her pillow for a handkerchief. "To think—" she said tearfully, "to think that I should live to see the day when my own daughter would begrudge the money for my doctor's bills. This will come home to you some day, Sabina, you'll see if it doesn't—" She wiped her eyes and lay back. "You can go now, Sabina. I know you want to go. If Claire were here, she would stay with me, she is much more sympathetic than you are."

God, thought Sabina, how long is it going to be like this? I can't stand it. I don't want to hate her, but how shall I be able to help it?

At first she went into her mother's room every morning before going to school but those visits upset her so that she never got over one during the day, and she soon discontinued them. When she came home in the afternoon she was too exhausted physically to want to do anything but fall on the bed and weep with self-pity. If she admitted to her mother that she was tired, Mrs. Frost would say, "You should thank God that He has given you the strength to work. I wish I could. It hurts me to be a burden on you, Sabina, but I'm just a helpless, bedridden old woman."

Sabina wanted to say, "It isn't you who are bedridden, it is the bed that is Janie Lee Frost-ridden." She was always thinking of cruel things to say to her mother, of vicious retorts; and she never went into the chemistry laboratory at school and saw the glass "retorts" there, filled with poisonous gases and brewing explosive mixtures without associating them with her own emotions. To her it was not a homonym or a very bad pun; there was an actual analogy that fascinated, yet repelled her.

And Mrs. Frost, instead of wasting away, seemed to become heavier as the weeks passed and her blood pressure mounted. She assured Dr. Mannering that she ate exactly what he told her to, and Lila May corroborated the fact. But one morning when Sabina came home unexpectedly from school because of a headache, she found Lila May taking an enormous tray upstairs. It contained the things on her mother's diet list: a thin slice of broiled chicken, a vegetable salad with lemon juice, stewed dried fruit and toast; but it also contained fried country ham, beans cooked with the hockbone, hot buttered rolls, spice cake and jam. Sabina wept, her mother wept; and after Dr. Mannering had finished talking to Lila May, she, too, was weeping. Sabina had got him on the telephone and he shouted so loudly at the darky that he could be heard by Sabina in the next room. "What are you trying to do, nigger, kill Mrs. Frost?"

"I ain't done nothin' but what she tole me to, Doctor— Lawd help me, I ain't—"

"You don't want to be responsible for her death, do you?"

"Suh?"

"I say, you don't want to be the cause of her dying, do you?"

"Nawsuh, nawsuh, I sho don't, Doctor—"

Lila May left the telephone and went to the kitchen grumbling, "Justs want to starve Miss Janie Lee to death, that's what he do; don't want 'er to have enough to keep a po little bird alive; makin' a fuss like that over a little dab o'ham and that tee-nincey little piece of cake. Miss Sabina, she just too stingy to pay for it, that's what—"

Sabina went to the kitchen door. "Lila May, that isn't true and you know it. If you ever say such a thing again—"

Lila May picked up her apron and blew her nose. "Yassum, I know it tain't so, Miss Sabina, but if de stuff's here and Miss Janie Lee wants it, I ain't got the heart to tell 'er she caint have it. Beside, if I don't take it to 'er, she come git it."

"She can't, Lila May."

"Humph! She done *is!* I seen 'er. That's how come I started carryin' it to 'er."

Sabina thought, A girl's best friend is her mother, and went to bed.

She rarely had time to look in the mirror these days and when she did, she was always surprised to find that her hair was not snow white. In addition to worrying about her mother and the nagging irritation of trying to teach literature to indifferent young savages, she spent restless nights besieged with unpleasant memories. When she was attempting to calm her mind, think of peaceful and pleasant things before falling asleep, there would come to her suddenly the memory of some humiliating childhood experience which she had deliberately and painfully made herself forget and had not recalled in many years. The scene would appear to her with its original vividness and poignancy: once when she had stepped out on the stage at the auditorium to play a piano solo at the "big girls'" recital (her body had always been small and delicate) she had heard a man in the audience say, "Look at those mockingbird legs! I don't see how they hold her up!" There was another similar experience; she was an adolescent when this occurred: one of the "big girls" in high school had extended her great fleshy legs in the aisle and said, "Put yours out, Sabina, and let's see whose are the biggest"—to the immense and ribald delight of the classroom.

She recalled still another humiliation that she had suffered; it was during her first year at college. At Christmas time she had bought a bottle of cologne as a gift for a wealthy room-mate who lived in Baltimore, and the shopkeeper offered to wrap and mail it for her. It was packed in sawdust and sent in a cigarbox, but Sabina did not know that until the room-mate mentioned it. "I opened it in the presence of the family and I didn't know what to think until I realized it was a joke. We gave it to one of the maids."

It was insufficient to say that these experiences were long past; it was not enough to tell herself that she, not her persecutors, had made Phi Beta Kappa at college, that the girl with the fleshy legs had married an indigent farmer and now lived in the country with her five dirty, towheaded children, that the girl from Baltimore had eloped with her family's chauffeur. The recollection of those incidents rankled anew as if it had never rankled before.

More recent was the remembered sound of Cousin Ella's voice as she had asked, "What is Janie Lee raising you for, anyhow, an old-maid schoolteacher?" And Claire's "Uh-huh, an old maid with forty cats, hiding your money under the planks in the floor." Claire had not specified where the money was to be obtained in the first place.

There was something about the very atmosphere of the room Claire had occupied that made Sabina unhappy and uncomfortable. When the room had been shut up for a long time it smelled ever so faintly of perspiration, for Claire's summer clothes were still hanging in the closet. There was one of her discarded corsets in a dresser drawer, the fabric and the strings were yellowed but it had a perverted fascination for Sabina. When she looked at it she thought of the word "woman" as opposed to "girl." It bespoke something so essentially feminine, or indeed, female; it suggested curves, rounded hips, flesh that was too exuberant and had to be confined. Sabina's own slender body had no need of restraint, it was a girl's body, and a potential spinster's. Clarissa's was that of a wife. Sabina would raise the windows (noticing as she did so that the paint on the sills had flaked and was peeling), she would let the cold air blow through the room for a while and the odor would be gone, but it retained still some quality of Clarissa's womanhood.

Sabina had suggested to her mother that those empty bedrooms might be rented; it was true that the house was old and the plumbing bad, that baths had to be ordered a half hour beforehand and there were other minor inconveniences, but it was not impossible that lodgers or boarders might be found. Mrs. Frost said that there had never been a lodger at Frost Haven and one would be taken in only over her dead body. If Sabina had no re-

spect for her departed ancestors, Mrs. Frost had. Moreover, people in the house would make her nervous, she
couldn't stand it for a single day, and honestly, it looked
sometimes as if Sabina lay awake at night thinking of
things with which to worry her.

But Mrs. Frost was even more shocked and grieved
when Sabina told her one afternoon just before the
Christmas holidays that the high-school principal was
coming that evening to call on her.

"You mean you have an engagement with him?" Mrs.
Frost's voice was weak with horror.

"Of course."

"Sabina Frost! You'd never have done a thing like that
if your father had been living. You don't know a thing in
the world about that man, about his family, his background—"

"But I do, Mother. They are in *The South in the
Building of the Nation;* there's a whole page about
them—"

"Probably paid to have it put in," said Mrs. Frost; "I've
known people like that. But I won't discuss it, Sabina, it
is simply out of the question. You'll have to call the man
and tell him you can't see him."

"But why, Mother?"

"Don't *you* know why? Think how it would look—
you downstairs entertaining a strange man and your
mother upstairs sick in bed."

"Well, I could ask Alice Hilton to bring her date
here."

"Alice Hilton! Sabina, that girl is as wild as Carter's
oats—"

"But Mother—" Sabina suddenly straightened. "I've

told him he could come and I'm not going to tell him he can't. Now what do you want me to do?"

It was some time before Mrs. Frost answered. "There is only one thing you can do. Telephone Cousin Ann Temple and ask her if she will come and chaperon you."

Cousin Ann came with her knitting and talked incessantly to the young man; he was bored and Sabina was bored. After that she decided that dates were not worth the effort they cost—which was probably what her mother had intended for her to decide. Sabina could, in fact, think of nothing that *was* worth the effort. Dr. Mannering told her she needed calomel—and a vacation, he added, when he looked closely at her. She could spend her Christmas holidays in Florida, lying out on the beach in the sunshine. Perhaps Miss Claire would stay with Mrs. Frost while Sabina was away.

CHAPTER XIII

SABINA WROTE TO CLAIRE AND THE ANSWER CAME TWO weeks later from Miami. Clarissa was terribly sorry but she herself had not been feeling very well and Barrett had insisted on her going to Florida for a few months. If Sabina could get someone else to stay with Mrs. Frost she might come on down to Miami, but it probably wouldn't be much fun for her since the Pages were expecting an heir in May.

One week of the holidays was gone when Claire's post card arrived. Sabina considered rushing madly up to Atlanta, buying resort clothes and hurrying down to Miami, then she realized that if she bought the proper clothes she wouldn't have enough money left for the trip—and she couldn't take the trip without them. For the first time in her life she wished that she could get drunk. In the dining room sideboard there was still some of her father's old sherry. She took the bottle to her room on New Year's Eve, along with some of Lila May's beaten biscuits, got her copy of Shakespeare's sonnets and spent the most delightful evening she had had in months. She went to bed at eleven, her head spinning, her heart pounding, and slept so soundly that she heard none of the wild celebration of the festivities, no car horns, no whistles, no bells.

The next morning she was awakened rudely by Lila May's tugging at the bedclothes. "Git up, Miss Sabina, you got to git up. Miss Janie Lee, she done had a heart attack and she say you just let her lay there and die—"

"Have you called the doctor?" Sabina could not keep her eyes open very well and the light hurt them dreadfully.

"Yassum, he on his way here now."

"Where's my bathrobe?"

"You got it on—you sho must-a been cold last night. Miss Janie Lee mad as a wet hen with you; she say she call you and call you last night and she rung her bell and still you ain't come. She say she could-a died for all you cared."

"Tell her I'll be there in a moment. Have you straightened up her room?"

"Yassum. Hits *ten* o'clock, Miss Sabina."

Her head felt heavy one moment and light the next; first it was filled with cement and then with bubbles. Suppose her mother had died—Sabina would have felt that she was responsible and her conscience would have hurt her as long as she lived—or would it? But Mrs. Frost wasn't going to die, ever, she would keep on getting fatter, spreading out over the bed until she completely covered it.

Dr. Mannering came running in with his bag and

stethoscope; his thin red hair seemed to be standing on end and his glasses almost falling away from his alert brown eyes. He put his head down and listened to the patient's heart; he made pencil marks on her chest and over her ribs and kept on listening. Finally, he asked her to get out of bed and hop around the room. Mrs. Frost was outraged and protested violently. Was the doctor trying to kill her? She might drop dead on the floor any minute.

He said nothing, only waited, and at length she began the laborious business while the room shook and Sabina expected to hear the crystal chandelier in the dining room come crashing down. Dr. Mannering said, "That will do," and bent over her again.

"Two large glasses of bicarbonate-of-soda water, Mrs. Frost. That will fix you up, I think. Now tell me what you ate for supper."

"Dr. Mannering, are you sure you know your job?"

"Quite sure, Mrs. Frost. What did you eat for supper?"

"Sabina knows, she brought it to me."

Sabina told him and he asked, "What else?"

"That's all."

"Except—" Mrs. Frost added after a moment, "except a little fruit cake. Just two or three slices, very thin ones. If I can't have fruit cake at Christmas time, Dr. Mannering, I might as well be dead."

"How did you get it? Did that nigger—"

"No. Lila May didn't bring it to me."

The doctor stood up and put his instruments in his bag. "Mrs. Frost, there is nothing the matter with your heart now except muscular weakness from lack of exer-

cise. You haven't any organic trouble but if you persist
in defying me and disobeying my instructions you will
have a serious one. This is final. If you aren't going to
do what I tell you, you can get another doctor. Good-
morning."

In the hall he paused briefly. "There are times in every
physician's life, Miss Sabina, when he wishes he hadn't
taken the Hippocratic oath. Good-bye and don't call me
again until I recover my temper."

"Old fool!" Mrs. Frost was saying. "I hate to say it, I
never used that word before in my life, but that's what
he is, a stubborn, pigheaded old fool. I reckon *I* know
when I've got heart trouble even if he doesn't—"

After that she persisted in talking about the "heart
attack I had at Christmas" but she was sufficiently frightened to be somewhat more careful about her diet.

Sabina became so accustomed to people saying, "Good-
morning, Miss Sabina, how is your mother?" that she
missed it when it was omitted; and if anyone had asked
her her name, she would have replied immediately,
"Sabina How-is-your-mother."

February was like March that year and March was
like April. From the bedroom windows the great old oak
trees could be seen laced with ropes of dripping wisteria
and the blooms from the oaks rolled into dried moss-like
balls and were pushed down the lawn by the wind. The
bloom on the peach trees had never been heavier, the
shimmering expanse of pink mist rose on the hillocks and
faded into the valleys. People drove out from the town
to see the orchards and were impressed as they were always impressed by masses of anything. Sabina thought
the orchards looked too artificial and monotonous, and

her friends said it was a "pose" when Sabina declared that she preferred a single wild tree blooming beside an old unpainted negro cabin. It was the contrast that she liked, she said, and the symbolism in the rich profligate artistry of nature foiled against the degradation of the work of man. "A pose," her friends repeated; "she just wants to be different."

Clarissa, who had gone back to New York, lost her baby that month and was told by the doctors that she could never have another. Barrett was upset about it, she said, but not so much as she was. A few weeks later she wrote that she was going to spend the summer in Maine and would Sabina like to come there for a visit? It probably wouldn't be much fun for Sabina, Clarissa said, because all she herself could think about and talk about was the loss of the baby.

Sabina agreed that it wouldn't be much fun, and besides, there was no one to stay with her mother. All the cousins who, during Mr. Frost's lifetime had received monthly checks from him were now too busy with their own duties to leave them. They implied that it was Sabina's and Mrs. Frost's own fault that they, the cousins, were now so busy.

Spring melted into the heat and stupefaction of midsummer, bringing with it one of the best seasons the Frost orchards had known in several years. It seemed to Sabina that no time at all passed between the day on which she saw the first truckload of darkies going to "thin" the hard green peaches, and the weeks when the roads were filled with packers and pickers. There was more dust during the harvest season, that was all. Mrs. Frost became more petulant and irritable as the heat grew more intense. She was not even pleased over the prospect of a successful crop; it was an indirect reflection on Mr. Frost's management, she asserted, and she believed Mr. Cox had simply tried himself in order to put his late employer in a bad light. Besides—Mrs. Frost never failed to add a "besides" that carried more sting than her original remarks—Henry Cox was making more money for himself than he was for the orchards, everything *he* made was clear.

Sabina never went into her mother's room when she could avoid it. She was no longer afraid of hating her; she knew that she already did so. This knowledge made her avoid other people lest they discover it for themselves, and made her think more constantly of herself. The simplest encounter with anyone on the street set up the most involved processes of thought within her. If the persons were acquaintances she wondered whether they were envious of her because she was Sabina Frost and beautiful, or pitied her because she had an invalid mother, and was fast becoming a traditional old-maid schoolteacher. If she decided that their reaction was one of pity, she usually spoke arrogantly to them, said her mother was doing nicely, and she herself was planning an extended trip. If, on the other hand, she suspected the acquaintances of being envious of her, her tone was one of self-ridicule, she laughed about the family finances, declared that soon they wouldn't know where their next meal was coming from, and proceeded to jeer at her mother's tendency toward ancestor-worship, asserting that one of them, she knew, had died in the Tower of London just in time to escape having his head chopped off by the king's executioners—that was Sir Henry Somebody, Lord Mayor of London. Another, she would declare, was a notorious pirate, and the remainder only came to America because there was a price on their heads. Yet, when Sabina finished her satirization of the Frost and Regis ancestors, she left her hearers convinced that they might have been ruthless and wicked but they were undoubtedly powerful noblemen whom rulers and emperors feared.

If she passed a stranger on the street one day she would say to herself, He doesn't know that I am Sabina Frost, that if I were not a "wage-earner, the sole support of my widowed mother," I could be writing exquisite verse, verses that would sing in the hearts of mankind long after I am gone. He doesn't know how classically perfect the lines of my verse and the lines of my body are.

The next day her feeling of superiority would have disappeared, followed by an anguish of self-condemnation; she would wonder if her skirt dipped in the back, if her stocking seams were crooked, if she looked as completely a down-at-the-heel school mistress as she felt herself to be. And so her moods fluctuated; she had no constancy of emotion or of self-appraisal. A roadside Buddhist contemplating his navel could not have been more occupied, or more out of touch with reality than Sabina was in the absorbing study of her own cerebral and emotional processes.

But in September she was rudely jolted out of this self-contemplation and Mrs. Frost was almost jolted out of bed. A cyclone could scarcely have shaken the Frost home with more force. Sabina had always laughed at Claire's habit of writing anything and everything on post cards. She had written on them about the prospective baby and Sabina had once said that if Claire were going to get a divorce she would break the news on a penny postal. It came, instead, by telegram, "LEAVING FOR RENO. WILL WRITE LATER."

Mrs. Frost said she would never hold up her head again. She had rather see Clarissa dead than disgraced like that; the word Reno was synonymous with Sodom and Gomorrah.

She sent for the telegraph operator, had him ushered to her room and threatened him with hell-fire and damnation if the news ever got out in Frost Haven. She seemed, actually, less disturbed by the fact itself than by the fear that Frost Haven would learn about it. "They must never know, Sabina, they must never know. Clarissa is not my own daughter" (thank God, her voice implied), "but we must protect her because of her father. She would never have done this if Mr. Frost had been living."

Sabina was wickedly and heartlessly glad. Claire had failed at something, that in itself was important; moreover, she had failed at being a wife. She had not said why she was getting the divorce and the letter which followed the wire was vague and casual. But if Claire ever came back to Frost Haven she would be a social outcast, her name would be mentioned in the Frost home only when it could not be avoided; she would no longer be "my daughter, Mrs. Barrett Page—the Boston Pages, you know." Clarissa the kind and sympathetic who would sit for hours with her invalid stepmother—in Mrs. Frost's imagination!

Barrett Page would be free. Sabina did not know what significance that fact had for her, if indeed it had any. The knowledge that he would soon be free to tell her he loved her, if he did, was so bound up with the fear that he would not and she would never see him again that she almost wished he had remained married. So long as he belonged legally to Claire, Sabina might pretend to herself that he cared somewhat for her. Now that he was at liberty to prove it, she was afraid. She began preparing her mind for the complete disappearance of Barrett Page from her life. It amounted to this: He will not come, I have no right to expect it. I was a fool once—I shan't be again.

And in spite of that she hoped—with all the desperation and longing born of the past year's suffering. She bought new clothes (no more black, she thanked heaven), and took care not to wear them when Mrs. Frost could see her. During the month of September she expected each day that she would have a telegram, or at least a letter, from Barrett. October brought no word from him, and she wore the new clothes defiantly now instead of jubilantly. He did not want to marry again, she told herself, especially another Frost. Or he would choose a Northern girl, they were not useless like Southerners. Had he not said, "Certainly, I'm crazy about the South. Nobody here ever does anything." He would never want to marry Sabina; Clarissa had told her so, ". . . no man wants to marry a revolving bookcase. There are plenty of public libraries in the world."

Mr. Frost had once said that Sabina had a terrible memory—she never forgot anything. She wished now that she could forget, forget the existence of Barrett Page, forget the things people had said to her and about her, forget, above everything, herself. The habit she had acquired in the past of putting aside things she did not wish to think about, refusing to recognize their actuality, helped her somewhat but not enough.

The rush of exaltation she had known when she first received the news spent itself, to be followed by doubt and finally by depths of bitter despondency. Her plight now seemed more hopeless than it had ever been before because previously she had been able to tell herself that Barrett Page would have chosen her instead of Claire if he had not already been married when he met Sabina. That last defense was gone, though it had served its purpose well enough for a time. She could not hate Barrett for failing to love her. But she could hate her mother as the immediate cause and source of all her present suffering.

She would watch the light of the late winter afternoon stealing over her mother's heavy face, over her forehead that was crossed with fine vertical and horizontal lines, over the thick pink lips that held their color preversely instead of becoming parched and pale as a sick woman's should, and finally slipped in a greenish glow down the plaited streaked hair and was lost among the bedclothes. As Sabina watched the light's slow progress down Mrs. Frost's face she began to wonder if that was the way death crept over a person's countenance. Did it come slowly, like a fading glimmer of winter sunlight, or swiftly—covering and obliterating everything at once? Wiping out the selfishness, the tyranny, the hypocritical piety—and leaving—what? Peace? Chagrin? Relief?

She began to brood over the things she could and would do if her mother were dead. Sometimes she would be halfway to New Zealand or walking down the Champs Elysées when Mrs. Frost would speak. "Laura Corliss came to see me today and brought me some angel-food cake and fruit gelatine. I can eat both of those things. She says Mr. Henry Caldwell has been seen with that little red-headed girl who works for him. I'd never know what goes on if people didn't come to see me occasionally. You never tell me anything, Sabina. And I hear Mrs. Weston has added a bathroom downstairs where her breakfast room used to be. It seems like that would be very inconvenient. Did you say something, Sabina?"

"No, Mother. I only stuck my finger with the needle."

"It's too late for you to be using your eyes. If anything were to happen to your eyes I don't know what would become of us."

"I was waiting to give you your drops." She would stand up, count the globules of liquid as they fell into the glass and wait until her mother had drunk them with a gulp and a shudder. Then Sabina would almost run from the room and stand outside the door thinking, How long, oh, God, how long? If she isn't going to get well, why can't she die?

The last Sunday afternoon in November was a damp and murky one but Sabina felt that walking in the cold mist over the hills would be infinitely preferable to staying in the house. She went into Mrs. Frost's room to mention the walk and find out whether her mother was going to make a scene about it, or only protest mildly.

Mrs. Frost seemed to be asleep, but when the doorbell pealed out downstairs she turned over in bed and opened her eyes. "Was that the doorbell or the phone, Sabina?"

"I think it was the bell."

"Is Lila May down there?"

"No, Mother, she always gets off on Sunday afternoon to go to church." Lila May did the church-going for the family these days.

"Well, you'll have to answer the door, and do hurry before they get away, I don't get to see many people—"

"Yes, Mother."

"And hand me my bed jacket before you go and punch up the fire. Does my hair look all right? I know I look a sight, but we can't afford a nurse—"

"Yes, Mother."

"Sabina, you didn't even look at it, but a lot *you* care," Mrs. Frost was saying as Sabina closed the door behind her.

The metal strips on the edge of the stair steps clacked as she went down and she thought, I hate those, too, I *hate* the steps, I *hate* the house, I hate my mother, I hate the town, I hate the school, I hate myself—

It made a sort of rhythm, a new hate with every stroke against the metal.

She went through the hall and living room to the great double doors where the pale glow of daylight broke in a wave through the fanlight above them. "Oh, how do you do, Mrs. Nixon? Hello, Miss Margaret, Miss Grace. It's so nice of you to come."

"Sabina, how *are* you, child? I was just saying the other day, I don't know *when* I've seen Sabina Frost." Mrs. Nixon ran over to a table. "Oh, Grace, do look at these hawberries, aren't they artistic? I love them in that brass vase, they look quite Chinesey, don't they?"

"We were beginning to think there wasn't anybody at home," said Mrs. Turner laughing, "we waited so long at the door. Of course, we were just joking, we *knew* somebody was at home." She lowered her voice and her expression became serious, "How is she, Sabina? Do you see any change?"

"Why, no, Miss Margaret, she's just about the same. Do you want to go up now and see her?"

"Let's sit down and talk with Sabina a moment," suggested Mrs. Nixon. "I want to know what the doctor says about Janie Lee. Oh, this lovely davenport! I'm always jealous every time I see it; and those drapes, just the thing for the room. But then, Janie Lee always was tasty; I've said to my husband many a time, 'I declare, I don't know anybody as tasty as Janie Lee Frost.'"

Mrs. Weston was running her fingers over a fiddle-back chair. "Rosewood, real rosewood, you know it's practically impossible to buy it nowadays at any price. I don't suppose—" she paused a moment, then went on, "Sabina, I hope you won't get your feelings hurt, but I've been thinking a long time that I'd ask you—with your expenses so heavy, and of course we all know that poor dear Mr. Frost—"

Sabina was surprised that she wasn't angry. "No, Miss Grace, we don't want to sell the chair."

"Well, I don't suppose there's any harm in asking—I just thought—"

"That's quite all right."

Mrs. Turner interposed tactfully, "I noticed today that there are still some redbirds around my house that haven't gone South. I think the birds have been sweeter this year than ever before."

"Oh, Margaret," said Mrs. Nixon stretching out her feet before the fire, "you say that every year."

"I reckon I do. My husband says I'm just a gypsy at heart. I love the out-of-doors, gardens and flowers and birds. I sometimes think we should all try to make our lives like a garden—where there is always something blooming." After a moment she added, "Even when we can't do it, it's a nice thought."

There was a silence, then Mrs. Nixon asked, "How is school, Sabina?"

"How is school? Oh, it's all right. Only it seems to tire me so much more to teach than it did last year."

"That's due to the strain you've been under; but you ought to go down on your knees every night and thank God he has given you the strength to work. Frankly, I didn't think you had it in you."

"Frankly, neither did I," Sabina laughed, "and I'm not sure yet that I have."

"Oh, you're just saying that, I know. Sometimes we don't know *what* we can do until an emergency arises, and then we—" she laughed gaily, "well, we sort of rise along with it. Tell me, Sabina, how is Clarissa getting along? I never hear anything about her these days."

"Oh, Clarissa is fine, thank you." Ah! she thought, if you only knew! Or do you know?

"I know Janie Lee told me she lost her baby last spring—it *was* last spring, wasn't it? My, how time flies, I simply can't believe Janie Lee has been sick that long. Let's see, it's been over a year, nearly a year and a half—"

"Fifteen months," said Sabina. "Father died on the sixth of August and she was taken a week later—the day," she added maliciously, "that Colonel Thibaut went over the business papers with us."

"That was a strange coincidence, wasn't it," said Mrs. Turner. "I remember it quite well, we'd been to a meeting of the board (D.A.R., you know), and Mrs. Corliss served such a nice plate, potato chips, frozen fruit salad, an olive, iced tea—and there was something else, I can't think now what it was."

"Wasn't it cookies, Margaret?"

"No, I don't think it was cookies, she served those when she entertained the Garden Club. They are mighty good; she puts black walnuts in them and I don't know what else; she got the recipe in Nashville and she won't give it to anybody to save their lives. Well, howsoever that may be (as the nigger preacher said), I remember I was coming home from Laura Corliss's and Horace Jennifer met me on the street. 'Have you heard about Janie Lee Frost?' he asked, and I said, No, I hadn't heard a word. 'She's had a stroke,' he said—you know how he loves to get there fustest with the mostest news. Don't talk to me about women gossiping! I never saw a woman yet as bad about it as Henry Jennifer. Where was I? Oh, I know. And I said right now, 'Horace, I don't believe it, it simply can't be true, it *can't* be—' "

"Yes," said Mrs. Weston, "we all thought then that it was a stroke. I came to see her the very next Sunday and I don't think I've missed one since, have I, Sabina?"

"No, I'm sure you haven't."

"Well, we have to look after her, she's a precious thing. We mustn't let her slip away from us."

"Really, Miss Grace, there's no danger of that. The doctor says she is getting along nicely."

"I'm afraid, Sabina, you don't realize how sick your mother is. Of course, she doesn't tell you, she doesn't want to worry you, but she tells *me*—"

Mrs. Frost's bell tinkled and Sabina went to the stair steps. "Yes, Mother?"

"Who was it at the door, Sabina?"

"Some friends of yours, they are coming up to see you."

Mrs. Frost's voice became much softer. "Oh, how nice! Ask them to come on up."

The ladies fluttered out of their seats, collected their gloves and pocketbooks. "Well, it's been nice having this little visit with you, Sabina."

Mrs. Turner paused at the drop-leaf table, picked up the books and began looking critically at their titles. "I just want to see what you've been reading, Sabina; I bet it's something naughty. *Ethics*, Spinoza, the *Consolation of Philosophy*, Boethius, *Journal of a Tour to the Hebrides*, Boswell—" She pronounced Spinoza to rhyme with mimosa and omitted the "e" in Boethius— "I declare they do give books the queerest titles nowadays. I simply don't have time to keep up with the new novels, I wish I did."

"Those aren't novels, Miss Margaret, and they aren't new, either."

"Well, I *thought* they looked dog-eared, but everything I get from the library looks that way. I suppose you are reading those things in connection with your school work. My Sarah says you certainly do know English literature but she wishes you wouldn't talk over the students' heads. They don't understand you half the time."

"Come on, Margaret," called Mrs. Nixon, "you and Sabina can finish your confab some other time. Just let two bookworms get together—" her gentle derisive laughter floated down from the landing. "My husband is like that, you never saw anybody so literary. He's read every poem Edgar Guest ever wrote and all of Zane Grey's books, or Jane Grey, which is it?"

"Mr. Weston likes Irvin S. Cobb," said Mrs. Weston; "he'll say, 'Grace, I wish you'd read this book. It's about down-to-earth ordinary people like you and me, no highfalutin nonsense. Yes sir,' he'll say, 'it's what I call a great book.'"

"They can say what they please about the South," declared Mrs. Nixon, "but we haven't lost our old cultural tradition. At our club we try to read a new book every month." She knocked softly on Mrs. Frost's door. "Anybody home? May we come in?"

Downstairs Sabina straightened the books which Mrs. Turner had left in a disorderly pile, and listened to the clock chiming four. She waited for seven more strokes in honor of her mother's illness; when they failed to come she went to the clock and opened the glass, exposing the face. She moved the hour hand until it struck the half-hour, then five, five-thirty, six. When it reached eleven and had struck, she caught and held the pendulum. For a while the ticking went on somewhere inside, back of the colored picture of Mount Vernon, below the eagle with outspread wings that had hovered there for more than a century. Finally, the ticking ceased and Sabina pushed the glass door to. "There," she said, "I reckon that'll l'arn you!"

She repeated to herself in whispers, "She's a precious thing, we mustn't let her slip away from us!" "I'm afraid, Sabina, you don't realize how sick your mother is!" "I just want to see what you've been reading, Sabina; I bet it's something naughty," and her mother's worn phrases, ". . . *you* never tell me anything," ". . . you must save your eyes, you must protect your ankles." Who ever looked at them?

Suddenly, she put her hands to her eyes. If only I could never see this house again, never see the library where those papers were spread out, or the piano where Barrett stood beside me, or the light falling through the window on mother's face. I've got to do something, I've got to.

The visitors would probably stay with her mother for some time. She could go for a walk and get back before five when Mrs. Frost had to have her drops.

She tiptoed upstairs to her room to get an old felt hat and a warm coat. As she started down again, her mother called, "Is that you, Sabina?"

She went defiantly to the door. "Yes, Mother, I was just going for a walk."

"In this weather? You'll catch your death o'cold, you haven't even got on any overshoes. You'll have sore throat and have to stay out of school and pay a substitute—"

"Oh, let her go, Janie Lee," said Mrs. Nixon, "the child needs to get out and mix and mingle with the young people."

"I wasn't going to mix and mingle," said Sabina looking at the fading iris in the vase by her mother's bed. "I only wanted some fresh air. I'll be back in a few minutes."

When she closed the heavy front door behind her it shut so firmly that the bell rang a little and the fanlight rattled overhead. It was always this way, she reflected, by the time she had managed to get away from her mother to do something, she was too tired to do it. She looked at the lawn, strewn with wet fallen leaves, and then thought of the dying iris in Mrs. Frost's room. "Lilies that fester smell far worse than weeds." Yes, there was a clean smell from the leaves and upstairs there was decadence, the odor of moral decay.

She went past Mrs. Nixon's car down the graveled driveway into the road, feeling a sort of ecstatic affection for the weeds that were crystalline with mist. Their dried, plumed fronds glittered on the banks of the ditch where a rope of muddy water curled by.

In front of her was a negro woman probably on her way home from church, and the darky walked heavily, her hips rising and falling like waves with each step, a wave on the right, a wave on the left. "The *Rise and Fall of the Confederacy*," thought Sabina; " 'They can say what they please about the South, but we haven't lost our old cultural tradition.' We can still find books in darkies' buttocks, poetry in Edgar Guest, and platitudes for everything."

The negress turned, looked back, and then stopped. "Ain't you Mr. Frost's daughter?"

"Yes, I'm Sabina Frost."

"Well, I declare, I'd a knowed you anywhere. If you ain't the spittin' image of old Miss Marie Antoinette, your papa's mama. I don't reckon you recollect her."

"No, I don't," said Sabina, "I've seen her pictures, of course."

"Course you ain't as pretty as she was." The old woman looked at her closely. "You ain't got no flesh on yo bones yet. How many chillun you got, hon?"

"I haven't any. I'm not married."

"Ain't? Lawd, that's a pity, a pretty thing like you. How come you ain't married, child?"

"Well—" began Sabina. She was wishing the old woman would go on her way, she was at a loss to answer her. It was a new experience to be stopped on a lonely road in the rain and asked why she wasn't married. There seemed, actually, to be no answer.

"That's all right, honey, don't you fret. You got plenty of time yet. How's your mama?"

"She's better, thank you."

"Tell 'er you seed old Aunt Viney." The darky shifted her bundles and walked on. "Tell 'er I ast about 'er. And you git some flesh on yo bones. You'se a pretty thing—"

"Thank you, Aunt Viney."

"The spittin' image of old Miss Marie Antoinette," the darky was talking to herself as she turned into a narrow path, "and she had lebben chillun—all gone now, God bless 'em. Ain't nobody left but old Aunt Viney—"

Sabina watched her trudging away, the mud spattering about her thick ankles as she walked. Yes, said Sabina, and some day I'll be stumbling along muttering, "Ain't nobody left but old Aunt Sabina." I'll have examination papers under my arm and somebody will ask, "Hello, Aunt Sabina, how's your mother?" and I'll say, "She's just the same, thank you."

Other people's mothers were killed in automobile accidents but Mrs. Frost never got into an automobile. Peasants came in from a hard day in the fields, sat down in a warm corner by the fire, and died. But Mrs. Frost's only acquaintance with fields was through the missionary society, the "foreign field" to which missionaries were sent.

It was impossible to fall in the bathtub and be killed when you were bathed in bed; there was no strain on your heart; and even lightning couldn't strike you there.

But there were drops of medicine that made you sleep. If four drops of medicine could make you sleep for four hours, how long would twenty drops of medicine make you sleep? Fifty hours—or forever? "Our little lives are rounded with a sleep." Was Mrs. Frost really awake and alive now? If she wanted to live, why did she not get up and do it? She preferred lying there and sleeping.

The trunks of the peach trees were black and glistening in the rain, like the bodies of snakes—no, not like snakes—God—not snakes—she had sworn on the day of her father's funeral that she would never think of that again. Barrett Page had put his hand over hers and she had taken it as a promise that he would help her not to remember. To not remember, that was a split infinitive, but it was more forceful, and she wanted to split something. What does an English teacher do on her day off? She goes out in the rain and splits infinitives—a capital offense, somewhat in the same category as bestowing upon one's mother the gift of perpetual sleep. Matricide? Headlines? Jail? Posing with her skirt above her crossed knees? Sitting in prison writing a new *De Profundis*, a better *Jerusalem Delivered*, another *Pilgrim's Progress?* Nonsense, she was Sabina Frost, and would she be to blame if her precious mother just slipped away?

The stalks of dead goldenrod by the roadside were bent down in the rain, dog fennel leaned wearily against them and Michaelmas daisies bloomed beside them both, blue, innocent, like the eyes of a child.

How did gorse look, and heather? How did moors

look in the rain, and were there really birds called plover, skylark and curlew? England had been there all these years and she had never seen it, never would, unless— something happened.

She came to an old stone bridge across the road and stood there watching the swollen tawny stream rush by. Tangled honeysuckle vines clambered on the banks, holding a plum thicket fast in its thongs; the gaunt trees held up their witch-like black boughs—but the vines climbed up into the very branches, holding the trees prisoner.

The rain dropped off the brim of her hat on to her shoulders and her stockings were like rubber wrapped around her legs. It meant a cold, laryngitis, more reproaches from her mother—

Tinkers lived in ditches and made tin cans to buy wedding rings, and Mrs. Turner was just a gypsy at heart.

Suddenly, Sabina turned and started homeward, her heart pounding. The women would be gone and the wind would be blowing drops of rain from the oak trees against the window panes. Who would ever know that Mrs. Frost had not poured the drops herself? Who would even suspect it? Had not Dr. Mannering himself said that he wished he had not taken the Hippocratic oath? Sabina had not taken it.

It was almost dark and she walked swiftly, not exultantly as she had hoped she would when this decision was made, but rather as if something outside her were pushing her along. Can I really do it, she kept asking herself, can I?

She was almost running now, the mud flew up and

stuck to her ankles, the housetop came into sight on the rise and she saw the light in her mother's room.

She would sell the house, the rosewood chairs, the grandfather's clock, the fanlight, the chandelier, the Hepplewhite dining-room furniture, the books, everything—no, not the books.

There was scarcely any light downstairs for the fire in the living room would be low, just a glimmer on the glass and polished wood. It was not at all the same house she had seen brilliantly lighted when her father died and she and Barrett Page came up the driveway together.

When she stepped up on the porch one of the planks gave way and she thought, That won't matter now. The whole floor can fall in.

She opened the door of the silent house and turned on a light in the living room. The shadows seemed to get up slowly, like old people, and move away just out of sight until they could creep back. Sabina felt that just as soon as her back was turned they would come again and settle into their accustomed places. It was like telling a dog to get down off the sofa. He would if you insisted, he'd lie panting on the floor until you were gone, then he'd jump up again and snuggle back as he was before.

She was tracking mud over the Aubusson carpet but she went straight on toward the stairs. "Is that you, Sabina?" came her mother's voice.

"Yes, Mother."

"I know you've caught your death o' cold. You'd better dry your feet."

"Yes, Mother. Just as soon as I give you your medicine."

She took off her coat and hat, hung them on the hall-tree, and glanced only briefly into the mirror. Her hair was wet and her cheeks glowing but she did not recognize the eyes at all—they were someone else's eyes. How many drops, fifteen or twenty? Fifteen—no, twenty. Mrs. Frost's bedroom door was ajar and Sabina was inside the room before her mother heard her. "It's after five, Sabina."

Sabina's heart stopped. "You haven't taken your medicine, have you?"

"No. I was afraid I would get it wrong."

There were the fading iris that had no right to bloom at this time of year, their petals were curled into purplish brown cocoons. "I'm going to throw these flowers out, Mother—"

"Oh, there are a few buds that haven't opened yet. Do save them for me, Sabina, I'll have something to think about, just watching them open."

"Yes, Mother."

"Sabina, your hand is shaking, you walked too far, you are tired."

"No, Mother, I'm all right."

Mrs. Frost raised herself up in bed and prepared to open her mouth for the medicine. Sabina looked at the thin plait of streaked hair over her mother's left shoulder, at the wrinkled sheets and shapeless pillow.

"Let me fix these for you first. Do you want a fresh pillow case?"

"No. It can be changed in the morning. That's better. Did you fix the drops?"

"I'm going to now."

She poured water into the glass, then she lifted the dropper, one, two, three, four—"Here you are, Mother."

Mrs. Frost shuddered and turned the glass up. "It's bitter."

"Not so bitter as it might be. Now I'll go change my shoes and stocking. Are you all right?"

"Yes. I'm all right."

Sabina fell sobbing across the bed in her room. God, God—!

Where had she ever got the idea that she could do such a thing, that she wanted to?

Heaven had protected the working girl—and her mother—this time, but would heaven always protect them?

Suppose she became obsessed with this idea again sometime and actually went through with it?

The sound of the doorbell rang loudly throughout the house. Had Mrs. Nixon forgotten her gloves, or was it Dr. Mannering stopping by, or Mr. Cox, coming on business? She wiped the tears from her face with her hands and went down the stairs making less noise this time because her shoes were so wet and muddy, then through the living room to the door.

She opened it and stood back crying, "Barrett! Barrett! It isn't you—"

"Of course it is, Sabina, what on earth is the matter?"

"Why didn't you come sooner? Yesterday, an hour ago—even a half hour?"

"What's happened, Sabina?" He closed the door and put his hat on the table. Then he started toward her, but she moved away, "No, don't touch me, Barrett—"

"Lord, such melodrama! Sabina, have you just married the villain to keep him from foreclosing the mortgage?"

She stood over by the piano looking steadily at him. "No, it's worse than that—"

Then he saw her muddy shoes and stocking. "Your feet, child! Where have you been?" He walked over to her, carried her to the sofa and took off her shoes. "I don't suppose you'll let me take off your stockings—"

"No."

He laughed then. "You're all right. I was beginning to be worried." He sat down close beside her and put her head on his shoulder. "It's nice to be here again, and nice seeing you, Miss Frost, but you do look awful."

"Do I?"

"Yes."

"Sabina, do you know why I came?"

"Yes."

"Oh, you do! Are you sure you are not jumping at conclusions?"

"No. I mean, yes, I'm sure." Suddenly, she looked up at him and put her hand on his cheek. "Are you real, Barrett? Are you really here?"

He held her closer and then he put his mouth down hard on hers. "Sabina—"

She felt exactly as she had on the night that she drank too much of her father's sherry. She wanted to go to sleep now, as she had then, and this time she hoped she would never wake up. Her eyelids seemed to be fastened down tight, but she had to open them, and she had to think. There were so many things to think about. She moved away from Barrett Page and rested her head on the back of the davenport. She began to be almost frightened by her sensations, she wasn't at all sure what they meant, or that she liked them.

She knew that Barrett was looking at her but she could not speak. For the first time in her life she was realizing that he was a man, and she knew nothing about men. He'd been a person to her up until now, a person whom she liked more than anyone she knew, and who liked her more than anyone else did. He'd been Barrett Page of the Boston Pages, with a fine social position and enough money, someone whom any girl would want to marry. But she had not thought beyond that. He was pleasing to look at, pleasing to talk with; she knew that he was tall, gray-eyed, dark-haired—and strong. Claire had said he was dangerous—was this what she had meant? He had held Claire in his arms just this way, kissed her; and how had Claire felt?

Suddenly, Claire was in the room between them, as she had always been.

Barrett had got up and was walking about the room. "Sabina, you've got to talk to me, I want to know exactly what you are thinking and feeling because it's important. A lot depends on it. There's so much we've got to talk about. I haven't asked you how your mother is, I haven't told you about Claire. You haven't even told me what was the matter with you when I came in. You haven't said, 'Hello, Barrett, how have you been getting along?' This is one time you can't just sit and think, you've got to do some talking—where are you going, Sabina?"

"Mother," she cried, putting on her shoes hurriedly. "I forgot all about her. I'll be right back."

"Could I see her?"

"No. No. I think she's asleep."

Sabina went as quietly up the steps as she could and opened the door softly. What should she say if Mrs.

Frost asked who was downstairs? But Mrs. Frost was sleeping soundly and Sabina returned quickly to the living room. "She really was asleep, Barrett."

"I believe you. Otherwise she'd have been listening at the door. Now, where were we?"

"Barrett, there's something I've got to tell you. You want to know what had happened just before you came in, and I'm going to tell you. You will probably never speak to me again—"

"Come over here and sit down by me, Sabina. You can tell me better there."

"No. I couldn't tell you at all. Barrett," she stood back of the davenport facing him squarely, "what would you say if I told you I was a matricide?"

"A what?" he exclaimed.

"A matricide."

"Sabina, Mrs. Frost is still living, isn't she?"

"Yes."

"And she's the only mother you have, isn't she?"

"Yes—but—"

"Then what the hell?"

"I—almost killed her."

"Just a moment. Do you mind if I sit down?"

"No. You see, I'd been for a walk—"

"So I gathered."

"Well, it goes back much farther than that, really. It goes back to the day you and Claire left. Barrett, she's never been really sick—"

"Your mother?"

"Yes. She's been lying there all these weeks and months and days, and there's never been anything the matter with her except her pride. She didn't want to be poor.

She wanted sympathy, but she wouldn't have pity. She was angry, angry because there wasn't any money and she couldn't be the *grande dame* of Frost Haven as she'd always been. Nothing I did pleased her. And she wouldn't get up. She said the doctor was an old fool because he wasn't taken in by her, she talked about her weak heart, and said I was an unnatural daughter because I had no sympathy with her. It was awful, Barrett—"

"I'm sure it was, Sabina. I didn't realize—"

"And the weather got nastier and gloomier, and she became more irritable. I got to thinking about things I didn't want to think about, spending the rest of my life in Frost Haven waiting on mother, being an old maid—"

"You didn't want to be an old maid—"

"No, it's a disgrace in the South. There's a saying here, 'There are worse things than being an old maid, but I don't know what they are.' "

"I see," he said gravely.

"And this afternoon I felt that if I stayed in the house another moment I'd go crazy. Some visitors came, bubbling over with cheerfulness and platitudes, and I went for a walk. That's when I decided to do it."

"To—kill your mother?"

"Yes. I was going to give her an overdose of her sleeping medicine, and then I could go to England, sell the house—"

"But you didn't."

"No."

"Why?"

"I don't quite know."

He was laughing, "Oh, Sabina, what a little fool you are. You had no more intention of doing that than I have.

You may have wanted to, and I don't blame you at all for that—"

"Do you think it's funny?" she asked.

"Yes. And rather sad, too. Child, I didn't know it had been so bad as all that."

"Do you feel sorry for me?"

"No, not at all. I think it's been good for you. I see a distinct improvement. In fact," he went on as she sat down facing him, "I never saw you so much alive before, you have more vitality, more—oh, call it personality, for want of a better word—you weren't like this when Claire and I were here."

"Claire," she said slowly. "No, I'm never like this when Claire is around."

"That's a strange thing to say, Sabina. Now why is that? Are you jealous of Claire, do you dislike her?"

"Perhaps, or perhaps it's something entirely different. I only know—that when Claire and I are in the same room I feel as if I might as well not be there, that even if I were to turn handsprings no one would notice me. When she speaks, it's enough for both of us—"

"No, I don't see that at all. I rather felt that there was just as much companionship in your silence as there was in Claire's conversation. And another thing, she always seemed to show up better, or rather show off more, when you were there—it's queer." He lighted a cigarette and said slowly, "Sabina, I've got to talk to you about Claire—"

"No," she cried, "I don't want to hear it." She pushed her hair back from her face, covered her ears and begged, "Please don't, Barrett—"

"But it concerns you so deeply, Sabina."

"How?"

"I thought you said you knew why I came."

"You came to tell us about Claire."

"I came to ask you to marry me, Sabina." He smiled suddenly. "After all, I don't want you to be an old maid."

"Did you, Barrett? You came all this way just to ask me that?"

"Certainly."

"Oh, a fine hostess I am! How and when did you get here? Have you had anything to eat? Do you want some sherry?"

He rose and stood before her with his back to the fire. "Sabina, will you marry me?"

"Of course I will," she said. "I've wanted to a long time."

"Why?" He did not take her in his arms; he went on, "Sabina, I'm not sure you know what this means. I wonder if, after all, I shouldn't adopt you instead of marrying you."

The living-room door opened and Mrs. Frost stood there in her dressing robe and slippers, her hair hanging down her back in a plait. "Well, if this isn't a pretty come-off! So that's what you do when my back is turned, Sabina—"

"Mother! What are you doing downstairs?"

"I was hungry. Tell that man to leave, Sabina, tell him never to come here again."

"Really, Mrs. Frost," Barrett Page said, "you can tell me yourself. I don't think Sabina wants me to go—"

"She doesn't know what she wants. Now I'll appreciate it very much if you'll just go. I'll speak to Sabina upstairs."

Sabina rose slowly. "No, Mother, you won't. Because I'm going with Barrett—I'm going to marry him—"

"Sabina Frost! You are not. I shan't allow it! He's ruined Clarissa's life, and now you're going to let him ruin yours—"

Sabina laughed. "What do you think it is now?"

Her mother's voice rose, "He's divorced—and it's a sin, you know that—no child of mine is ever going to marry a divorced man—Sabina, I'm going to faint, my heart—"

"Your performance falls flat, Mother, it isn't up to your usual standard. Go ahead and faint. Have a heart attack, too, if you want to. Don't mind us, we are just leaving."

Barrett looked at Sabina. "Do you mean it?"

"Of course I do." She ran into the hall to get her coat and hat.

He picked up his own hat from the drop-leaf table. "Good-night, Mrs. Frost."

They closed the door and Sabina caught his arm. "Barrett, I'm frightened. Where are we going?"

"South Carolina," he said. "Do you like South Carolina?"

"I like Charleston, they have lovely shrimp Newburgh there."

"We'll go to Charleston."

"Do you think mother will die?"

"No such good luck," he said. "She'll be at the missionary society next Friday."

"It meets on Monday. Barrett, I'm worried about mother, I can't leave her this way. What can we do?"

"Do you want to go back? If you do, you'll never leave."

"No. I'm not going back."

"We could stop at the doctor's and ask him to go to see her, but I don't think that's a good idea. If she has an audience she'll stage a scene. If she's alone, she can't."

"I know—we'll get Lila May. We go right by her house."

He opened the car door and when she was seated he said, "Sabina, do you know what you are getting into?"

"No, but I know what I am getting away from."

"Listen, Sabina, I love you. I don't think you know very much about love, and you know nothing about men and marriage. I tried to tell you in there—but there were interruptions. Are you sure you won't be sorry?"

"It's going to be an experiment, isn't it—like the day you wanted to kiss me—"

"Yes. You see, Sabina, you've got a lot of growing up to do yet."

"I—I want to try it, Barrett."

"So do I. Kiss me, Sabina."

It was exactly like having drunk too much sherry.

"Barrett, do you feel like Lochinvar?"

"No, I feel rather like a fool. I don't like getting married this way. The first time Claire and I had to keep it secret; now you and I are having to elope. The next time I marry I'm going to have a church wedding with a white satin bride, green chiffon bridesmaids, candles and lilies and rice."

"Where are you going to get another wife? There aren't any more Frost girls."

He laughed. "Your mother is a widow."

The peach orchards were lost in the darkness as they rushed past, and the rain beat across the windshield in silver strips. "Now, Sabina, you've got to listen while I tell you about Claire," he said.

"Tomorrow."

"It'll be too late tomorrow. You'll be married to me then."

"That's what I was thinking. That's why I said it. To-morrow."

She could see him smiling in the darkness. "Very well," he said, and added, "You see, I'm just as afraid to tell you as you are to hear it."

CHAPTER XIV

BARRETT PAGE LEFT HIS CAR IN THE GARAGE AND DECIDED to go for a walk before he went home to Sabina. She wouldn't be standing at the window looking for him, or listening for his ring at the door. In fact, it would make very little difference to Sabina whether he came home at all or not, unless she preferred that he didn't; in which case she could finish her book. It would not be a book on Pre-Natal Care, or The Care and Feeding of Children as it should be. Most likely she'd be reading the *Analects* of Confucius, John Donne's *Biathanatos*, or Aristotle's *Poetics*.

He sighed as he walked along in the soft May air. The river was grayer than usual today, a dirty, muddy gray, and crowded with small commercial craft, barges, trawlers, freighters, an occasional flag-bedecked boat carrying sight-seers up to Bear Mountain and Poughkeepsie. Over on the Jersey side were the huge billboards whose messages he knew by heart: the superlative virtues of tooth-

[286]

paste, lard, chewing gum; and the perennial carnival was already aglow with twinkling lights.

There was no use going into the question of who was to blame for the present situation. He had covered that ground so many times and it got him nowhere. He always began by blaming himself, saying that he should never have allowed Claire to divorce him in the first place. From the way Claire had talked you would have thought the Pages were a royal family who had to have an heir to the throne, or he, Barrett, a Napoleon to put aside Josephine and marry an Austrian princess to secure the succession. It was fine of Claire to feel that way, his family had appreciated it; but he saw now that a man wanted to live his own life, not his children's. He missed her warmth and gaiety, her quick responsiveness, her frankness. You knew what Clarissa was thinking and feeling, and she made you think that whatever she thought and felt was centered about you. Oh, she had her faults—he could name them over callously: she drank too much, she was extravagant, she liked superficial and amusing people, queer artists and radicals. There'd been one man—no use thinking of that now. And Claire had laughed when he had asked her about the man. "Oh, darling, I do love you," she had said, stretching out her arms, "but I simply feel too good these days to be true." There had not been a scene about that, the scenes had come later when Claire accused him of being in love with Sabina.

"You've got ideas about her," Claire had said, "and I can't have ideas for a rival. Oh, I don't mean the kind of ideas that an old roué gets when he sees a chorus girl's legs. I could fight that, but Barrett, the truth is, you think

Sabina needs you. And I don't. You know I could get along very well without you. You want to be needed, it appeals to your masculine vanity, you want to play Sir Galahad and rescue her, you want to try to mould her into something you've got in your mind. You'll never be happy until you try it." He had allowed Claire to convince him because he had wanted to be convinced.

The cars whipped past him on the driveway to his right and he found that he was almost within sight of Grant's tomb. Dr. Fosdick's pseudo-Gothic cathedral loomed at the crest of the slope in proof that the rich as well as the poor were entitled to the comfort of religion. Warmth, that was what people wanted and sometimes tried to buy—and he now wanted the warmth of Claire's arms.

It wasn't Sabina's fault. He should have told her before they were married that women frequently had children and men nearly always wanted them. Or her mother should have told her. It wasn't so much the actual fact of children as it was the whole question of sex. He did not know now whether Sabina was abnormal, or whether her reactions had been due to her mother's training.

He had thought on the night when she showed sufficient spirit to defy her mother and elope with him that she had "grown up," was fully awake to life and its responsibilities. He had soon learned that she had only been driven by desperation. It was obvious now that he should have told her then why Claire had got the divorce. Instead he had put it off until—until it was too late.

At the top of the rise he paused and sat down on one of the park benches overlooking the river. The trees were pale and shimmering green with their new leaves.

Nursemaids and children passed before him, old men with books under their arms, students and pert, painted young girls. He watched them go by without actually seeing them.

All he could see was the look on Sabina's face in the mornings, during those first days of their marriage. Was she a narcissist? He had seen her standing before the mirror to see what had happened to her body. He had seen the color suffuse her face when she met him at breakfast and watched her pathetic attempts at friendliness. When he came home at night she seemed to be afraid to talk to him, afraid that he would read into her words a meaning she had not intended, and equally afraid that he would say things to her that had a double meaning. The ease of their former conversations was gone; once she had told him that in gaining a husband she had lost the only friend she'd ever had.

Friendship—that was what Sabina wanted. When he had tried to be kind to her she had drawn away from him into herself, misinterpreting his motives. There had been times at first when he hoped, when he almost believed that she had got over her sense of shame, or repulsion or whatever it was, when he suspected that she was beginning to respond to his love. And then she had become pregnant.

That was when he had told her about Claire, how Claire wanted him to have a child—and it had been the wrong time to tell her.

He'd found her white and limp on the bed in her blue and silver room, the pale blue ruffled curtains whipped by the winter wind, the silver jars and brushes gleaming on her spotless dressing table.

"I suppose you are happy now," she had said bitterly, and he'd replied, "No, not unless you are. Are you?"

"I hate it. I can't stand it," she had screamed; "why did you marry *me* for that? I'll kill myself—I'll go crazy—"

She hadn't killed herself but she had tried the other. She had begun telling him at breakfast that she had dreamed about snakes, about her father's death; and it was possible that she had. As the months passed she had deliberately done queer things to make him think that she was unbalanced. Then one day she'd got hold of an almanac in the kitchen—the cook had been studying astrology—and in the almanac was an old folk tale about a Bavarian peasant girl who had been driven from home by her parents because of her supposed pregnancy. The girl in the story eventually reached a hospital, was operated on, and a serpent was removed from her abdomen. Sabina had become obsessed by the story, she had insisted that that was what her own dreams meant. She could feel it crawling, she contended. It took the doctor and the psychiatrist exactly a week to get her over that. He'd not been afraid of Sabina's producing a serpent instead of a baby, but he was still apprehensive lest she bring forth a book.

In the meantime Sabina was unhappy and so was he—and there was nothing he could do but wait for the birth of the child. He had staked everything on that; it *had* to "humanize" Sabina. October—that was a long time to wait.

Wearily he got up and started walking homeward, wondering in what sort of mood he would find Sabina. He wished that he did not love her quite so much—perhaps he was too patient and considerate. And yet, Sabina would hate a man who was less so; whatever their relations now were, she did not actually hate him.

Perhaps Claire would be there, she'd been over several times since her return from California. He wanted to see her, and yet he dreaded the effect of her visit on Sabina. It was a strange thing that when he'd been married to Claire she had thought he was in love with Sabina; and now that he was married to Sabina, *she* suspected him of being in love with Claire.

Youngsters on roller skates passed him, and he went past the popcorn and peanut vendors. Always there was the constant stream of students, confident young people —wearing horn-rimmed glasses and carrying loads of books in their arms. He wanted to stop them and tell them that there was either too much learning in the world or too little; he wasn't sure which. But he was certain that the present proportion was all wrong. The softness of the spring air, the tender green leaves and the cooing of pigeons seemed to indicate that no learning at all was quite sufficient; Herrick had been right, and Alexander Pope, and especially the Cromwellians who forbade education for women.

Barrett turned into the apartment building and walked slowly to the elevator. "Good-afternoon, Hopkins," he said to the attendant.

"Good-afternoon, Mr. Page. You're late today."

"Yes. I suppose I am." He was in no mood to discuss baseball scores with Hopkins today.

The elevator door closed behind him at the fourth floor and he went down the corridor to 4D. He wished that just for once Sabina would meet him at the door and throw her arms around him, cry, "Darling, at last you've come," or something equally dramatic. But she was afraid to put her arms around him, afraid that he would want to make love to her.

He wished that she would say just once, "Let's go dancing tonight, or see a play," instead of sitting there like a lady and discussing the principles for which the South had fought during the Civil War, or the deplorable present state of literature in America.

He put his key in the lock and the door flew open. "Oh, hello, darling—" it was Claire, and she was lifting her face for a kiss— "we thought you'd never come. We have the most marvelous letter from Lila May."

He took her in his arms and kissed her hard, as much for his own pleasure as for Sabina's discomfort. "It's so nice to see you, Claire. Hello, Sabina."

For just a moment there was a gleam in Sabina's eye that he hadn't seen since the night they left Frost Haven. He thought she was going to come up to him and kiss him as Claire had. Then the gleam died. He could almost hear her thinking, "No, that would be cheap."

"Hello, Barrett. You look tired."

"I went for a walk."

"What we all need—" began Claire.

"Is a drink," he supplied. "I quite agree with you. Claire, you're looking fine."

"I feel too good for my own good," she laughed. "Let me help you with the drinks."

"Hilda makes them better than I do, I'll ask her to do it. Sabina, you won't have one?"

"Yes," said Sabina, "I think I will."

He stopped halfway to the kitchen. "But you really shouldn't—"

"No," said Claire, "you mustn't, Sabina."

Sabina got up and walked over to the window. "What difference does it make?" she asked.

Barrett raised his eyebrows and looked at Claire. "I think she can have one, just this once."

When he returned Claire was standing by a parallel window looking out. "Nice view you have here."

"Yes," Sabina answered, "looks like quite a little city, doesn't it? Oh, Barrett, you must read Lila May's letter, it's wonderful."

"I'd love to," he said. "You know, Claire, Mrs. Frost doesn't consider that Sabina and I are legally married. She hasn't written us a line, but Lila May keeps us informed."

"I always thought Lila May was just as intolerant as mother—"

"No, her religion is more flexible. But her social standards are as adamant as ever. Where's the letter, Sabina? And let's sit down, you two."

The letter was serving as a bookmark in the third volume of Montaigne's *Essays* which he knew Sabina had been reading. She took it out, noting the number of the page and sat down. " 'Dear Miss Sabina—' You'll just have to imagine the way she spells. 'We been havin' mighty hot wether lately, but come Mancipation Day, hits sho to rain. Hit ain't never faild yet. I got me a new pupple and green dress to ware that makes me look reel fair, almost like I was a high yaller.' "

"Isn't that lovely?" Claire sat down between him and

Sabina, because she always had to be in the center of everything. "I can see Lila May looking like a high yaller. Go on, Sabina."

" 'Yo momma enta—' she started to write entertained there, then decided not to—'had the U.D.C's last Wensdy. We served strawberry shortcake and coffy, hit want very good. I like a sallid plate better. Miz Nixon plaid yo pianner, Miss Sabina, and sed hit was outer tune, but I think hit was the way she plaid it.' I'll bet it was, too," Sabina commented. "Oh, here are the drinks."

Barrett looked about the room and tried to understand what had happened to it. It was the same room he came home to every night, handsome and sedate with fine old pieces from the Boston house; there were the same Oriental rugs and hand-blocked linen draperies; but now he suddenly found that he did not want to go out and leave it. It contained everything he wanted—and what did that mean?

" 'Yo momma's been hittin' it up on country ham and green tomayto pickle agen. That Mr. Cox has been sendin' her hams, extry speshul that he raised. But she don't like him much as she do his hams. She say he makin' too much money for heself—they got a good crop this year, and the urly peeches fetchin' a high price. Miss Janie Lee she mad, say ain't but one way out. I reckon she gwi fire 'im. She don't like him gittin' half of all that money.' "

Sabina's face was quiet and wistful, it looked almost as if she wished she were back there with Lila May and the peach orchards and the U.D.C. He recalled something Mr. Frost had said to him once: "Claire has no roots. Sabina has." And then he recalled with a start a scene

from that same summer. They'd been sitting on the side
piazza at Frost Haven, the four of them, sipping lemonade—why in hell did anybody want to drink lemonade?
—and talking about the dance to which he would take
both Sabina and Claire. They had laughed about bigamy
and Mr. Frost had looked intently at him as if he suspected Barrett Page of being a potential bigamist, with
designs on both his daughters. What had it meant? What
was the meaning of his realization a moment ago that this
room contained all he wanted? He had not been happy
with Claire alone, nor with Sabina alone. He was not a
bigamist, he was not promiscuous; if he had to choose
again between them he'd take Sabina, because she needed
him, because she was the most appealing girl he'd ever
known and when she looked at him his heart turned
over; he wanted to get down on his knees to her. And
yet—there was Claire. It was like saying, "Before Eve
there was Lilith."

Claire was looking at him now over the rim of her
cocktail glass as if she were amused by his preoccupation.

" 'The Cummins' house is been rented,' " Sabina read
on, " 'to a family as like the Cumminses as two pease in a
pod. I be dog if I know where all the po-whites comes
from.' "

"They find 'em in heads of cabbage," said Claire.
"Don't they, Sabina?"

"I was always partial to the stork theory, myself,"
Sabina answered without looking up from the paper. "I
haven't read the rest of this, do you want to hear it?"

"Yes, yes, do go on."

" 'We had some news about Bud Cummins last month.
They got him for somethin' in Flarrida and they was

goin' to send him back hear for trial but he got away and noboddy knows where to. They ain't heard of him sinst. That's all, Miss Sabina, cept we sho does miss you and we'll always be yo lovin' servant, Lila May Hilliard.' 'P. S. Later—Miss Sabina, you better come home quick, somethin' awful's bout to happen.' Now what on earth?" cried Sabina. "Why would Lila May end a letter like that? What could happen? Is mother going to be ill again?"

"I'm sure it's nothing to worry about, Sabina," Barrett told her. "If anything awful had happened you would have heard about it before now. You can't afford to get upset over a darky's vague predictions."

"She said for me to come home quick—"

"Really, Sabina, you're not going to be absurd, are you?" asked Claire. "Barrett, I want a cigarette."

"Certainly, Claire." Before Eve there was Lilith, and Lilith probably had red hair above mocking brown eyes; she probably wore her fig-leaf frock shorter than Eve's, and had it lower in the neck. Damn it all, he wanted Claire, he wanted to see the amusement in her eyes change to—something else.

"Dinner is served, Mrs. Page," said Hilda from the doorway.

"Oh, yes. Thank you, Hilda."

"Dinner? Good heavens, is it that late?"

"You're staying, of course, Claire."

"Oh, no, I can't really. Some people are coming over to my place. Let me get my hat—"

"I'll get it," said Sabina, going into the bedroom.

"Claire, please stay," Barrett begged, "I want to talk to you—"

"I couldn't possibly. Don't, Barrett. Sabina will see you—"

"I'll take you home."

"No."

"Sabina, let's take Claire home," Barrett said.

"Dinner's ready—"

"Nobody's hungry. Come along."

"We could call a taxi for her."

"She hates taxis."

"No, Barrett. I'm not going. You do as you like."

Was she being noble, or just contrary? And was he glad she was not going, or sorry? The telephone rang and he picked up the receiver. "Yes?"

"There's a telegram for Mrs. Page. Shall I send it up?" It was the boy at the reception desk. "Yes, please do." He turned to Sabina. "A telegram for you."

"For me? Nobody ever sends me telegrams."

"It isn't your birthday?"

"No."

"I really must go," said Claire, "but I want to know what's in the telegram."

"It's that bad news Lila May was anticipating," said Sabina, "I know it is—"

"Here's the boy now." Barrett tipped him and took the envelope. "Do you want me to read it, Sabina?"

"Yes, please, Barrett."

"Do hurry," said Claire, "I'm simply dying—"

She was looking over his shoulder but Sabina was holding to the library table. He tore open the envelope and cried, "Good Lord, Sabina! Listen to this—'MRS. FROST MARRIED THAT MAN YESTERDAY. I'M QUITTING. LOVE, LILA MAY.' What man? What is she talking about?"

"It's Mr. Cox, of course," cried Sabina; "good heavens, how could she do it?"

"Mr. Cox? Holy cats! *Why* should she marry him?" asked Claire.

"Well, I'll be everlastingly damned." Barrett sat down in the nearest chair. "I would have staked my last cent on Mrs. Frost's upholding the traditions of the old aristocracy down to the last syllable of recorded time. I don't believe it. There's something fishy about it—"

"No," said Sabina, "it's true all right. That's what Lila May meant when she quoted mother as saying 'There is only one way out.' She married Mr. Cox because it was the only way to get the money he was making, and he is probably the best money-maker she knows. I'm sure he'll be a good provider."

"I still don't believe it," declared Barrett. "Let's call up and find out." He picked up the receiver. "Long distance, please—get me Frost Haven, Georgia. Mrs. Ellison Frost—" He could hear the conversation between the operators, "No one answers at Mrs. Frost's residence. Mrs. Frost is out of town. Shall we try again tomorrow?" When the operator reported to him, he said, "No. It's no use. Thank you."

"Honeymooning!" said Claire, and then she began laughing. "Mother is honeymooning—oh, my God!"

"It makes me lose my faith in human nature," said Barrett. "I can't stand it. Nobody could have persuaded me that Mrs. Frost would be untrue to the Confederate Army. I'm hurt. I'm appalled. She's taken my last illusion away from me—Mrs. Frost of *all* people! The Benedict Arnold, the Esau—oh, God, let's have another cocktail!"

Claire was already drinking her second one. "I've got

to go—but I never left such an interesting situation in all my life. I can scarcely tear myself away."

Sabina went into her bedroom and closed the door.

"If you're going to take me, Barrett, come along," said Claire. "I'm late already."

"Just a minute." He went to the kitchen door. "Hilda, see that Mrs. Page eats her dinner. And you'll stay with her until I get back, won't you?"

"Yes, sir, if you ain't out too late."

"Don't leave her for a moment. Promise me—"

"What time you coming back?"

"In about an hour, or an hour and a half. You can take a taxi home."

Hilda lifted her blonde head. "Who's going to pay for it?"

"I am."

"All right, sir. But I still don't like it."

Then Barrett rapped on his wife's door. "Sabina?"

"Yes?"

"I'll come back just as quickly as I can, but I've got to talk to Claire. Are you all right?"

"Of course. I understand, Barrett."

What did she understand? Something that wasn't true at all, probably. He hated to leave her—but Claire was waiting.

Sabina heard the entrance door close and then she got up and went to the kitchen. "Hilda, I don't want any dinner. You may go as soon as you like."

"But I can't, Mrs. Page. Mr. Page made me promise to stay here."

"I want you to go, Hilda."

"I'm sorry, Mrs. Page, but I can't. He told me not to leave you."

"Hilda, I'm asking you to go. You must do as I say, or —we'll have to get someone else."

"Yes, Mrs. Page. I'll go just as soon as he comes back."

Sabina could not keep the tears back. "Oh, Hilda, I'm dreadfully sorry, I didn't mean to speak to you like that."

"That's all right, Mrs. Page. I understand—"

Sabina went back to the living room where there was room to walk about and told herself she must think. Her husband was in love with his first wife—not with his second; her mother had sold her birthright for a mess of pottage. There were worse things than being an old maid, and having a baby was one of them. There was the physical indignity, there were the pain and the revulsion —there were too many things to think about.

There was one thing certain: she would not be here when Barrett returned. She could go to Frost Haven— the house would be empty while her mother was off honeymooning with her middle-class breadwinner. There was a train at nine-thirty or ten; she had time to pack her things if she only felt like doing it.

She went to her room and got her bags out of the closet. Claire had given her her chance and she had failed. The cocktail was making her as drunk as a lord. She could lie down for a while and still have plenty of time. Her head was going round like a carrousel, a carrousel—

Barrett and Claire were looking at each other over their drinks at a speak-easy in Greenwich Village.

"Claire, you don't understand," Barrett was saying,

"you are deliberately misinterpreting everything I have tried to tell you."

"I think I understand only too well."

"But you don't," he shouted. "I'll start over."

"Not so loud, Barrett. Everybody is staring at you."

"Let them stare—what do they matter?" He looked at the men with their affected garb of flowing ties and peasant berets, at their Vandyke beards, the girls with their smocks and short straight hair, older women in flowered chiffon dresses and dirty white Oxfords, fat old men scribbling or drawing on the tablecloth, and all of them talking, talking, talking. Settling the problems of art, politics, economics, straightening out the world over their glasses of synthetic gin. They got in his way, he had his own world to patch up and he wanted to do the talking.

"Waiter—two more dry Martinis, please."

"Yes, sir."

"Now listen, Claire, and try to get this straight. I grant you that a man can be in love with two women; possibly every man needs two women, I don't know. He needs one who needs him, to make him feel strong and masculine; he needs another to go to when he wants to put his head on her shoulder and confess that his responsibilities are too much for him. He wants one who's as pure and chaste as the virgin moon, and another who will love him with joy and abandon. But that's got nothing to do with it."

"Oh, it hasn't!" said Claire.

"No. It hasn't. I was sitting there tonight looking at you and Sabina and I knew that in that room there was all I wanted in the world. Not you alone, nor Sabina alone, but you two together."

"Bigamist, that's what you are."

"But I'm not. That's just it, that's what I've been trying to tell you. Listen, Claire," he held his glass midway in the air, "I've just found out what's been worrying me for two years. You and Sabina are not two women, you are one. One person. Now tell me I'm crazy. Go ahead and laugh."

Claire set her glass down hard on the table and her face was as dead white as the piqué collar on her printed silk dress. "Barrett," she whispered, "why did you say that?"

"Because it's true," he cried.

"Hush—Barrett, did you—did you ever hear of a case like that before?"

"No. Don't you think it's funny?"

"No." She pushed her chair back from the table. "Let's go."

"I'm not ready to go. I've just got started. What's the matter, Claire."

She leaned back, still limp and white. "Do you really want to know?"

"Of course I do."

She took up her cigarette from the ashtray and spoke slowly. "That's—exactly what father said once. He said Sabina and I were antipathetic but integral parts of the same personality and we ought to be put in a basket and shaken up until we made one fully rounded person."

He cried triumphantly, "Don't you see? It's true! That proves it. Oh, Claire—"

She was shaking. "I wonder if it is true—"

"Of course it is. Don't you see, Claire?"

"Let's go—"

"All right. Waiter, our check, please." He put his arm around her when they got to the door. "Claire—you *will* call those people and tell them not to come—"

"They've probably already come and gone—"

The street was not too light and standing before a bookshop he bent down to kiss her. "Claire—"

She put her arms around his neck crying, "Oh, Barrett, I've missed you so terribly—it's like—like coming home—"

"Where did we leave the car?" he asked after a moment.

"I don't know—it was somewhere near here. We were right at the Square, I remember because somebody was making a speech. I—don't exactly feel like walking, Barrett."

"I know. There's a speech going on over here at this corner under the trees—let's see if that's the same one—"

Suddenly, she clutched his arm. "Barrett, do you see what I see?"

"No," he said, "you've had too much to drink."

"But look, Barrett, that girl and that child—"

He looked then, and standing by the side of the speaker he saw a girl in a pink gingham dress holding the hand of a deformed child whose head rolled foolishly about on his shoulders. "Daisy Cummings," he said, "and Tippy."

"It *is*, Barrett! Come on!"

They joined the crowd then and at length got where they could see the man on the soap box. He was dressed in the robes and turban of a Hindu and at his feet was a coiled serpent. With one hand he was gesticulating, the other arm was amputated just below the elbow. "I wish," said Barrett, "we hadn't drunk so much. Do you see any pink elephants, Claire?"

"Hush, Barrett, and let's listen to what he is saying."

"And friends," the man cried, "if you think Marx was the first socialist, that's where you're dead wrong. It goes a heap further back than that. The first socialist warnt nobody but the Lord Jesus Christ. It was Jesus that first proclaimed the great doctrine that all men are equal, that lifted up the low and humble and told the rich to divide with the poor. It was Jesus Christ, friends, and I'm appealin' to you in His name, the name of our Lord—"

His voice was a sonorous, singing monotone, the voice of a Holy Roller preacher.

The throng was constantly increasing, and the accents of Harvard joined with those of Missouri. "Isn't that lovely?" "I think he's wonderful!" Chuckles came from the throats of Irish tenors and Bavarian contraltos.

"His own people heard Him not—they laughed, too, my friends, just as you are laughing now, but his words lived on—and come to flower—not in Russia, but in America. Right here in these same United States—I don't know much histry, friends, I ain't pretendin' that I do— but I do know this. Listen close, friends, I'm talkin' to you—" his long finger pointed to first one laughing spectator, then another, "and you—and you. Hit was on the shores of Virginia that socialism first came to flower. in that brave little colony at Plymouth. 'No work, no eat,' that was their motto. They had a common storehouse where the food was kept, and each man had his job to do—"

"I'll be damned," said an Indiana voice, "I never thought of that—"

"And what happened to that brave litle colony? What did Virginia become? A state of slaveowners, men holding other men in bondage."

"He's ruining his own argument," said Barrett. "He has proved that socialism can't last—"

"And the bondage ain't over, friends, not by a long shot. The Civil War didn't end it. Hit just changed the color of the slaves, that's all. They're white now instead o' black. Po-whites, that's what they call 'em all over the South. Po-whites. Help 'em today, brethren and sistren, they're your brothers and your sisters just the same as mine. Drop your money in the hat, friends, the girl in the pink dress is goin' to pass it around and give you all a chanct. She's one of 'em, brothers, and you see that po deformed little thing beside her—I'm askin' you in Jesus' name to help 'em—"

"Barrett," whispered Claire, "he's Bud Cummings, I know it, I know it—"

"Yes, I think you're right, Claire—"

"And Tippy—Barrett, Bud Cummings is Tippy's father—"

"Yes, you stay here, Claire, I'm going to get a policeman—don't let him get away."

"Friends," cried the exhorter, "we want to sing while the hat is bein' passed around. Let's all sing, 'Stand up, stand up for Jesus' "

"We'd rather hear you talk," cried someone near the front and the others laughed.

"This ain't nothin' to laugh about," the speaker cried angrily, "this is God's business, and yours and mine—"

Claire pushed up closer and someone said, "We're not laughing at what you say, but at the way you say it. It sounds so funny to hear a Southern accent coming out of a Hindu dress—"

"Take his robes off," cried a man, "let's see what he looks like underneath."

The speaker drew back but someone caught at his robe and jerked it. "Stop it! This ain't no way to treat a servant of the Lord!" The robe fell about his feet and there were the overalls and faded blue shirt of an indigent farmer. "It's Bud," Claire said to herself. "I knew it—oh, why doesn't Barrett come?"

"Take his turban off," shouted a girl. "The turban next—"

Bud Cummings turned and looked about for Daisy. He could not see her, evidently, for he reached down for his robe and started to run. "Stop him," cried Claire, "don't let him get away, that man is a murderer—"

The crowd was now in an uproar. "Grab him! She says he's a murderer—"

"He killed my father," Claire was screaming, "don't let him get away—"

Suddenly, she saw him close to her, he had come around the left fringe of the crowd and in the shadows of the trees he was half-hidden. "There he is!" she cried, "over by the elm tree!"

She heard the sound of a shot and thought it was a policeman shooting Bud Cummings. Then something hit her chest. She called, "Barrett, Barrett—" and fell back against the strangers who were crowding around her. Women began screaming and there was the long shrill of a policeman's whistle.

"Claire," Barrett cried, "where are you?"

"I guess she's here, mister," someone said.

He came running. "Get that man, don't let him get away—"

"They've got him," he was assured, "he won't get away now."

"Claire—" he called again; then he saw that the crowd were moving back from a very still figure on the ground. Before he looked down he knew that it was she.

Sabina was vaguely conscious that the telephone was ringing in the next room but she knew that she was not going to answer it. It would be Barrett calling to say— well, it made no difference what he would say.

Then she heard Hilda's voice. "Yes, Mr. Page—oh, how awful! No, sir, she's asleep, do you want me to wake her?"

Hilda knocked on the door. "Mrs. Page, Mr. Page wants to speak to you, there's been an accident—

"An accident? Is he all right, Hilda?"

"Yes ma'am, I suppose he is. He is telephoning—"

"Hilda, are you sure?" She did not intend running to the telephone but it seemed such a long way across the living room. "Barrett, are you all right?"

"Yes, I'm quite all right, Sabina."

"Where are you? You sound so far away, Barrett. Were you in the car? What happened?"

"It's—Claire, Sabina. I'm down at the hospital."

"Do you want me to come?"

He was silent for so long that she thought they'd been disconnected. She repeated, "Barrett, I'll come immediately—where is she? Which hospital?"

"It's—no use, Sabina."

"No—use." Somehow she could not make her voice clear, it was only a whisper. "You mean—she's been—killed?"

"Yes."

After a moment she asked, "Barrett, were you driving?"

"No, we weren't in the car at all. I'll tell you just as soon as I get home—I'm coming now, Sabina. Are you all right? Will Hilda stay with you until I come?"

Sabina looked at Hilda, and the girl nodded.

"Yes, she'll stay, Barrett."

"Let me speak to her."

She heard him saying, "Hilda, give Mrs. Page some ammonia, a teaspoonful in some water—" and then everything began turning black. She lay down on the davenport thinking, I'm going to lose the baby—I'm going to lose Barrett's baby—I didn't want it, anyhow. But he did.

She forced her eyes to stay open. No, I won't, I won't—

"Tell him I'm all right, Hilda," she said firmly. "Tell him I'm fine."

Clarissa had lost her baby but Sabina was not going to lose hers. After all, her grandmother Marie Antoinette had had eleven. Eleven little Pages would be almost enough to make a book.

Suddenly, she began laughing. "Hilda, I just thought of the funniest thing—"

"Here," said Hilda, handing her a glass, "you drink this."

CHAPTER XV

Down in Frost Haven, Georgia, the darkies are celebrating their emancipation, for it is May twenty-ninth, and if there is some doubt among them what they are celebrating, they are at least quite sure of the verb itself. Lila May is complaining to her friends that she has "developed 'the body trouble' from going up and down all them steps at Miz Frost's," but she is gay in her purple and green dress and gets along easily in felt bedroom slippers while she carries her patent leather pumps in her hand.

Taxis from Atlanta and Macon are so thick around the "square" that they get in one another's way but they are all loaded to the brim with darkies, and barkers with megaphones hang over the fenders shouting, "Everybody rides, nobody walks—all the way to Lincoln Park, ten cents, one measly little dime! Everybody rides, nobody walks!"

The streets are a turgid stream of nobodies walking.

The courthouse lawn is a swarm of black ants, and every hot-dog stand, every "pink lemonade" booth, every photographer's kiosk is so jammed with patrons that the flies are having to crowd closer in order to make way. There are balloons, walking canes, pennants, United States flags and Confederate flags, long flybrushes made of gaudily colored strips of paper. There has never been so much color since the last twenty-ninth.

There are wagon loads of darkies sitting in straight, hickory-bottom chairs, grannies in gingham or calico dresses and sunbonnets, boys uncomfortable in new long trousers and stiff shoes, pickaninnies in sashes and pigtails, cooks and hoe-hands in the castoff finery of the whites, pert young gals from the city wearing rouge, earbobs and sto-bought clothes. And there's the parade, God bless 'em, led by the head men in silk hats, mind you, and long-tailed broadcloth coats—the hats and coats came out of the Georgia House of Representatives when Governor Joe Brown went out. There's the band in uniform, there's braid and there's noise and sweat and color and the odor of food; the smell of dust, of straw hats, of cheap liquor and lollipops and niggers.

There's a speaker on the courthouse lawn, talking from the base of the Confederate monument, but he's only a minor speaker from some academy. The main ones are at Lincoln Park or New London, watching the dinner being spread out on the long tables under the trees and wondering if those shipped watermelons are fit to eat. Anybody knows a watermelon ain't good before the fourth of July.

Out from town, in the orchards, the fruit hangs heavy on the trees; it is the color of gold and blood, a savage, untamed fruit, this "Persian apple," this middle-Georgia peach.

Sabina Page pauses by a pond in the old Frost orchards and says to her husband, "Look at the waterlilies, Barrett, aren't they lovely? And sometimes at dusk a wild crane or a heron stops by, and wades in the water at the edge. It's an enchanting sight."

"Yes, it is. What were you saying before that, Sabina?"

"Oh. That Southerners are a strange people. They'll do anything for you when you're in trouble, but they can't stand for you to be prosperous. The South itself doesn't stand prosperity very well; I think we were rather gallant and admirable in our poverty, but this new flourishing commercial South is crude, it's brash, it's blatant—because we hadn't the background for it. Mrs. Turner says we haven't lost our old cultural tradition, and it's true—because we never had any—not as you did in New England. We had a slight impulse toward it just before the War (the Civil War, of course), but it never got beyond social urbanity and a certain leisure for contemplation."

"Sabina," said Barrett Page, "let's dismiss the class and sit over there under the pine trees."

She laughed. "All right. Once a schoolteacher, always a schoolteacher, I suppose."

"No," he said, putting down his coat for her to sit on, "you're not a schoolteacher and I'll wager you were an awful one when you tried it. Sabina, do you know what you are?"

"No," she answered, "tell me."

He whispered in her ear, then he lay back against a pine tree with her head resting on his shoulder.

She smiled happily. "Do you mind if I beam with honest pride?"

"No, I love you to beam with honest pride."

"Oh, Barrett, do you really think—that—about me?"

"I'm sure of it." But there were other things about which he wasn't sure. Was his discovery on the night Claire was killed the result of too many cocktails, or was there some truth in it? Had Sabina actually become a different person since then, was she beginning to take on some of Claire's characteristics, was she two people? Or had Sabina simply been envious of Claire all her life, afraid of Claire's charm, her ability to make friends, her spontaneity? Had Sabina always been afraid to undertake anything because she might fail at it, afraid to give herself lest she lose herself, afraid to be herself lest someone else be more attractive?

A breeze whipped through the orchards and blew the curtains in the living room at Frost Haven.

"Yes," said Janie Lee Cox, to Mrs. Nixon, "it was an awful thing. And do you know, I'm at an utter loss to know what to put on her tombstone—I don't know whether it ought to be just Clarissa Frost, or Clarissa Frost Page."

"Or Clarissa Frost Page Frost," said Mrs. Nixon. "She took her name back, didn't she?"

"Yes," said Mrs. Cox with asperity, "but she didn't add it again."

"It looks to me like Mr. Page would have wanted her buried with his people—after all, she *was* his wife—"

"He did. But I said, 'No, Barrett, if I knew Clarissa, and I think I did, she would have wanted to be buried by the side of her father.' "

"Yes, I suppose you are right. Where *were* you when you got the message, Janie Lee?"

"We were at Mr. Cox's old home in Ohio, going through the old family Bibles and graveyards. He's getting up his papers, you know."

"You mean he's going to join the Sons of the American Revolution?"

"Of course."

"How nice," said Mrs. Nixon flatly. "If he can get in—the requirements are much stricter than they used to be."

"Mr. Cox's grandfather was a major in the War of 1812, and his great-grandfather on his mother's side was a lieutenant colonel in the Continental Army. It's quite an old family, they—"

"Came over on the *Mayflower*, I suppose."

"Yes—there's the coat of arms above the library table," said Mrs. Cox reaching for a fan, and leaning back in her rocking chair. "Hasn't it been hot today?"

The breeze pulled at the draperies and grew into a wind that brushed the oak trees against the freshly painted house. The dust spiraled and billowed, settled on rose petals in the garden, on peaches in the orchards and on the sweating bodies of festive darkies. Then the first great drops of rain spattered into starry shapes where the dust lay thickest. It always rains in Frost Haven on the twenty-ninth.

THE END